The Economics of Fintech

Sahoko Kaji · Teruo Nakatsuma ·
Masahiro Fukuhara
Editors

The Economics of Fintech

Springer

Editors
Sahoko Kaji
Faculty of Economics
Keio University, Tokyo, Japan

Teruo Nakatsuma
Faculty of Economics
Keio University, Tokyo, Japan

Masahiro Fukuhara
Institution for a Global Society
Corporation, and Faculty of Economics
Keio University, Tokyo, Japan

ISBN 978-981-33-4912-4 ISBN 978-981-33-4913-1 (eBook)
https://doi.org/10.1007/978-981-33-4913-1

This Springer imprint is published by the registered company Springer Nature Singapore Pte Ltd.
The registered company address is: 152 Beach Road, #21-01/04 Gateway East, Singapore 189721, Singapore

Contents

Chapter 1
An Overview of Fintech

Sahoko Kaji

1 The History of the Development of Fintech

The word "fintech" was first used in the 1980s as an abbreviation of "financial technology." It is generally believed to have been coined by Peter Knight, then editor of the Sunday Times Business Newsletter.

However, it was only after the financial crisis of 2007–08 that it became a household word. Around this time, the balance sheets of financial institutions, especially in the United States, began to be severely affected by financial products in which subprime loans were integrated in a complicated way. Then one day in September 2008, Lehman Brothers filed for bankruptcy. (It is based on this incident that the global financial crisis as a whole is known as the "Lehman Shock" in Japan.)

In an attempt to prevent the financial crisis from spreading around the world and causing a large-scale global economic meltdown, the U.S. Department of the Treasury established the USD 700 billion Troubled Asset Relief Program (TARP). The U.S. government and taxpayers would eventually benefit from this injection of public funds, but initially, people were very angry that their hard-earned tax money was being injected into the very same financial institutions that had triggered the crisis. As a result, starting from the West Coast of the United States, there spread a

Many thanks to all the companies that provided support to the Centre for Finance, Technology and Economics at Keio (FinTEK), as well as to our course "The Theory and Practice of Fintech (a)," which provided the materials for this book. Many thanks also to the speakers who took time out of their busy schedules to give lectures as part of the course and to write the chapters of this book.

S. Kaji (✉)
Faculty of Economics, Keio University, Tokyo, Japan
e-mail: kaji@econ.keio.ac.jp

S. Kaji et al. (eds.), *The Economics of Fintech*,
https://doi.org/10.1007/978-981-33-4913-1_1

movement in favor of fintech, which was aimed at creating an economic system that did not rely on financial institutions.[1]

Today, there is a diverse array of services covered by the word "fintech," some of which are not even directly related to finance. The word is now used as long as the service is provided online via computer or smartphone and uses the latest technology. This book also deals with fintech in this broad sense.

Fintech, therefore, signifies a diverse range of things, but they all have the following three common characteristics.

The first characteristic of fintech is its effect of democratization, which can also be called "atomization" or "localization," as it does away with the need for people to come from various places and physically congregate in a single location, given that individual transactions can be conducted electronically in the cloud. As mentioned above, fintech originated with the desire to cut out the middleman, i.e. financial institutions, and eliminate the need for a central bank among tech-savvy people angry with the government for injecting public funds into financial institutions.

As we will learn in this book, blockchain-based cryptocurrencies set up by private organizations fall outside the purview of the central bank's control. Private economic entities that issue cryptocurrencies for use as mediums of exchange and lending also do not yet come under the supervision of financial regulatory authorities. With fintech, friends can lend to, borrow from, or pay each other on the spot using a common application installed on their smartphones, without going through banks or using currencies issued by the government. Fintech also gives rise to the possibility that people will be able to pay lower health insurance premiums if they are known to be safe drivers and take good care of their health.

The second characteristic of fintech is exclusivity, which may appear to be in conflict with the first one at first glance. This is because software programs that support fintech are written in computer languages. While some programming languages like Python are relatively easy to learn, most are incomprehensible to anyone who has not spent the time and money necessary to become fluent in them. In fact, there is not much opportunity for ordinary users of fintech products to even see the programs, so they are left with no choice but to trust the providers or creators of these products.[2]

---

[1] Of course, Wall Street, which is the financial nerve center of the U.S., is on the East Coast, and this initially created a geographical divide between those who supported the rising trend of fintech and those who supported conventional finance. Eventually, the financial institutions on the East Coast would also proactively adopt fintech, through acquisitions and other means. However, at least in the beginning, the rising trend of fintech was in conflict with traditional financial institutions. This promoted competition and spurred on innovation to a degree not seen in Japan and Europe, with no clear divide as the one between the East Coast financial institutions and West Cost technology firms in the U.S. Apart from the U.S., it was easier for a new business area like fintech to grow in countries where communication infrastructure and financial systems were not well developed. Iwasaki (2018) and Fujita (2018) discuss the state of fintech in Southeast Asia and China in detail. Takasaki (2017) provides a concise summary of the state of fintech in Africa, and is useful as a reference.

[2] On November 27, 2018, the Japanese government released a list of seven legal guidelines based on which companies entrusting their decision-making to artificial intelligence (AI) software would

The provision of fintech services requires specialized education and training. It also requires large-scale computing and communication infrastructure capable of instantaneously handling large calculation volumes, and of storing and analyzing the resultant data. Because of this, companies that have an edge on others in terms of the scale of their operations are at an advantage.[3] The services offered by GAFA (Google, Apple, Facebook, Amazon) have become daily necessities for people around the world, making it difficult for others to catch up to them in the areas of social media, communications equipment, information provision, and online shopping.

Meanwhile, the Chinese mobile payment market is almost completely dominated by WeChat Pay and Alipay, provided by technology giants Tencent and Ant Financial, respectively, and their user bases are said to surpass that of Apple Pay. These large technology companies are accumulating enormous volumes of data ("big data") including both personal information as well as information on the transactions and behavior patterns of their users, which puts them at an advantage in developing AI.[4]

The third characteristic of fintech derives from its first and second characteristics, and it is that it shatters conventional wisdom. Public versus private, foreign versus domestic, consumer versus producer, supply versus demand, real versus virtual, man versus machine—fintech has fundamentally changed and even blurred the lines between these dichotomies that were previously believed to be universal and immutable.

This is clearly a major development and the reason why fintech is hailed by some as the fourth industrial revolution. Of course, no one has been able to explain why, compared with previous industrial revolutions, fintech has not resulted in an increase in productivity, but it has certainly had a broad and deep impact in terms of turning conventional wisdom on its head. The changes taking place in economic systems as a result of fintech, including through the use of AI, are unprecedented, and there seem no limits to the extent by which it could improve the convenience of people's lives. At the same time, the development of fintech also makes cyberterrorism, theft,

---

be required to explain those decisions. It should be emphasized here that the mechanisms of AI are intuitively comprehensible to anyone who has studied economics. "Optimization" is something a student of economics understands as a matter of course, and the least squares method is taught even to first- and second-year students. Students of economics should, therefore, be confident about understanding the idea of AI. As a concept, there is nothing difficult about it whatsoever; rather, it gives the impression of a concept patented in economics but utilized in a different field. Even if one cannot write the program itself, this knowledge of the thought process behind AI, which is increasingly catching up with human intelligence, will prove very useful in navigating the global economic systems of the 21st century.

[3]This is an "increasing returns industry," to use economic jargon, and it is very easy for such industries to descend to a state of monopoly or oligopoly. Some startups are leaving Silicon Valley because the big technology companies manage to lure away all the talented people with high salaries.

[4]It is becoming clear, however, that simply possessing big data is not sufficient. For instance, Alibaba used the data it had accumulated to introduce Sesame, a consumer credit rating application, but as of 2018, the application had not been put to use in making loan-related decisions. In Japan, again, companies like LINE and NTT have introduced screening services for loan applicants, but to little avail. Thornhill (2018) has explained quite usefully that there is a difference between "big data" and "strong data."

and fraud that much easier, and even gives rise to the possibility of wars and killing based on AI-guided weapons.

It is inconceivable that people living in the 21st century, especially young people who are just embarking on their journey as adults, will go through their entire lives untouched by fintech in the broad sense. Even now, people are using AI in their daily lives without even being aware of it. This is a fact that applies to everybody, whether they work in the public or private sector, no matter what kind of organization they work for, whether they run their own business, or are stay-at-home moms/dads. The only way to remain unaffected by fintech and AI is to renounce the world and go live in the wilderness.

However, until 2017, Keio University did not offer any courses that focused on fintech. This is despite the fact that a significant proportion of its graduates are employed by the financial sector every year. Then, in June 2017, with the support of companies that shared our alarm at this, the university established the Centre for Finance, Technology and Economics at Keio (FinTEK), which began to offer several fintech-related courses from the Fall Semester of the same year.

2 Structure of This Book

This book is based on the lectures given as part of the course "The Theory and Practice of Fintech (a)," which is offered every year in the Spring Semester. It comprises the following chapters.[5]

This chapter, provides an overview of fintech. In the first section above, we briefly went over the history of its development. Section 3 below surveys how fintech is changing a variety of businesses from a microeconomic point of view. This is followed by Sect. 4, which looks at fintech's macroeconomic and policy implications.

In Chap. 2, Dr. Naoyuki Yoshino, dean of the Asian Development Bank Institute (ADBI) and professor emeritus of Keio University, explains the role of financial systems in modern economics and discusses fintech from a macroeconomic perspective. Chapter 3 is by Professor Naoyuki Iwashita of the Kyoto University School of Government (former head of the Bank of Japan (BOJ) FinTech Center). This chapter discusses the relationship between cryptocurrencies and central bank digital currencies. In Chap. 4, Division Manager Tomohiro Senda and Assistant Manager Miwa Takemura of the Personal Marketing Department of Mizuho Bank, Ltd., take a consumer-side perspective to explain how fintech affects consumer behavior and how this is changing financial marketing.

In Chap. 5, Deputy General Manager Kazuhiko Tajimi of the Mizuho Financial Group Inc.'s Digital Innovation Department discusses the impact of fintech on existing financial institutions. Chapter 6 is by Masahiro Fukuhara, founder and CEO

[5]The authors' affiliations and titles are as of the time of the publication of this book in Japanese, August 2019. By its nature, the pace of change of all matters related to fintech is very rapid. We ask readers to keep in mind that the lectures behind these chapters were given in 2018.

of the Institution for a Global Society Corporation, who is jointly in charge of this course as Project Professor. Dr. Fukuhara discusses what it means to set up your own business in a world where fintech is on the rise. Chapter 7 by Mr. Spyridon Mentzas of HiJoJo Partners Inc. contemplates the impact of fintech on the international capital markets.

Mr. Masakazu Masujima, a partner at the law firm Mori Hamada and Matsumoto, explains the legal aspects of fintech in Chap. 8. In Chap. 9, Mr. Junpei Miwa, Director, Fintech and Innovation Office, Policy Planning Bureau, Financial Services Agency, and Mr. Yusaku Matsui, Chief of Financial Informatization, Financial Services Agency, Currently Chief, Planning and Management Division, Policy and Markets Bureau, Financial Services Agency, discuss regulation and international cooperation in fintech.

Chapters 10 through 13 deal with four different aspects of technological innovations that support fintech. These include (1) blockchains and cryptocurrencies, (2) AI and machine learning, (3) high-frequency trading (HFT), and (4) robo-advisors. Chapter 10 on blockchains is written by Dr. Fukuhara and myself, while Chaps. 11 through 13 are written by Prof. Teruo Nakatsuma, who is FinTEK's director and also in charge of this course.

Chapters 14 and 15 are about new risks that are arising as a result of fintech. Assistant Manager Yuta Miyauchi of the Mizuho Financial Group's Data Management Division, Cyber Security Team, discusses cyber security, while Rissho University Professor Kazuhito Ikeo (professor emeritus of Keio University) discusses the destabilization of financial systems.

3 Microeconomic Implications of Fintech

Fintech products and services fall into the following four broad categories.

Payments	(E.g., electronic payment, money transfer among friends, sharing of expenses, Internet of Things (IoT)
Infrastructure	(E.g., blockchains, cryptocurrencies, social networking services)
Customer services	(E.g., robo-advisors, HFT, insurtech)
Platforms	(E.g., crowd funding, sharing economy, open banking)

It would be impossible to comprehensively list all the fintech services provided in the above areas, but let us take a brief look here at some examples. Several of these will be discussed in greater detail in the subsequent chapters.

Of the above, social networking services (SNS) have a relatively long history. Google first came into being in 1998, Facebook has existed since 2004, and Twitter since 2006. However, their payment services, Android Pay (which later became Google Pay) and Facebook Pay, were introduced only in 2015, and

Twitter does not provide any payment services.[6] The earliest "financial technology" services to emerge were electronic payments, blockchain-based cryptocurrencies, robo-advisors, and HFT.

When electronic payments were introduced following the collapse of Lehman Brothers, it was thought that the use of cryptocurrencies could give rise to an economic system independent of central banks and financial institutions. However, cryptocurrencies have turned out to be used mainly as stores of value or for speculation seeking capital gains; at present these currencies have very limited use as mediums of exchange in the trade of goods and services.

Blockchains are what provide credibility to cryptocurrencies. The bockchain that supports Bitcoin is shared and maintained by a public network of users, but there are now also blockchains that are created exclusively by entities sharing information. The use of blockchains has expanded far beyond cryptocurrencies.[7] For this reason, blockchains and cryptocurrencies should be thought of as separate infrastructures. Ever since its dawn, humankind has faced a choice between dictatorship and democracy, and blockchains now offer this choice in the area of currencies. It is useful to comprehend that, in addition to a model where each country has a single currency-issuing entity, models on the other extreme are also possible. Analyzing this idea may provide interesting hints for voting and collective decision-making.

Electronic payment enables not just payments from consumers to providers of goods and services, but also among consumers themselves. We are also rapidly approaching an age in which our refrigerators and cars can place orders and make settlements using IoT.

New online services that write assignment papers are an example of infrastructure causing headaches for university professors. On the other hand, there are services that use AI to expose plagiarism. However, students could still pay someone to write a whole new paper for them, and it would be difficult to expose such treachery. We may one day have a robot that can instantaneously sniff out online sales contracts for school assignments, but it would be difficult to balance the activity of such a robot with the protection of our right to privacy. Perhaps our only hope is to count on divine intervention against those who graduate on the strength of grades obtained with fake assignments they have passed off as their own work.

Consumer services including robo-advisors and HFT emerged relatively early. The use of HFT began to expand starting around 2006 and had grown to account for over 60% of all stock trading volume in the U.S. by 2009.

HFT, as is evident from the name, is trading that takes place at rapid speeds, and is implemented not by people but by computers (programs). Making the transaction a few milliseconds faster than your competitor allows you to snap up the small residual margin. Even if each individual margin is miniscule, the large volume of such transactions means that the trader can make a big profit. This is another example

[6] As of 2018. Also, though not SNSs, Apple was established in 1976 and Amazon was established in 1994, while their payment services Apple Pay and Amazon Pay were introduced in 2014 and 2007, respectively.

[7] This will be discussed in more detail in Chapter 10, but Okina et al. (2017) goes into greater detail.

of the "atomization" that is possible as a result of fintech. Instead of traders gathering under a single roof on the trading floor and yelling across the floor to find trading partners, individual computers silently and rapidly execute transactions in the cloud.

In the past, HFT was implemented in parallel with transactions on the trading floor. But now New York stock market transactions are all conducted in the data center in Mahwah, New Jersey, and the famous trading floor scene seen on TV and other media is not much more than advertising material for companies that list on Wall Street.[8] But of course, the attractiveness of HFT declines with the decline in margins. The decline in margins could be short-lived if it is due to a decline in market volatility, but could be more protracted if it is due to more intense competition as more companies introduce HFT. Add to this the cost of computers and computer programs, and some even say that the golden age of HFT is behind us.

However, this does not signify a reversal of the trend of computers replacing traders. The Goldman Sachs Group, Inc., for instance, slashed the number of traders it employed from 500 to three, but now employs 9000 engineers instead.[9]

Consumer services that are expected to expand in the coming years include insurtech and robo-advisors. Insurtech is an abbreviation of "insurance technology" and stands for technologies or platforms that help optimize insurance services. About 75% of insurtech services are retail (targeting individual customers) non-life-insurance services. Globally, 46% of insurtech services are concentrated in the American market, with another 40% in Europe, the Middle East, and Africa. Only 14% of the insurtech market is in the Asia Pacific region, so there is scope for expansion here.[10] It is natural to consider that risk-averse people should not have to pay the same insurance premium as risk-seekers, so there is plenty of scope for an increase in demand for insurtech in Japan.

Robo-advisors are (AI-operated) robots that give asset management advice, and they were introduced for the first time in 2008. As of the end of 2016, the outstanding amount of investments made using robo-advisors in the U.S. was estimated at approximately USD 83 billion.[11] The figures for Europe have not yet been officially released, but some 2018 estimates suggest an outstanding amount of USD 15.5 billion.[12] In Japan, robo-advisors were introduced for the first time in 2016, and as of the end of February, 2018, the outstanding amount of asset investments using robo-advisors was no more than a combined total of JPY 122 billion for the big four domestic asset investment companies. It is noteworthy, though, that the amount had more than quadrupled within a year.[13]

---

[8]Meyer et al. (2018).

[9]Basak and Palmeri (2018).

[10]Catlin et al. (2017).

[11]Higashiyama (2018).

[12]https://www.statista.com/outlook/337/102/robo-advisors/europe (viewed on January 2, 2019). For a detailed analysis of asset management in the European Union including through robo-advisors, see European Union (2018).

[13]According to the March 24, 2018, *The Nikkei Online Edition*, https://www.nikkei.com/article/DGXMZO28548230U8A320C1EA1000/ (viewed on December 31, 2018).

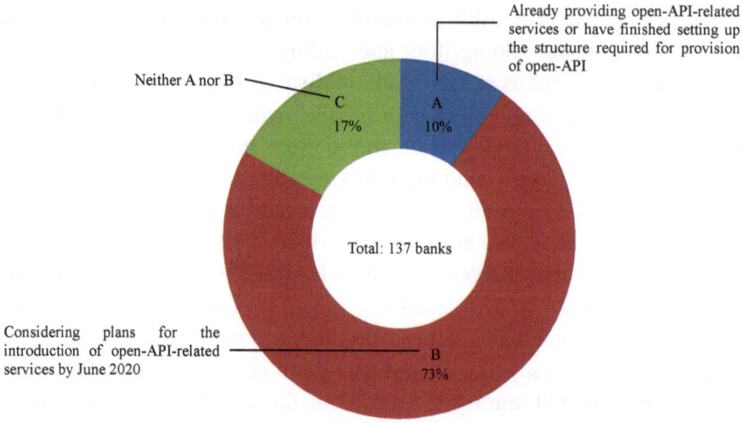

Note: Of the 137 Japanese banks that responded to the survey, 114 (83%) were either already providing, had finished setting up the structure for provision of, or considering plans that would enable the provision of open-API-related services by June 2020.

Source: Reproduction of a chart created by the Nippon Institute for Research Advancement (NIRA; http://www.nira.or.jp/outgoing/highlight/entry/n181218_912.html) based on an article entitled "Status of Initiatives Undertaken by the Japanese Bankers Association Toward the Advancement of Settlement Systems" by the Japanese Bankers Association.

Fig. 1 Results of a survey on the status of open API introduction or introduction plans by various banks (December 2017)

Let us move on to the fourth category—platforms. As part of its Future Investment Strategy 2018, the Japanese government included the formulation of "rules in response to the rise of the platform business model" as one of its "bold regulatory and institutional reforms" toward realizing a data-driven "Society 5.0." Specifically, it stated:

> As digital platform continues to dominate the market, the rise in businesses with platform business models has brought a need to sustain a competitive business environment. Data portability on selected platforms and open APIs ensure a transparent and level playing field inclusive of SMEs and venture firms. Fundamental principles regarding this new business model shall be finalized and rolled out during this year to ensure fairness to users and clarify corporate social responsibility of platform businesses. Deregulation aimed to stimulate innovation (relaxation of entry requirements, etc.) will be also considered.[14]

In the extract above, API stands for Application Programming Interface, and "open APIs" became available in some banks following the establishment of the Act for Partial Revision of the Banking Act, etc., in 2017 (Fig. 1).[15]

---

[14] The Prime Minister's Office (2018). "Platform businesses" include the aforementioned GAFA and other technology companies that provide platforms.

[15] For those who read Japanese, the website of the Japanese Bankers Association (link to the article in question provided in the bibliography) provides an easy-to-understand explanation of open APIs in banking. For more information on "open banking" to which open APIs pave the way, see Okina (2018).

Subsequently, in November 2018, the Ministry of Economy, Trade and Industry (METI) released an interim report (draft) compiled by the Study Group for the Improvement of the Trade Environment Involving Digital Platform Businesses, and simultaneously announced that it would compile a wide range of opinions based on the results of interviews of businesses and comments from the public.[16] Other examples of platforms include crowdfunding, the practice of funding projects by raising small amounts from a large number of people via the Internet, which has now become common in Japan. The sharing economy is a similar concept, and there is even an association for it in Japan called the Sharing Economy Association, Japan.[17] The idea of share houses, which is popular especially among young people, or share parking spaces, which are parking spaces shared by one or two cars, is no longer uncommon. However, while fintech services such as ridesharing and AirB&B are gaining great popularity the U.S. and countries that do not yet have fully-developed social infrastructures, there are arguments both for and against their spread in a country like Japan.

The various categories of fintech explained above all embody the three characteristics of fintech. The final section of this chapter deals with the macroeconomic implications of fintech, where again, the three characteristics will stand out.

4 Macroeconomic Implications of Fintech

This section will consider the macroeconomic aspects of fintech, from the perspective of the Abe administration's "three arrows" of economic policy. The section also alludes to some related potential future research topics and implications of fintech for security and the overall stability of the economy and society.

Let us first look at fintech's impact on monetary easing, which is the first of the three arrows. This relates to the effectiveness of the zero interest-rate policy (ZIRP) and the high usage of cash payments (low usage of electronic payments) in Japan. In a talk given at the University of Zurich in Switzerland on November 13, 2017, BOJ Governor Haruhiko Kuroda mentioned the "reversal interest rate" theory of Brunnermeier and Koby (2018), according to which, lowering policy interest rates beyond a certain level reverses the intended effect of monetary easing by negatively impacting financial intermediation.[18]

---

[16] METI (2018). METI had also released "Japan's FinTech Vision" in May 2017, the details of which are available in METI (2017). In 2016, the Strategic Council for AI Technology was established, the details of which can be found on the Cabinet Office website (link provided in the bibliography).

[17] https://sharing-economy.jp/ja/ (viewed on December 31, 2018).

[18] Bank of Japan (2017). Mr. Kuroda stated that "In Japan's case, financial institutions have a solid capital base and credit costs have fallen sharply, so that at present their financial intermediation function is not impaired. However, because the impact of the low interest rate environment on financial institutions' soundness is cumulative, the Bank will continue to pay attention to this risk as well."

According to the reversal interest rate theory, because the interest rate on deposits cannot be lower than zero (this would lead to people simply keeping their money in cash as the interest rate on cash is zero), the narrowing profit margin between the interest rate on deposits and the interest rate on loans would put bank lending operations in jeopardy and cancel out a low policy rate's expansionary effect on the economy. The economist John Maynard Keynes called this the "liquidity trap," and the problem has also come to be known by the term "zero lower bound" (ZLB) in recent years.

Assenmacher and Krogstrup (2018) consider the possibility that this situation could be ameliorated by the fact that the interest rate on cash (notes and coins) turns negative with the increased use of electronic money. By contrast, Tomura (2017) says, "If banks are charged an excessive fee on their reserve deposits following a deepening of the negative interest rate, city banks could shift to large private settlement systems that use government bonds as security."[19]

In connection with monetary policy in general, if cryptocurrencies were to become more widely used and the private sector were to become involved in supplying money to the economy, this would naturally give rise to many old-yet-new questions, namely, should the rate of increase in money supply be maintained at a fixed percentage or change according to circumstances (rules versus discretion), would there be an upper limit to the amount of money that could be supplied as in the case of the Bitcoin, how would exchange rate stability be maintained, and so on.

While not directly related to monetary policy, there is also the question of who would, based on what legal grounds, be the lender of last resort. In this day and age, when non-financial private-sector corporations provide payment "interfaces" and "settlement mediums," it is becoming increasingly important for financial supervision and regulation to be function-based rather than entity-based.[20]

In connection with fintech's implications for fiscal policy, the second of the three arrows, recall the policy right after the 2019 consumption tax hike, through which those who used electronic payment methods were paid back the equivalent of the increased tax in the form of "purchasing points" and cashbacks. Crowdfunding sites have already simplified tax filing procedures related to tax-deductible donations and Hometown Tax schemes. Whether or not fintech facilitates tax evasion and/or the avoidance of inheritance tax is an interesting topic for research.

---

[19] According to Tomura (2017), "Ordinarily, the central bank's operating expenses come from the profit margins on short-term government bonds and cash. If there is no cash, the central bank would become dependent on the government to provide its budget, which could hurt its independence in implementing monetary policy." Costa and De Grauwe (2001) also makes the same point.

[20] As discussed again below in connection with security, in order to analyze scenarios where payment methods issued by private entities are used internationally, it is important to consider payment "interfaces" and "settlement mediums" separately. It must be noted here that the first financial supervisory body in the world to point out the need for function-based regulation rather than entity-based regulation was Japan's FSA. For details regarding these points, see Kaji (2018) and Kaji (2019). Carstens (2018) explains these concepts using a "money flower," which highlights four key properties on the supply side of money, namely issuers, forms, accessibility, and transfer mechanisms.

When it comes to fintech's impact on deregulation, the third of the three arrows, technology has given rise to "reg tech" (regulation technology). According to NIRA (2018), in addition to bringing down administrative costs, regtech has the potential to lower the cost of complying with regulations. It could also enable feedback from the private sector as to how to optimize regulations. Here again, the fixed notions of "public versus private" are obviously being shaken up.

In connection with economic stability overall, the concept of "singularity" is well-known in the context of fintech's impact on employment. For instance, even when the government implements expansionary fiscal policy (public works), the new jobs created may be performed by AI, preventing an increase in human employment.

One must take care to correctly understand the meaning of singularity. Alpha Go is famous as an AI program that has already surpassed humans as a Go player. However, AI is still far from surpassing human intelligence when we take into account the various human capabilities including metaphysical knowledge regarding our own physical or mental state. Still, thanks in part to big data, AI can replace humans when it comes to jobs that can be coded in the language of a computer program, and this could have very grave implications for the issues of wealth distribution and income inequality.

From the perspective of economic policy effectiveness, when privately issued currencies begin to coexist with currencies issued by the state,[21] all the questions that economists have traditionally dealt with still apply. For instance, how effectiveness of policy is affected by whether a fixed or floating exchange rate system is adopted; whether or not a region using the privately issued currency is an optimum currency area (OCA); which of several parallel currencies would be the key currency (competing currencies, "bad money drives out good"); and so on. In the context of OCAs, the macroeconomic impact of an app (payment interface) rather than a currency (a settlement medium) being shared internationally has not yet been studied.

In fintech, one of the interesting implications of currencies being issued by private entities is the separation of a currency's "medium of exchange" versus "store of value" functions. The separation of these two functions was seriously discussed in Europe following the European sovereign debt crisis in an attempt to avoid bringing financial intermediary functions to a standstill caused by balance-sheet impairment resulting from asset mismanagement. In the end, such a separation was not realized. However, considering how severely financial crises can impact economic activity, it might be helpful to attempt the separation using electronic methods of payment. Consider, for instance, a digital currency that is not allowed to be held for more than a day, and is used only as a medium of exchange, never as a store of value. Such a currency could be similar to the US Dollar in Japan before the revision of the Foreign Exchange and Foreign Trade Act in 1980—a currency that cannot be obtained without providing proof that it is to be used for the purpose of a transaction.

---

[21] According to Dabrowski and Janikowski (2018), looking back at the history of privately issued currencies, such currencies have never supplanted the state-issued currency except in times of hyperinflation, financial crises, political turmoil, wars, and other emergencies. However, according to Prof. Naoyuki Iwashita, the author of Chapter 3 of this book, cryptocurrencies are not currencies but IOUs.

The procedures for verification could become too onerous to be practical, but perhaps they could be simplified through the use of AI and fintech.

Another idea could be to locally issue currencies that can be used only for the purchase of daily essentials. When it comes to local currencies used for small transactions, there already exist examples such as Pasmo and Suica, which have an upper limit of JPY 20,000 on payments. A time may come when it becomes difficult to believe that we ever had large-scale and systemically important financial intermediaries and used currencies as mediums of exchange and stores of value at the same time.

Note that even in the case of currencies that are used merely as mediums of exchange, the possibility of capital gain/loss in terms of their relative value compared with commodities or other means of storing value cannot be ruled out. In a crisis, the exchange rates between currencies used as mediums of exchange and those used as stores of value would fluctuate wildly. Whenever an economy receives a shock, some variable (often the price) inevitably acts as a shock absorber and suffers volatility in order for the economy to arrive at a new equilibrium.

Even if we succeed in stabilizing the macroeconomy, there would be no point to the exercise if our lives and livelihoods were at risk due to threats to our security. Fintech is capable of causing fundamental changes in this area too. As already mentioned, it is very easy to weaponize AI. For instance, loading an extremely small drone with a deadly toxin, flying it into a crowd, and releasing the toxin would enable the killing of several, or in some cases, large numbers of people without having to use massive weapons. It would be similarly possible to commit mass murder by hacking into the brains of self-driving cars and other vehicles. If such things became possible, the ability to dominate the world would shift from the hands of countries that have conventional military power, to high-tech companies (or countries) with advanced AI technology. This would be tantamount to the creation of a major military industry, totally independent of the existing defense industry, which has close ties to the Pentagon. Moreover, unlike in the case of missiles, AI-based weapons would not need enormous silos or launch pads. Just as the fintech industry evolved in protest against the financial industry in the East Coast of the U.S., it is not unthinkable to see a high-tech industry evolve in protest against the policies of a reigning government. Attacking one's own government would result in a coup d'état or a civil war, but attacking another country is an equal possibility. War with the Islamic State (IS), an unrecognized proto-state, is already a reality. It is possible that the wars of the future will more commonly take place not between nations but between entities that have the requisite technologies, or between a nation and an entity with the technologies.

There are other types of potential security threats. The election outcome of the head of a country can be influenced by external agents through the use of social media trolls, by emotionally manipulating voters. There is no guarantee that these tactics could not be used to elect military regimes that 49% of the people did not want.

It is also possible, without the use of weapons, to deliver a catastrophic blow to a country's economy by taking control of the currency that is its medium of exchange or of its health-care systems. If currency is supplied electronically, transactions and economic activity can be brought to a standstill simply by "switching off" the currency app or the supply of cryptocurrency.[22] Because of this, it will become necessary to regulate foreign funding and ownership of private entities that supply cryptocurrencies as mediums of exchange or provide apps that act as payment interfaces, in the same way that core infrastructure industries are regulated.

Even if such services are provided by domestic companies, regulations regarding their acquisition by foreign enterprises will become necessary. In this way, there will arise an increasing number of restrictions of the free movement of capital that economists generally advocate. There will also be additional points to be considered when it comes to free trade. In 2018, the United States Department of Defense banned the use of security cameras made in China due to concerns that these cameras may have secret built-in mechanisms for sending back to China the images captured in sensitive security locations.

In the area of health, the use of AI in cancer detection is becoming more popular, but if the people developing the AI software had malicious intent, it would not be impossible for them to, say, develop a program that failed to report the presence of cancer in specific racial groups. The same can be said regarding food safety. Before we worry about the ethicality of AI, it is important to think about how we can make sure there are no problems with the ethicality of the people writing these AI programs.

Finally, some thoughts on income inequality and redistribution of wealth in the context of singularity discussed above. Will broad-based use of fintech widen disparities and worsen the capitalistic impasse, or will it help narrow the disparities and lead to a breakthrough? This is a very important question. Depending on the extent to which fintech turns conventional wisdom on its head, ideas that had never before seen the light of day or activities that had never before been considered economically viable could become the source of high incomes, status, or fame. On the other hand, people who cannot afford the education or training needed for jobs that cannot be replaced by AI could become alienated and dissatisfied, leading to economic and social destabilization.

There is no question that learning about fintech now will have a significant impact on one's life going forward, as will continuing to learn about fintech for life.

---

[22]As Kaji (2019) explains, there are two aspects to financial intermediation, one being to provide an "interface" for transactions and the other being to provide the "medium of settlement." Cash (currency notes and coins) has both of these aspects. In the case of electronic settlements, the app is the interface, while the cryptocurrency used for the transaction is the medium of settlement. The greater the number of alternatives available in terms of both the interface and the medium, the smaller the impact when the provision of one or other is stopped. For instance, people would have a way out if they could pay by credit card in the event of their smartphone app not working. The threats to security are the greatest when a large part of a country's financial settlements is administered through a single interface, using a single medium of settlement, especially if both these services are provided by a single foreign company.

5 Epilogue—The Importance of Trust[23]

Legend has it that young Matsudaira Takechiyo and Zen master Taigen Sessai had the following conversation sometime in the Sengoku Period (1467–1615 C.E.). Sessai told Takechiyo that, when asked by a disciple about the nature of polity, Confucius explained that a nation must have weapons, food, and trust. The disciple had asked Confucius which one he would abandon if he could have only two of the three, and Sessai posed the same question to Takechiyo. Takechiyo's response was "weapons," the same as Confucius' response. Sessai then asked which one Takechiyo would abandon if he had to choose one of the remaining two – food and trust. Remembering his hungry days of captivity in Owari province when he had to share a small amount of food with two other children, Takechiyo replied that he would choose food over trust. Sessai then taught him that "trust" was the only reason the three children had been able to share the food and survive. With food but without trust, human beings would descend to the level of animals in the wild.

This story about the importance of trust is quite famous, and is frequently framed and hung up on walls. However, the word "trust" would seem to have a wider connotation for those of us who pursue abstract, invisible things for a living. Of weapons, food, and trust, trust is the only one that is invisible.

As of 2018, we are already seeing jobs being taken over by increasingly sophisticated AI. The jobs that are being replaced by AI have a common feature—they involve tasks easily encoded as AI programs as well as big data availability. For instance, a soldier's job formulating strategies to defeat opponents, or food service industry jobs that involve developing recipes, procuring ingredients, cooking, and waiting on or billing customers.

The question, then, is—is AI capable of thinking about invisible things? The answer at present is no, and it will probably remain no even in the year 2030. AI is not capable of discovering tasks that have not been given to it. Why am I here? What is the purpose of life? What can I do to make the world a better place? What can I do that will contribute to the improvement of society? These are examples of questions AI is incapable of asking or answering, so jobs that require thinking about these invisibles are unlikely to be taken over by AI. In fact, AI may be forcing us to rethink what it is to be a human.

In future, AI may become capable of thinking about invisible things on its own. If and when this happens, humans and AI must work together to understand the importance of invisible things and put them to good use for the well-being of humanity (and of AI). The task is up to us.

It is for this reason that we continue to teach, in direct and indirect ways, the importance of the invisibles to our students, who are expected in a few years' time to work in a world of profit maximization and cost minimization.

[23]This section is a reproduction, with the kind permission of the TM Forum, of an opinion piece titled "AI-IoT Society 2030 as I See It" in the TM Forum bulletin. Takechiyo is the childhood name of Shogun Ieyasu Tokugawa.

References

Assenmacher K, Krogstrup S (2018) Monetary policy with negative interest rates: decoupling cash from electronic money. IMF Working Paper WP/18/191. https://www.imf.org/en/Publications/WP/Issues/2018/08/27/MonetaryPolicy-with-Negative-Interest-Rates-Decoupling-Cash-from-Electronic-Money-46076. Accessed 3 Jan 2018

Bank of Japan (2017) Quantitative and qualitative monetary easing and economic theory (Japanese translation of lecture given at the University of Zurich, Switzerland). https://www.boj.or.jp/announcements/press/koen_2017/ko171114a.htm/. Accessed 3 Jan 2019 (in Japanese)

Basak S, Palmeri C (2018) A goldman trading desk that once had 500 people is down to three. https://www.bloomberg.com/news/articles/2018–04-30/goldman-trading-desk-that-once-had-500-people-is-down-to-three. Accessed 2 Jan 2019

Brunnermeier MK, Koby Y (2018) The reversal interest rate. https://scholar.princeton.edu/markus/publications/reversal-interest-rate-effective-lower-bound-monetary-policy. Accessed 3 Jan 2019

Cabinet Office (date of publication unknown) Strategic Council for AI Technology. https://www8.cao.go.jp/cstp/tyousakai/jinkochino/index.html. Accessed 3 Jan 2019. (in Japanese)

Carstens A (2018) Money in the digital age: what role for central banks? https://www.bis.org/speeches/sp180206.pdf. Accessed 3 Jan 2018

Catlin T, Lorenz JT, Münstermann B, Olesen B, Ricciardi V (2017) Insurtech–the threat that inspires. McKinsey & Company, Mar 2017. https://www.mckinsey.com/industries/financial-services/our-insights/insurtech-the-threat-that-inspires. Accessed 30 Dec 2018

Costa CS, De Grauwe P (2001) Monetary policy in a cashless society. https://www.researchgate.net/publication/4752639_Monetary_Policy_in_a_Cashless_Society. Accessed 5 Jan 2018

Dabrowski M, Janikowski L (2018) Can virtual currencies challenge the dominant position of sovereign currencies? http://bruegel.org/2018/12/can-virtual-currencies-challenge-the-dominant-position-of-sovereign-currencies/. Accessed 3 Jan 2018

European Union (2018) Distribution systems of retail investment products across the European Union. https://ec.europa.eu/info/sites/info/files/180425-retail-investment-products-distribution-systems_en.pdf. Accessed 31 Dec 2018

Fujita T (2018) Chinese Fintech reaches a turning point. RIM: Pacific Business and Industries, 18, Nos. 68–69. https://www.jri.co.jp/MediaLibrary/file/report/rim/pdf/10458.pdf. Accessed 31 Dec 2018 (in Japanese)

Higashiyama M (2018) Hints for popularization in Japan from robo-advisor users in the US. Nomura Research Institute. http://fis.nri.co.jp/ja-JP/publication/kinyu_itf/backnumber/2018/01/201801_6.html. Accessed 31 Dec 2018 (in Japanese)

Iwasaki K (2018) Emergence of Fintech in Southeast Asia and expectations for the resolution of fiscal issues. RIM: Pacific Business and Industries 18(68). https://www.jri.co.jp/MediaLibrary/file/report/rim/pdf/10320.pdf. Accessed 31 Dec 2018. (in Japanese)

Japanese Banker Association (date of publication unknown) What is Open AI? https://www.zenginkyo.or.jp/article/tag-g/9797/. Accessed 31 Dec 2018 (in Japanese)

Kaji S (2018) Electronic settlements and financial regulation, Paper presented at the 2nd CAG-KGRI Workshop, Tokyo

Kaji S (2019) Electronic settlements and financial regulation, forthcoming. In: Kikuchi T, Sakuragawa M (eds) Financial Cooperation in East Asia, RSIS Monograph, S. Rajaratnam School of International Studies

Meyer G, Bullock N, Rennison J (2018) How high-frequency trading hit a speed bump. Financial Times, 1 Jan 2018. https://www.ft.com/content/d81f96ea-d43c-11e7-a303–9060cb1e5f44. Accessed 30 Dec 2018

Ministry of Economy, Trade and Industry (2017) FinTech Visoin. http://www.meti.go.jp/press/2017/05/20170508001/20170508001.html. Accessed 31 Dec 2018 (in Japanese)

Ministry of Economy, Trade and Industry (2018) Draft interim report of the Study Group on the Improvement of the Trade Environment Involving Digital Platform Businesses. http://www.meti.go.jp/press/2018/11/20181105005/20181105005.html. Accessed 31 Dec 2018 (in Japanese)

Nippon Institute for Research Advancement (NIRA) (2018) RegTech: The dawn of a new direction for regulation. https://www.nira.or.jp/pdf/vision35.pdf. Accessed 30 Dec 2018 (in Japanese)

Okina Y, Yanagawa N, Iwashita N eds (2017) The future of blockchains—How will finance, industry and society change? Nikkei Publishing Inc. (in Japanese)

Okina Y, Yanagawa N, Iwashita N (2018) Banking in the open banking era. NIRA Opinion Paper. http://www.nira.or.jp/pdf/opinion35.pdf. Accessed 31 Dec 2018 (in Japanese)

Prime Minister's Office, Japan (2018) Future investment strategies 2018—Changes towards a society 5.0 and data-driven society. https://www.kantei.go.jp/jp/singi/keizaisaisei/pdf/miraitousi2018_zentai.pdf. Accessed 31 Dec 2018 (in Japanese)

Takasaki S (2017) Fintech will change the future of Africa. JETRO Area Report. https://www.jetro.go.jp/ext_images/_Reports/01/b65e34cd54825211/20160116.pdf. Accessed 31 Dec 2018 (in Japanese)

Thornhill J (2018) Lessons from history on the dangers of data. Financial Times. https//www.ft.com/stream/33a9ea49–00d8-4bff-9b83-8ca7ebcle614. Accessed 31 Dec 2018

Tomura H (2017) Electronic payments and the finance system from the perspective of the economics of payments. Internal Lecture Meeting by External Experts at the Policy Research Institute, Ministry of Finance, 14 Nov 2017. https://www.mof.go.jp/pri/research/seminar/fy2017/lm20171114.pdf. Accessed 4 Jan 2019 (in Japanese)

Chapter 2
Understanding Fintech from a Macroeconomic Perspective

Naoyuki Yoshino

1 Growth of Fintech and Need for Data Analysis

If students of economics or finance want to work in financial technology (fintech), they must first acquire at least a basic understanding of statistics and econometrics. They must also know about and correctly understand the state of the economy, the efficacy of economic policies, and so on. Further, in addition to the flow of capital within the country, they must understand why foreign exchange rates fluctuate on a daily basis in the international financial markets and how this is driven by flows of trade and capital. Without this, they cannot invest in foreign assets.

Below, I will first discuss how fintech is changing the method of evaluating companies. Following that, I will discuss the current state of the Japanese economy and the effectiveness of its policies, and finally reveal why it is necessary to seek investment opportunities abroad.

In the past, doctors used stethoscopes to listen to the internal sounds of our bodies, and a good doctor was one who was skilled at telling where the malaise was simply by listening to those sounds. However, medical science has now advanced to the extent that doctors can use endoscopes inserted into our bodies to actually see what is going on inside and diagnose disease.

A very similar phenomenon is taking place in the financial world as well. In the past, it was important for banks to use their judgement in determining whom to give loans to. A bank official would, for instance, meet with the president of a small- to medium-sized enterprise (SME), find out about the company's management policies or the details of its business, evaluate the company's future potential, and determine whether or not to provide a loan. Further, having given the loan, the bank would have to track the company's business performance by checking on its factories' production status, keeping an eye on its customers' behavior, and generally making sure it is

N. Yoshino (✉)
Economics, Keio University, Tokyo, Japan
e-mail: yoshino@econ.keio.ac.jp

S. Kaji et al. (eds.), *The Economics of Fintech*,
https://doi.org/10.1007/978-981-33-4913-1_2

doing well. The way banks screened companies was very similar to how doctors used a stethoscope. They used their sense of judgement to determine whether or not to give a loan, and if yes, then for what period and at what interest rate, how much collateral the borrower should pledge, and so on.

However, in the age of fintech, with the large amount of data that has become available, even a scholar such as myself, who specializes in finance but is not a financial industry professional, can look at the data collected and evaluate the performance of a company to some extent. Even scholars such as myself have become capable of understanding the state of a company through data analysis.

Another development is that financial institutions have begun to employ a large number of people with science and technology backgrounds. Such people use their understanding of quantitative models to invent new financial products and investment methods. However, not many of them have a clear understanding of how the economy works. This is where those with a background in economics come in. Since many students of economics also have an understanding of mathematics, they are in a good position both to understand the analyses of their mathematically oriented colleagues and also to translate what customers seek from financial products into abstract mathematical terms for them. People with economics backgrounds possess the ability to connect people with engineering and humanities backgrounds, and using this ability will help strengthen Japanese finance.

As an example, I am currently conducting joint research with scholars from the science and engineering faculties of The University of Tokyo. As you may know, Japan has won the contract for India's first high-speed railway project. My research involves studying the economic impact of investing in infrastructure such as bullet trains and roads, and my colleagues from the Tokyo University Faculty of Engineering are estimating the same using a different method. However, because of my economics background, I have a better understanding of economic variables and can point my colleagues in the right direction in terms of suggesting which economic variables should be included in the analysis. This results in very productive collaborative research.

In the future, I hope that students of economics such as yourselves can serve to bridge the gap between science and humanities professionals in whatever career you choose, whether in the financial industry or elsewhere. And to that end, I urge you to study econometrics and statistics well, in order to communicate effectively with colleagues from science and engineering fields.

Let us use an example to see how big data enables credit rating even for SMEs. Traditionally, bank officials had to rely on their experience and judgment to evaluate SMEs as candidates for loans in terms of whether they were performing well, what their future prospects were, and so on.

However, with the enormous amount of data now available and the development of fintech, it has become possible to more-objectively analyze the performance of companies seeking loans. In Japan, there are companies that gather corporate information and build credit risk databases (CRDs) to analyze the credit risk of borrower companies. These databases include millions of data points, which are then analyzed to compute a company's probability of default (PD). Financial institutions must make decisions on whether or not to lend to a particular company based on whether that company is a safe borrower or a likely defaulter, because lending to companies that are likely to fail will negatively impact the financial institution's own performance. The collected data is analyzed using multivariate analysis techniques such as probit, logit, or cluster analysis.

Having analyzed the data, the next step is to understand the results. In other words, even after a data scientist has analyzed the data and produced results, you still need to understand the method of analysis used before you can evaluate a company based on the results. It is in such contexts that the ability of economics graduates to act as bridges between science and humanities graduates comes into play.

In the past, in the financial industry, it often happened that managers, who tended to have humanities backgrounds, could not really understand the mathematical analyses performed and reported by data scientists. Moreover, there was even a time when some top-level managers of regional banks were critical of data analysis, asserting that statistics had nothing to do with banking.

Let us take a slightly detailed look at an example of corporate analysis using big data.

Chart 1 shows 11 variables including assets, cash, sales, and profitability gathered from corporate data (not pertaining to Japanese companies).

No.	Symbol	Definition	Category
1	Equity_TL	Equity (book value)/total liabilities	Leverage
2	TL_Tassets	Total liabilities/total assets	
3	Cash_Tassets	Cash/total assets	Liquidity
4	WoC_Tassets	Working capital/total assets	
5	Cash_Sales	Cash/net sales	
6	EBIT_Sales	Ebit/sales	Profitability
7	Rinc_Tassets	Retained earnings/total assets	
8	Ninc_Sales	Net income/sales	
9	EBIT_IE	Ebit/interest expenses	Coverage
10	AP_Sales	Account payable/sales	Activity
11	AR_TL	Account receivable/total liabilities	

Notes: Retained earnings refers to the percentage of net earnings not paid out as dividends, but retained by the company to be reinvested in its core business or to pay debt; it is recorded under shareholders' equity in the balance sheet. Ebit refers to earnings before interest and taxes. Account payable refers to an accounting entry that represents an entity's obligation to pay off a short-term debt to its creditors; the accounts payable entry is found on a balance sheet under current liabilities. Account receivable refers to money owed by customers (individuals or corporations) to another entity in exchange for goods or services that have been delivered or used, but not yet paid for; receivables usually come in the form of operating lines of credit and are usually due within a relatively short time period, ranging from a few days to 1 year.

Chart 1 Eleven variables gathered from corporate data (Yoshino and Taghizadeh-Hesary 2016), "Analysis of Credit Ratings for Small and Medium Sized Enterprises: Evidence from Asia," in *The Asian Development Review*, Vol. 32, No. 2, pp.18-37). *Source* Yoshino and Taghizadeh-Hesary (2019)

Variables (Financial Ratios)	Component			
	Z1	Z2	Z3	Z4
Equity_TL	0.009	0.068	0.113	**0.705**
TL_Tassets	−0.032	**−0.878**	0.069	−0.034
Cash_Tassets	−0.034	−0.061	**0.811**	0.098
WoC_Tassets	−0.05	**0.762**	0.044	0.179
Cash_Sales	**−0.937**	0.021	0.083	0.009
EBIT_Sales	**0.962**	0.008	0.024	−0.004
Rinc_Tassets	0.014	**0.877**	0.015	−0.178
Ninc_Sales	**0.971**	−0.012	0.015	0.014
EBIT_IE	0.035	0.045	**0.766**	−0.098
AP_Sales	**−0.731**	−0.017	−0.037	−0.016
AR_TL	0.009	−0.041	−0.104	**0.725**

Chart 2 Results of a factor analysis conducted using 11 variables. *Source* Yoshino and Taghizadeh-Hesary (2014)

Chart 2 shows the results of a factor analysis conducted using these 11 variables. Variables with eigenvalues of 1 or more are considered statistically significant, so in this example, the four components Z1 to Z4 are statistically significant.

The important variables, highlighted in bold, are the main constituents of each component, and in the case of Z1 (the first component), Sales are an important constituent variable. Tassets (total assets) are an important constituent of Z2 (the second component), Cash (liquidity) is an important constituent of Z3 (the third component), and TL (total liabilities) are an important constituent variable of Z4 (the fourth component).

Figure 1, which uses components Z2 and Z3 from Chart 2 to divide companies into various groups, shows the results of a cluster analysis.[1] This is an example of how big data is used for corporate analysis. Group 1 shows safer SMEs, while Group 3 shows risker SMEs. Thus, big data analysis provides a certain statistic evaluation and grouping of SMEs that financial institutions could take into account in their loan-making decisions.

2 Japan's Expanding Fiscal Deficit Problem and Theoretical and Empirical Analyses Aimed at Solving It

Evsey Domar's Domar condition,[2] which compares the current interest rate and the economic growth rate, is often discussed when talking about how a country can

[1] Yoshino and Taghizadeh-Hesary (2014).

[2] A theorem that proposes a condition for debt sustainability. According to it, economic collapse can be avoided if the nominal GDP growth rate exceeds the nominal interest rate in a condition where the primary balance is in equilibrium.

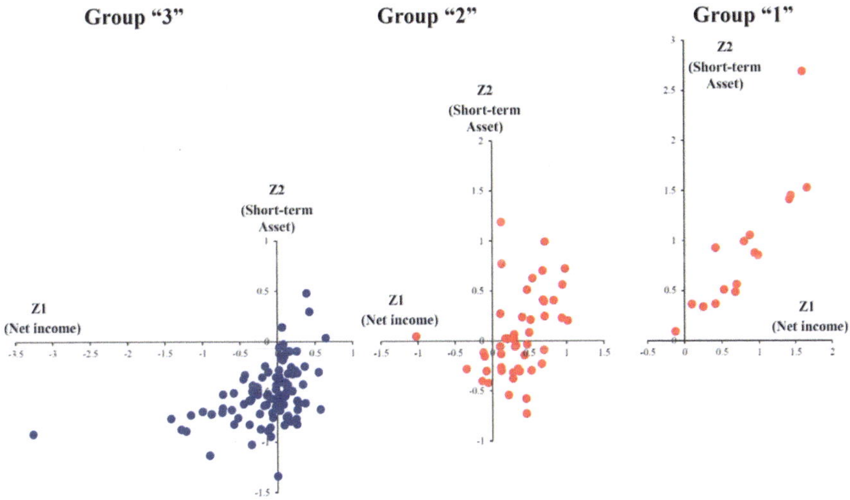

Fig. 1 Grouping based on principal component analysis (Z1–Z2). *Source* Yoshino and Taghizadeh-Hesary (eds) (2020), *Unlocking SME Finance in Asia*, Routledge. *Note* Group 1 = healthiest SMEs; group 2 = in-between SMEs; group 3 = least healthy SMEs

avoid economic collapse despite a growing fiscal deficit. The Domar condition can be calculated using the government's budget constraint (Eq. 1 in Fig. 2) and is derived solely based on the condition of government bond issuance (by the government) as a consequence of a fiscal deficit

The Domar condition in Eq. (2) of Fig. 2 shows that if the interest rate (r) is larger than the growth rate of the economy (η), the budget deficits will keep on rising, leading to budget explosion. On the other hand, if the interest rate (r) is lower than the growth rate of the economy (η), the budget deficits will converge. Thus, Domar

The Domar condition and Bohn's condition are often used to determine whether budget deficits are sustainable or not. The Domar condition is obtained from the government budget constraint as follows.

$$G_t + r_t B_{t-1} = \Delta B_t + T_t \qquad (1)$$

Equation (1) states that government spending (G_t) + interest payments ($r_t B_{t-1}$) = new issue of government bonds (ΔB_t) + tax revenue (T_t).

Dividing equation (1) by GDP (Y_t) and rewriting equation (1), we obtain the Domar condition:

$$b_t - b_{t-1} = \frac{(r_t - \eta_t)}{1+\eta_t} b_{t-1} + g_t - t_t \qquad (2)$$

where $b_t = B_t / Y_t$, $\eta_t = \Delta Y_t / Y_t$, $g_t = G_t / Y_t$, and $t_t = T_t / Y_t$.

Fig. 2 Derivation of Domar condition (Yoshino et al. 2019), "Optimal fiscal policy rule for achieving fiscal sustainability: the Japanese case," in *Global Business and Economic Review*, Vol. 21, No. 2) compares the interest rate and the growth rate of the economy to judge the stability of the national budget.

There is an assured global demand for U.S. Treasury securities because the U.S. dollar is the world's key currency and investors around the world have confidence in the American economy. Furthermore, US Treasury securities have a thick secondary market that attracts investors from around the world. In other words, Treasury securities can be issued to a certain extent without worrying about the level of demand for them within the U.S. itself. This is the reason Domar derived the condition for government bond market stabilization from the government's budget constraint, which expresses the condition for government bond issuance.

Many scholars and economists use the Domar Condition to measure the possibility of a country going bankrupt and defaulting on its debt as its government bond rating becomes lower as bond issuance expands. In Fig. 2, the right-hand side of Eq. 2 compares the current interest rate (r) and current economic growth rate (η)—i.e., interest rate minus economic growth rate (r- η)—and derives the condition that a country's economy will collapse if its interest rate is higher than its economic growth rate. However, in the case of countries other than the U.S., the level of demand for their bonds plays an important role in stabilizing their government bond markets.

Figure 3a, b compare the Japanese Government Bond (JGB) and Greece Government Bond (GGB) markets based on supply and demand trends.[3] The y-axis represents the interest rate while the x-axis represents government bond supply and demand. The vertical lines represent the issuance of government bonds. If there is a fiscal deficit, the government has to issue bonds regardless of how high or low the interest rate is. This is why the issuance of government bonds is represented as vertical lines.

Given that the y-axis represents the interest rate, the demand for government bonds will tend to be a positive slope. In other words, the higher the interest rate on a bond, the stronger the demand for it from economic entities. Graph (a) represents the JGB market, while Graph (b) represents the GGB market.

Figure 3 shows the supply and demand trends of both JGB and GGB. In the case of Japan, interest rates are declining because the demand for JGBs continues to rise. By contrast, the demand for GGBs declined sharply following the crisis, when foreign owners sold GGB and fled to other markets. This dealt a significant blow, given that the foreign ownership ratio in the case of GGBs is quite high compared with JGBs—around 70% in 2013. The graph reflects the increase in interest rates as compensation for risk amid a decline in demand for GGB from investors.

In the case of Japan, JGB issuance is increasing, but demand for JGBs is increasing even faster, so the interest rates are declining. Until recently, banks, insurance companies, and pension funds were major buyers, but recently, the Bank of Japan (BOJ) has been buying up large volumes of JGBs, pushing demand further to the right and causing the interest rates on JGBs to become negative.

[3] Yoshino and Yamakami (2017), pp. 133.

a

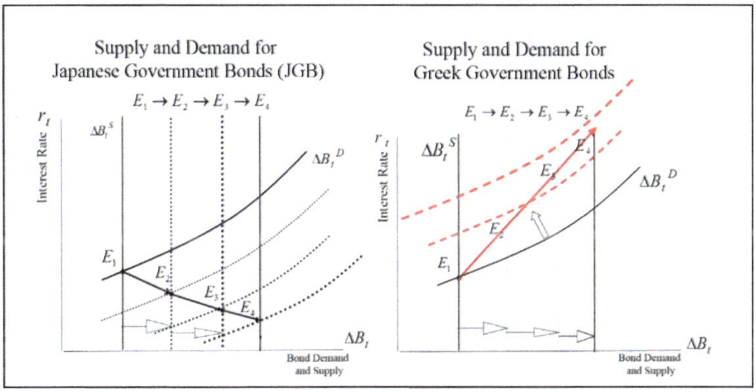

b

Holders of Japanese Government Bonds	% of Total	Holders of Greek Government Bonds	% of Total
Bank and postal savings	45	Overseas investors	33
Life and non-life insurance	20	Domestic investors	21
Public pension funds	10	European Central Bank	18
Private pension funds	4	Bilateral loans	14
Bank of Japan	8	Social pension funds	6
Overseas investors	5	International Monetary Fund	5
Households	5	Greek domestic funds	3
Others	3		

Fig. 3 **a** Government bond markets of Japan and Greece, **b** Holders of Japanese and Greek Government Bonds. *Source* Yoshino et al. (2019)

In the case of Japan, close to 90% of JGBs are owned by domestic investors in recent years. Consequently, the JGB market is stable, thanks to the sufficient domestic demand, which has maintained low interest rates.

Meanwhile, as Fig. 3b shows, close to two-third of GGBs are owned by foreign investors. When there emerged concerns that the Greek government might be unable to repay its debts, foreign investors simply sold off their GGB holdings. This resulted in a decline in demand for GGBs, as the graph (Fig. 2a) shows, shifting the demand curve to the left, causing the GGB interest rate to rise sharply, and pushing Greece into an economic collapse. Figure 4 shows the government bond interest rate trends in Greece and Japan. Note how the sharp rise in GGB interest rates contrasts with the stability of JGB interest rates.

Henning Bohn proposed an important condition for fiscal sustainability. Under this condition, it is considered important to monitor the trend of the primary balance (the difference between the government's income and expenditure, excluding interest

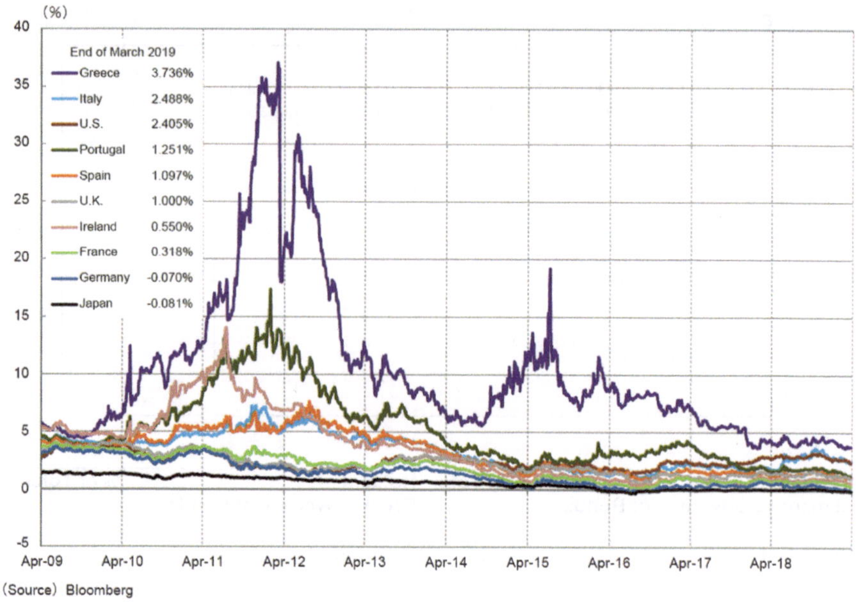

Fig. 4 Sharp rise in GGB interest rates versus stability of JGB interest rates (Debt Management Report, 2019, Ministry of Finance Japan)

rate payments). To put it differently, Bohn's condition is the condition for preventing the primary balance from straying onto a divergent path and is derived, again, from the equation related to government bond issuance (i.e., the government's budget constraint [Eq. 1 of Fig. 5]), without taking into account the demand for government bonds.

By contrast, a model that considers both the supply of and demand for government bonds would draw the conclusion indicated in Fig. 5, that fiscal stability cannot be maintained unless government income and expenditure (including interest rate payment expenditure) are considered as simultaneous equations.

Figure 5 shows how considering the (G_t-G_{t-1}) and (T_t-T_{t-1}) equations as simultaneous equations can help achieve fiscal stability. Variables including (i) outstanding government debt as a ratio of GDP, (ii) annual fiscal deficit as a ratio of GDP, and (iii) the GDP gap, which expresses the state of the economy, need to be taken into

$$G_t - G_{t-1} = \alpha_1 (B_t - B_t^*) + \alpha_2 (\Delta B_t - \Delta B_t^*) + \alpha_3 (Y_t - Y_t^f)$$

$$T_t - T_{t-1} = \beta_1 (B_t - B_t^*) + \beta_2 (\Delta B_t - B_t^*) + \beta_3 (Y_t - Y_t^f)$$

The Revised Bohn's Condition is as follows:

$$PB_t - PB_{t-1} = (\alpha_1 - \beta_1)(B_t - B_t^*) + (\alpha_2 - \beta_2)(\Delta B_t - \Delta B_t^*) + (\alpha_3 - \beta_3)(Y_t - Y_t^f)$$

Fig. 5 Considering the condition for fiscal stability through simultaneous equations that take into account both government income and expenditure

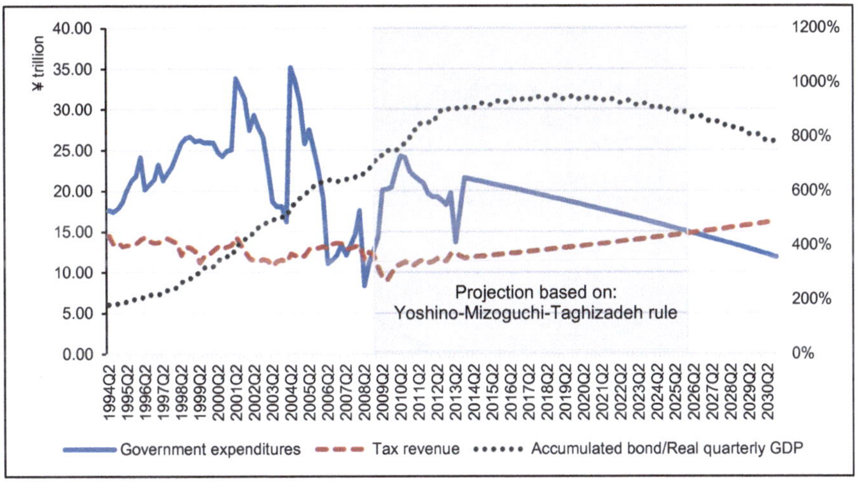

Fig. 6 Government expenditure and tax revenue (quarterly data). *Source* Yoshino et al. (2019). *Note* The gray shaded area indicates the projected values based on the Yoshino et al. (2019). The left-hand axis indicates government expenditures (primary expenses) and tax revenues, both in quarterly values, and the right-hand axis indicates the accumulated bonds/real quarterly GDP

account in implementing fiscal policies. The idea is to consider income and expenditure simultaneously while doing so. In other words, income and expenditure must be taken as a set, as for instance in terms of (a) policies aimed at raising taxes so that the government's social welfare services may be expanded or (b) policies aimed at lowering government expenditure on social welfare services in order to avoid imposing heavier taxes.

Doing this will help achieve fiscal stability, as shown by the simulation in Fig. 6.[4] Bohn's Condition is also expressed as an equation that subtracts expenditure from tax income as in Fig. 5, and the conclusion is that fiscal policy must be implemented taking into account outstanding government debt as a ratio of GDP, annual government bond issuance amounts as a ratio of GDP, and the GDP gap, in order to lower the primary balance.

3 Decline in Fiscal and Monetary Policy Efficacy as Society Ages

Macroeconomic textbooks generally explain fiscal and monetary policies using models that assume that everyone works—not taking retirees into account. Under the conditions assumed by such models, economic recovery can be achieved through the implementation of fiscal and monetary policies.

[4] Yoshino et al. (2019).

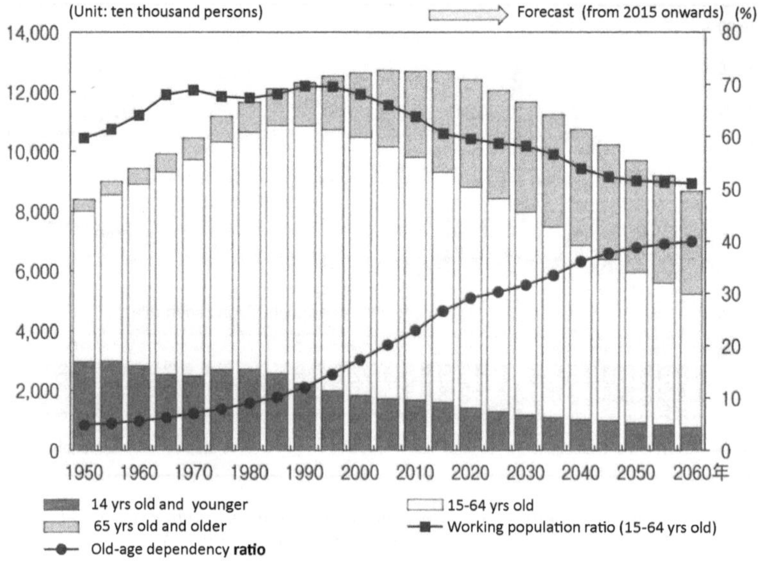

Fig. 7 Old-age dependency ratios (%) (ratio of those who are 65 years and older to the working population (15–64 years). *Source* Ministry of labor and Welfare

However, in the case of Japan, the population of retirees (older people) is increasing rapidly—a situation that is not analyzed in ordinary textbooks. In this section, I want to show how fiscal and monetary policy efficacy declines when one incorporates the rapid increase in the retiree (older) population into a macroeconomic model (Fig. 7). Let me give you some of the details of the joint research I am conducting with Dr. Hiroaki Miyamoto, an economist at the IMF. We created a new model by incorporating the working and retired populations into the Dynamic Stochastic General Equilibrium (DSGE) model and studied how the efficacy of fiscal and monetary policies would change with an increase in the retired population as society aged.[5]

Monetary policy aims to stimulate the economy by increasing the money supply and lowering the interest rate. Lower interest rates encourage companies to borrow more, thereby stimulating corporate investment. Textbooks explain that greater investments lead to more income, which boosts consumption and leads to an economic recovery. It is true that people working in companies enjoy higher incomes and increase their consumption accordingly, but retirees depend on social welfare and pensions for their living expenses, so their incomes do not increase as a result of monetary policies, and their consumption appetite remains unaffected. As society continues to age, a larger number of people will remain unaffected by monetary policy measures.

[5] Yoshino and Miyamoto (2017).

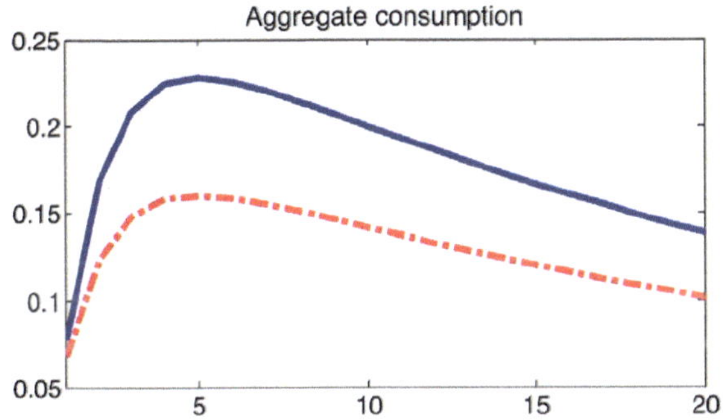

Fig. 8 Aging of society lowers stimulatory effect of monetary policy on consumption. Total consumption (Yoshino and Miyamoto 2017), "Declined effectiveness of fiscal and monetary policies faced with aging population in Japan," in *Japan and the World Economy*, Vol. 42, pp. 32–44). Labor participation rate 85% (upper line). Labor participation rate 55% (lower dotted line)

Figure 8 compares two scenarios—one in which the labor participation rate is 55% and another in which the labor participation rate is 85%. The efficacy of monetary policies—their stimulatory effect on consumption—progressively declines with the decline in the labor participation rate.

Next, we studied the effect of Keynesian fiscal stimulus measures (public works), as shown in Fig. 9. Keynesian fiscal policy involves providing employment to the unemployed through public works, thereby giving them an income, which boosts consumption and expands total demand, thereby stimulating the economy. This is because the unemployment rate was quite high in Keynes' time, and a large number of people had no jobs.

However, an aging society is one in which there is a progressive increase in the number of retirees living on social welfare and pensions. Retirees are neither

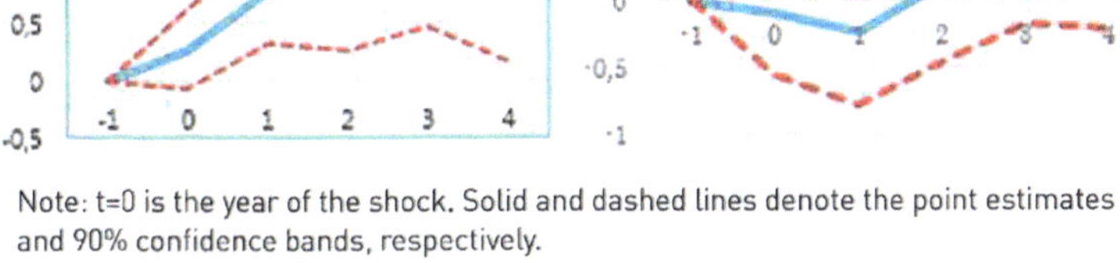

Fig. 9 Aging of society lowers stimulatory effect of public works on the economy (lower multiplier in aging economies compared with non-aging economies) (Yoshino and Miyamoto 2020), "How does population aging affect the effectiveness of monetary and fiscal policy," in *Global Solutions Journal*, Issue 5, pp. 249–255)

working nor looking for work. In such a society, expanding public works will only result in a labor shortage, making it difficult for companies to secure the manpower they need. As Fig. 9 shows, the effect of public works on production (the multiplier effect) is smaller in aging economies compared with non-aging economies. In aging economies, the multiplier is only about 0.5, while non-aging economies show about 1.5.

What kind of policies, then, are necessary in an aging society? By analyzing the DSGE model, we arrived at the conclusion that structural reforms, as outlined below, are necessary. If the retirement age is increased and wages are set based not on seniority but on productivity, consumption and GDP will both increase as shown in Fig. 10. By enabling older people to continue working alongside their younger colleagues, the government can reduce its social welfare spending. This will eliminate the need to increase taxes, resulting in more disposable income for younger people, and thereby boosting consumption. If older people were able to continue working and earning incomes in accordance with their productivity, it would reduce social welfare spending and the tax burden on the young generation. If young people feel that their future income will be higher and increase their spending, this would help expand overall demand today. In fact, questionnaire surveys conducted in Japan have revealed that people would like to remain in the labor force for longer if possible. Figure 10 shows that aggregate consumption, hours of work and aggregate investment would increase if the retirement age was postponed and a productivity-based wage rate system was simultaneously introduced.

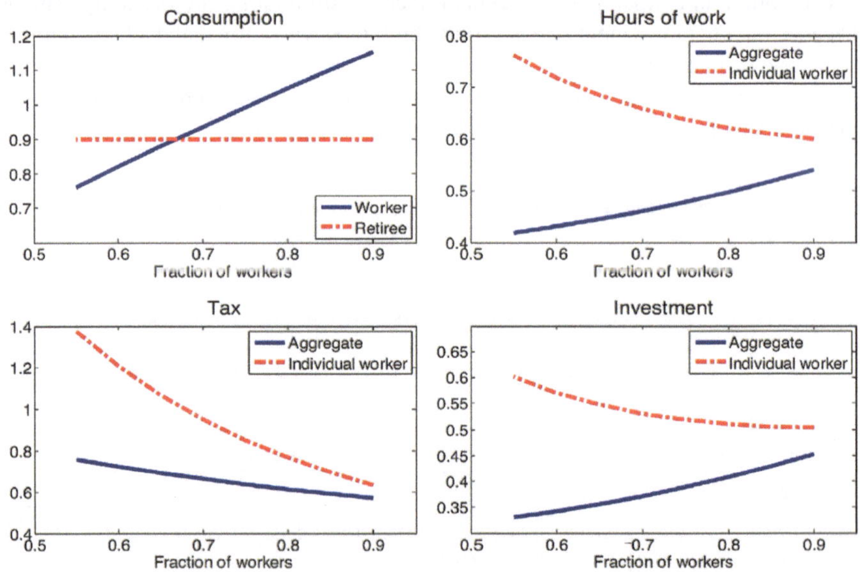

Fig. 10 If the retirement age is increased and people are allowed to continue working for wages based on productivity. *Source* Yoshino and Miyamoto (2017), *Japan and the World Economy*

It is important for companies to establish wages for older workers in accordance with their productivity and make good use of their experience and knowledge as they work alongside younger workers.

The conclusion arrived at from our DSGE model is that it is not for the lack of fiscal or monetary policy efforts but because of the aging of society that the Japanese economy is on the decline.

4 Investment in Japan Compared with in Other Countries

Lastly, I would like to compare the state of investments in the U.S., the UK and Japan. As Fig. 11 shows, financial assets in the U.S. increased by 3.11 times in the 20 years between 1997 and 2015, and those in the UK increased by 2.27 times during the same period. It is obvious at a glance how high the return on investments in these countries is.

By contrast, financial assets in Japan have increased by a mere 1.47 times over the same 20-year period. In an aging society, if people cannot invest the assets they have accumulated to obtain a high level of returns, maintaining the standard of life can become quite difficult. Japanese investors need to look beyond domestic investments and diversify by investing in the U.S., Europe, Asia and other regions. Investment yields in Japan are unlikely to increase given the Japanese economy's low rate of growth, but there are many rapidly growing countries in the rest of Asia. Japanese

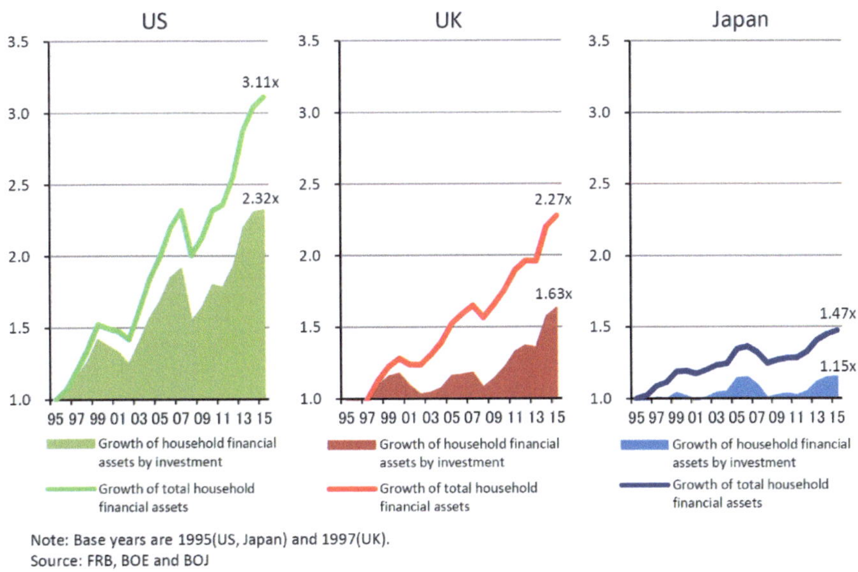

Fig. 11 Comparing investments in the U.S., the UK, and Japan. *Source* Strategic Direction of Policies, Financial Services Agency

investors would do well to study the causes of exchange rate fluctuations and become capable of investing their assets abroad.

References

Yoshino and Miyamoto (2017) Declined effectiveness of fiscal and monetary policies faced with aging population in Japan. Japan World Econ 42:32–44

Yoshino and Taghizadeh-Hesary (2014) Analytical framework on credit risks for financing small and medium-sized enterprises in Asia. Asia-Pacific Dev J 21(2), UnNESCAP

Yoshino and Taghizadeh-Hesary (2016) Analysis of credit ratings for small and medium sized enterprises: Evidence from Asia. Asian Dev Rev 32(2):18–37

Yoshino and Taghizadeh-Hesary (eds) (2020) Unlocking SME finance in Asia. Routledge

Yoshino, Mizoguchi and Taghizadeh-Hesary (2019) Optimal fiscal policy rule for achieving fiscal sustainability: the Japanese case. Global Bus Econ Rev 21(2)

Yoshino and Miyamoto (2020) How does population aging affect the effectiveness of monetary and fiscal policy. Global Solut J Issue 5:249–255

Chapter 3
Crypto Assets (Cryptocurrencies) and Central Bank Digital Currencies

Naoyuki Iwashita

1 Rise and Fall of Crypto Assets

Bitcoins, which drew attention worldwide after their price soared in 2017, began to be seen as a high-risk investment after crashing in 2018. But a byproduct of the Bitcoin, blockchain technology, is drawing attention as a leading next-generation technology, and pilot studies for various applications of this technology are being conducted. Having said that, the only examples of the large-scale application and social acceptance of blockchain technology so far are bitcoins and other crypto assets (cryptocurrencies).

Blockchain technology was developed using already existing technologies such as digital signatures based on public key cryptography and hash chains, which are successive applications of hash functions. It has as many as 3.6 million users in Japan alone, even if their use of it is mainly for the purpose of dabbling in crypto assets, because, at its peak, the economic value of crypto assets being traded was tens of trillions of yen. In that sense, this phenomenon represented the social deployment of information security technology on an unprecedented scale.

However, the rise of the Bitcoin is not an unalloyed story of success. Early investors made economic gains from the bitcoins they had purchased for extremely low prices when the price of the currency shot up. However, this rise in the bitcoin's market value was owing to the fact that they were beyond the reach of financial regulators and could be traded anonymously in the international market, and with their rise, they have been used for purposes such as international money laundering and terrorism financing, causing disruption to the global financial order.

Meanwhile, those who invested in the currency in 2017 or later have suffered losses as the price of the currency plummeted following several cases of the hacking of bitcoin exchanges and the theft of bitcoins. From the perspective of information

N. Iwashita (✉)
School of Government, Kyoto University, Tokyo, Japan
e-mail: iwashita.naoyuki.7e@kyoto-u.ac.jp

S. Kaji et al. (eds.), *The Economics of Fintech*,
https://doi.org/10.1007/978-981-33-4913-1_3

security technology, these incidents were fresh reminders of how difficult it is to securely manage the safety of private keys, a security essential when it comes to digital signatures.

The key to the success of the Bitcoin was to use the Proof of Work (PoW) system, a consensus mechanism that increases the safety of a transaction even in the absence of a trusted third party. As the market value of bitcoins soared, it became possible to make enormous profits by mining bitcoins using the PoW function. This resulted in massive investments in Bitcoin mining facilities, enough to distort global resource allocation and intensify global environmental problems.

The creator and developer of the Bitcoin in its early days, Satoshi Nakamoto, designed it as a form of electronic cash that could be used for pseudonymous financial transactions among strangers over the Internet. However, the currency has deviated significantly from what Satoshi seems to have intended, and his original plan never came to fruition. How did this deviation take place, and is it possible to return to the original plan?

2 Birth and History of the Bitcoin

There is no evidence to show that a person named Satoshi Nakamoto actually exists. It is not even clear whether this is the name of a specific individual, but if it is, the identity of this person is shrouded in an aura of mystery. However, let us not worry about that for the moment. Going by the paper[1] published under this name, it is hard to imagine that its author had envisaged the Bitcoin to be what it has become today.

The title of this paper is "Bitcoin: A Peer-to-Peer Electronic Cash System." Regarding electronic money (e-money) that can use digital data to function on open networks such as the Internet exactly in the same way as cash does—as a medium of money transfer or payment—and that can also protect the privacy of the participants by ensuring the anonymity of the transaction, various ideas have been proposed since the 1980s.[2,3] The studies behind such ideas are relevant even today in the application of encryption technology, and they have spawned diverse proposals for electronic payment systems around the world, some of which are in actual use. In Japan, e-money is widely used in the transport and retail sectors.

However, most such utilitarian forms of e-money are regulated by the financial authorities as debts of the issuing entities, and the transactions are not anonymous. Satoshi would have seen this as being far from ideal. He proposed the Bitcoin as a system of electronic payment that allowed transactions to remain anonymous and could take place without a trusted third-party intermediary.

---

[1] Nakamoto (2008).

[2] Chaum (1982).

[3] Okamoto and Ohta (1989).

Technologically speaking, the Bitcoin is no more than the merger of two previously existing projects. One was Surety.com's electronic record authentication service,[4,5,6] and the other was the Hashcash[7] project. The Bitcoin was no more than a combination of the latter's PoW concept with the former's system of linking hash functions to make it difficult to falsify data. Based on the fact that it enabled online money transfers without going through a third-party intermediary, the Bitcoin came to be known as a form of electronic cash.

We will not go into the details of the principle behind the Bitcoin, but the important thing to note is that there exists no organization, such as an issuing company, that supports the Bitcoin. What supports the Bitcoin system is, essentially, a computer-generated resource exchanged among individuals who endorse the concept of the Bitcoin or want to profit from it. Bitcoin transactions are not governed by specific contracts or legal frameworks, but merely by a code (a computer program). Even that code is publicly accessible and can be freely modified (subject to peer review and testing) by developers on a voluntary basis.

The code has important economic consequences (such as crypto asset price changes or the settlement of leadership struggles among traders). The emergence of this kind of a world dominated by code was predicted right from the time the Internet was born, but the prediction came true earlier than expected, and the fact that it took the shape of a crypto asset worth tens of trillions of yen was enough to astound people.

3 Jolted Awake by the Cyprus Financial Crisis

The Bitcoin system used its own monetary unit, bitcoin (BTC), which did not have a fixed rate of exchange with legal currencies such as dollar (USD) or yen (JPY). Even e-money that comes with a guarantee from issuers that it can be used at the same rate as legal tender for making purchases took time to gain the trust of users and be widely accepted. No wonder, then, that crypto assets, which have unique currency values that make them difficult to use either for purchases or as a means of storing value, were not accepted by the public—until the Bitcoin emerged.

As bitcoins began to be increasingly exchanged among and mined by enthusiasts, BTC's rate of exchange with legal currencies began to rise. In the beginning, it had almost no worth, but by 2012, it had become worth around USD 10. But it was the outbreak of the Cyprus financial crisis on March 28, 2012, that transformed the Bitcoin from a game for enthusiasts to a practical investment option (see Fig. 1). When banks in Cyprus, a small Mediterranean island country, temporarily suspended operations during the financial crisis there, bitcoins were used, and gained widespread

[4]Haber and Stornetta (1991).
[5]Bayer et al. (1993).
[6]Haber and Stornetta (1997).
[7]Back (2002).

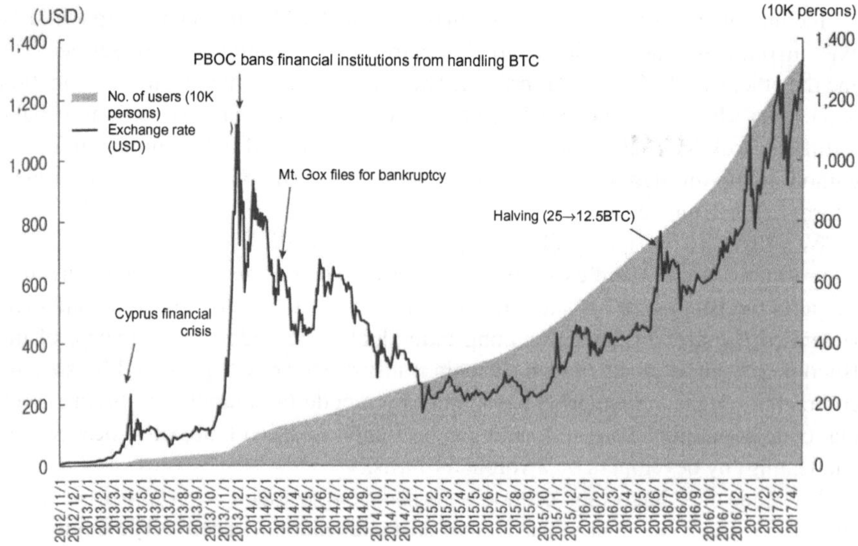

Fig. 1 Bitcoin price trends and user statistics (2013–16). *Source* blockchain.info

attention, as a means of transferring funds abroad. As a result, the price of BTC, which had been around USD 20 before the crisis, rocketed to nearly USD 200. Of course, the rate went down again once the crisis ended, but the incident highlighted the ability of bitcoins to be used for international fund transfers, causing it to gradually strengthen.

The next wave came toward the end of 2013. When a Chinese e-commerce site enabled payment in bitcoins, it triggered a bitcoin speculation fever in the country. The market overheated and BTC quickly shot up to USD 120.

Concerned about the overheating, the People's Bank of China (PBOC) banned domestic banks from paying out bitcoin purchase funds at the end of 2013. This caused the currency to plummet to half its previous price, to USD 600. Shortly thereafter, the largest bitcoin exchange in the world, Japan-based Mt. Gox, filed for bankruptcy, setting off a downward trend for BTC. By 2015, BTC had returned to its former price in the vicinity of USD 200.

It remained at that level for a while, but began to recover once again in 2016. Several explanations are offered for why this happened, such as that the potential of blockchain technology began to draw attention internationally or that more individual investors were buying BTC for speculation purposes, but it is not clear which of these explanations is correct.

Even if a commodity is not backed by the government or supported by business confidence, it can have value if there is a possibility that somebody might buy it from you for a high price, and this value changes based on people's expectations. In particular, in this era of monetary accommodation around the world, the target policy interest rate of central banks in the major economies has been close to zero.

Undoubtedly, this excessive monetary accommodation has also had a hand in creating an abnormally big market for crypto assets.

4 Rise of 2017 and Fall of 2018

The price of BTC began to rise rapidly at the start of 2017. The currency, which was being sold at around USD 1000 in January 2017, had appreciated as much as twenty times by the end of the year, hitting USD 20,000 at one point in December 2017 (see Fig. 2). Every time the price hit a new milestone, there was wide media coverage, and an increasing level of public attention was inevitably directed at the rates.

This soaring of BTC prices was a phenomenon that surpassed the expectations of finance professionals. Economists who place importance on economic fundamentals have been declaring that crypto assets, which are not backed by either government or business confidence, have an intrinsic value of zero and will eventually converge at that price. Professional traders, who place importance on market trends, have also avoided investing in crypto assets, being unable to calculate their theoretical price and not liking that there are no safeguards in place against broker accidents or bankruptcies. Investments in crypto assets, therefore, are entirely the preserve of individual investors, who are amateurs, and they were the only ones who benefited from the soaring of BTC in 2017.

In 2017, the prices of other cryptocurrencies rose even more dramatically than that of BTC, and the total value of all crypto assets in circulation for the entire year

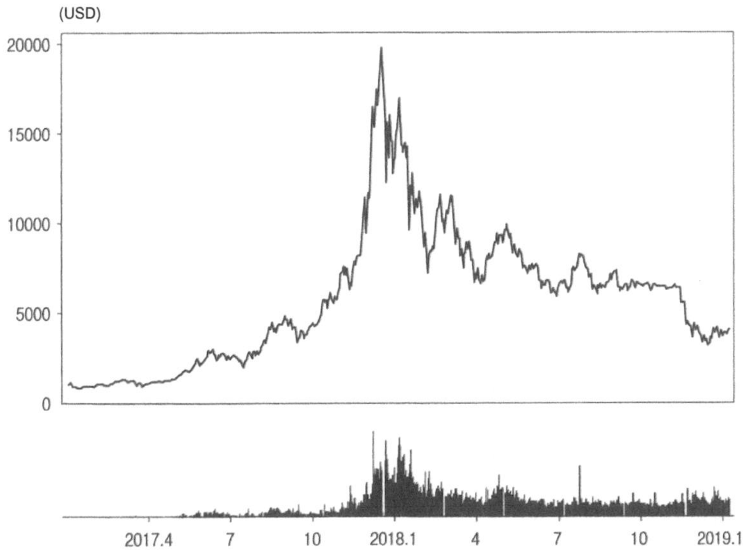

Fig. 2 Bitcoin price trends (since 2017). *Source* coinmarketcap.com

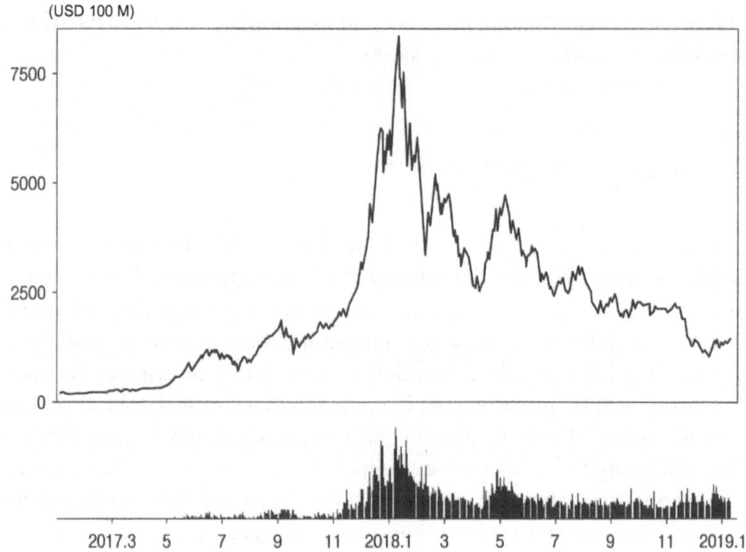

Fig. 3 Aggregate market value trends of all cryptocurrencies (since 2017). *Source* coinmarketcap.com

was almost 50 times greater than that for the previous year (see Fig. 3), expanding from JPY 2 trillion (USD 1.77 billion) to JPY 90 trillion (USD 83 billion). This is an amount equivalent to the currency in circulation in Japan (JPY 100 trillion) or the aggregate market value of stocks listed on the First Section of the Tokyo Stock Exchange held by individual investors. The rise in the price of cryptocurrencies was so dramatic that many senior central bank and finance ministry officials in major developed economies began to voice extreme concern over it.

And then in January 2018, crypto asset prices entered an adjustment phase. The price of BTC plunged to below 10,000 USD on January 18 and subsequently began to fluctuate wildly. However, this was a natural correction to be expected following a rapid increase in price, and many market participants remained bullish on the currency.

What poured cold water on the enthusiasm was an incident of the theft of crypto assets in Japan. Coincheck, the largest domestic bitcoin exchange, lost the entirety of customers' NEM crypto assets in its custody to theft. The assets were worth a total of JPY 58 billion. Coincheck confessed that its security measures had been inadequate and compensated customers for their losses, but was forced into a long-term suspension of operations and was given two business improvement orders by the Financial Services Agency (FSA). Following wide media coverage of the incident, the price of BTC fell again and has not risen over USD 10,000 since April 2018 (as of the writing of this book).

Having fallen to USD 6000 in June, BTC remained relatively stable between USD 6000–8000 until mid-November, but it fell sharply again between mid-November and

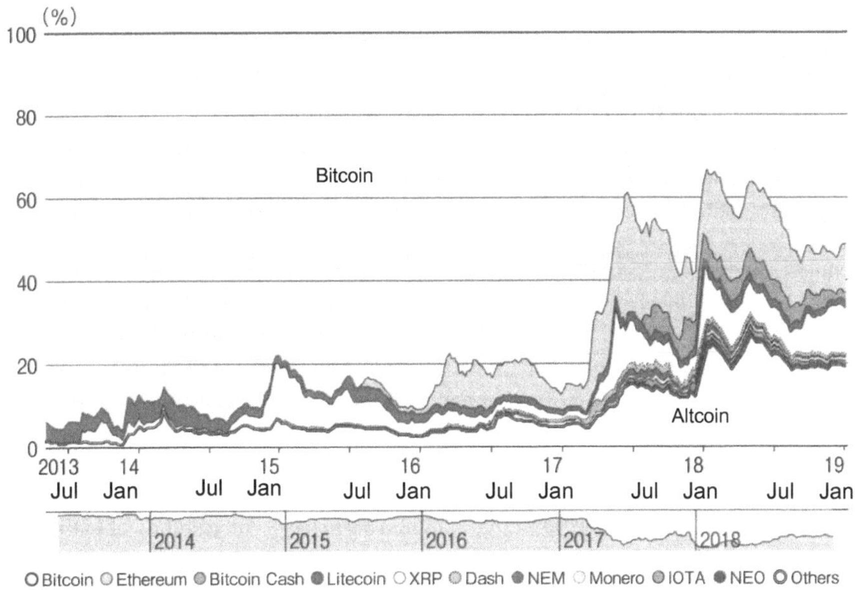

Fig. 4 Currency-wise composition trends of the distribution value of crypto assets (past five years). *Source* coinmarketcap.com

early December, ending the year at USD 3800, a fifth of the peak price posted barely a year before.

5 A Magic Wand Called ICO

The price of BTC soared by 20 times over the course of 2017. Meanwhile, the total value of all crypto assets soared by 50 times during the same period. As a result, the share of BTC in the larger crypto asset market more than halved, from about 85% to under 40% (see Fig. 4). This change took place over an extremely short period of time, having started only in May 2017. Before that, the share of BTC in the crypto asset market had never been lower than 80%. Therefore, in order to understand what happened in the crypto asset market in 2017, it is important to look not just at the Bitcoin, but also at other crypto assets (collectively termed "Altcoin").

It is thought that the driving force behind the expansion of the cryptocurrency market in 2017 was the Initial Coin Offering (ICO). An ICO "collectively means an activity to raise funds from the public using a digital token issued by a company or an individual."[8] The mechanism of an ICO warrants some explanation.

[8]From "Initial Coin Offerings (ICOs)—User and business operator warning about the risks of ICOs," posted on the FSA website dated October 27, 2017.

The total value of ICOs undertaken in 2017 amounted to JPY 400 billion, which is 40 times the amount of the previous year. The total value of ICOs organized in 2018 amounted to JPY 2 trillion.

Most ICOs are based on the crypto asset platform Ethereum and are issued in the form of digital crypto assets called ERC-20 tokens. One needs Ethereum to buy such tokens, so with an increase in ICOs, the demand for Ethereum increases, and so does its rate of exchange. Again, although the money paid toward obtaining ICO tokens is not reimbursed, because these tokens are Ethereum denominated, their dollar value goes up when Ethereum appreciates. As a result, the price of the tokens in the secondary market rises, further invigorating ICO activity. This kind of positive feedback loop is thought to have been behind the rapid rise in the amount of ICO tokens issued and in the price of Ethereum from May 2017 (see Fig. 5).

Let us take a look at the reality behind ICOs, which became the engine driving the rise of crypto assets in 2017, and the various arguments related to their regulation.

ICOs are sometimes characterized as Initial Public Offerings (IPOs) using digital assets, but in fact, there is another difference. The entity planning an ICO need not be a corporation. It could be an individual who comes up with a somewhat attractive plan for a small new business he or she hopes to set up with friends, or a group of people who have gathered together for this purpose over the Internet. The first thing such people create is a business plan called a "white paper."

This document, which is on average several dozen pages long, is sometimes explained as being similar to the prospectus for a stock or bond initial or secondary offering, but in reality, it is much more random. A prospectus is issued for the

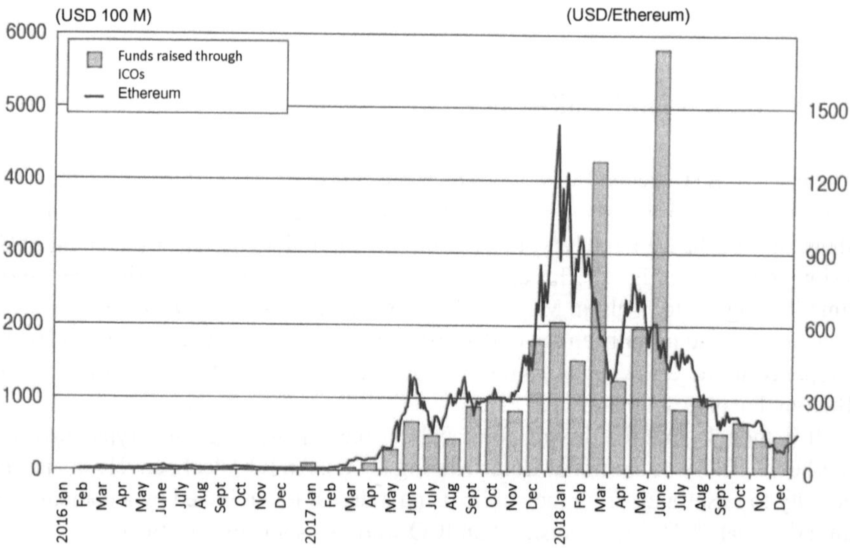

Fig. 5 ICO-based fundraising and Ethereum price trends. *Source* www.coinschedule.com, www.coingecko.com

purpose of providing information on the basis of which investors can make investment decisions. It covers certain standard topics and is liable for damages if found to have misrepresented the facts. By contrast, ICO white papers are not governed by the law, nor are their contents standardized. They are often rewritten subsequent to the implementation of the ICO.

Tokens issued during ICOs are also different from stocks and bonds. Token owners, unlike shareholders, do not have the right to receive dividends or participate in the management of the company, nor are the tokens, unlike corporate bonds, repayable upon maturity. The tokens merely come with something like discount coupons, called "utility tokens," that can be used to purchase the products or services of the business operated by the token-issuing entity. As a result, the entity making the ICO can raise funds in exchange for tokens with almost no obligations.

Common sense would seem to dictate that, like stocks or bonds, tokens issued for purposes of fundraising would be better received if they bound the issuing entity to paying some form of dividend or repayment of the principal. However, ICO tokens would risk being seen as marketable securities governed by the securities laws of the land if they were to commit to paying out dividends or repaying the principal. And the act of issuing marketable securities to the public would make the issuing entity subject to disclosure requirements and various other behavioral regulations under the securities act. This is why token-issuing entities issue utility tokens, which are a type of "wildcat securities," in an effort to circumvent the aforementioned regulations.

It is surprising enough that anyone would be willing to buy such "worthless" tokens, but the fact is that these ICO tokens were so popular that the websites of issuing companies ended up crashing due to excessive traffic from would-be investors. Why did investors buy these tokens? They did so because they wanted to sell them in the secondary market and make a profit on the sale. In fact, investors who bought ICO tokens issued during January–March and April–June 2017 and held them until the end of the year made profits that were, on average, 18.3 times and 3.5 times the invested amount, respectively.

Although the number of times by which the price increased obviously fell during the second half of the year, the rumor that buying ICO tokens in the primary market and selling them in the secondary market was profitable spread like wildfire among crypto asset investors, resulting in a huge surge in the popularity of ICOs, thereby causing the price of crypto assets also to soar.

If the fundraising entities were to make good use of the craze to develop sterling products or services that contribute to economic growth, then perhaps ICOs could be acknowledged to have some value. However, there is no guarantee that those who raise money through no-obligation utility tokens rather than by taking loans or issuing stocks will put that money to effective use.

In a paper titled "Digital Tulips? Returns to Investors in Initial Coin Offerings" published in May 2018, Boston University research scholars Hugo Benedetti and Leonard Kostovetsky analyzed the behavior of token-issuing entities following an ICO. They did this by counting the number of tweets made from the twitter accounts of projects for which funds had been raised through an ICO and conjecturing that a project had expired when the tweets died down.

ICO issuer category	Number of issuers	Number remaining after 120 days	Number gone by 120th day	Disappearance rate at 120 days (%)
No funds raised, no tokens listed	694	118	576	83
Funds raised, but no tokens listed	420	200	220	52
Funds raised and tokens listed	440	369	71	16
Total of all categories	1,554	687	867	55.8

Chart 1 ICO issuer disappearance rate by 120th day after the issue. *Source* From Benedetti and Kostovetsky (2018); some figures estimated by author

Since community management through dialog with ICO token buyers is an important business activity, twitter is often used as a means to conduct such dialog, so Benedetti and Kostovetsky's approach is persuasive. Their paper analyzes the official twitter feeds pertaining to as many as 4003 ICOs that were either implemented or planned. Table 1 summarizes the knowledge gleaned through their study (the paper itself presents the data as running text, but I have presented it in a chart here).

It is understandable that 83% of the projects that failed to raise funds would have disappeared by the 120th day. By contrast, only 16% of the projects that had both been able to raise funds and list tokens had disappeared within 120 days. Having said that, companies that list their stocks on the market through an IPO rarely ever disappear (go bankrupt or close down) even if they are venture firms, so a 16% disappearance rate within four months should be seen as quite a high rate.

Entrepreneurs who set up venture firms work very hard for business success so that they can return the borrowed capital and become wealthy. By contrast, if someone can obtain large sums of money simply by writing a white paper, it is unsurprising that their motivation to work hard in pursuit of business success is not too strong. As for those who invest in these ICOs, they are happy so long as they can resell their tokens in the secondary market for a higher price, because whether or not the business ultimately succeeds is no concern of theirs. Consequently, the contents of white papers tended to be vague and sloppy, sometimes not even complete as documents, and yet this did not seem to affect the sale of ICO tokens in 2017. Since the end of 2017, of course, many ICOs have ended unsatisfactorily, without selling many tokens, but the enthusiasm of issuers who hope to procure funds with no strings attached remains strong.

The mechanism of an ICO is like an enormous game of Old Maid. While both the issuer and the primary market issuers make a killing, investors who buy these tokens at high prices in the secondary market are ultimately left holding worthless tokens. Even in a scenario where the issuer's business project succeeds, the fruits of that success are not shared with the token owner, so it is almost certain that the tokens will be worthless once the overheated market cools down. In this sense, the whole thing is an extremely unethical setup.

Regulatory authorities around the world have begun to attempt regulating this problem-ridden practice of ICOs.

The U.S. Securities and Exchange Commission (SEC) has expressed the view that some ICOs are equivalent to the sale of marketable securities in the open secondary market as defined by the Securities Act. It is also pushing for the prosecution of those who conduct ICOs that are patently fraudulent. There also exist ICOs that are deemed similar to private placements under the Securities Act and regulated to offer only to accredited investors. However, there is information to show that such ICO tokens are then being resold to the general public, something that is not technically allowed under the law, and it remains to be seen whether the regulations can function as intended. In this way, the general trend in the U.S. is in the direction of regulating ICOs as a whole under the Securities Act.

Meanwhile, China banned ICOs in September 2017. A joint statement issued by various Chinese financial regulatory authorities sternly pointed out that ICOs had destroyed economic and financial order. It is said that there were as many as 65 ICO platforms in China at that time, and that an average of 10 ICOs were being held each week. According to local reports, the authorities had to step into regulate the market after it overheated to the extent that elderly people began to invest their retirement funds in bitcoins without even understanding what they were. Under the new regulations, issuers were forced to return the funds raised to the investors even in cases where the ICO had been conducted before the regulations had been promulgated.

In Japan, too, the FSA issued a warning about the risks of ICOs in October 2017 (see Fig. 6). Unusually for a document published by an administrative authority, the warning utilizes strong language, such as "become worthless suddenly" and "potential for fraud." Japan launched a system for the registration of crypto asset

Initial Coin Offerings (ICOs)

- User and business operator warning about the risks of ICOs -

October 27, 2017
Financial Services Agency

1. What are ICOs?

O In general, an ICO collectively means an activity to raise funds from the public using a digital token issued by a company or an individual. It can also be known as a token sale.

For users: Risks of ICOs

O A digital token issued in an ICO has the following high risks;

✓ Price volatility
The price of a token may decline or become worthless suddenly.

✓ Potential for fraud
ICOs usually provide a white paper. However, there are possibilities that the projects in the paper are not implemented, or the goods and services planned are not offered in reality. Frauds taking advantage of ICOs are reported in the media.
(Note) A white paper is the document which puts together the use of funds collected in an ICO, the content of the ICO project, the way to sell a token, etc.

O You should have a deal at your own risk only after understanding enough the risks as above and the content of an ICO project if you buy a token. https://www.fsa.go.jp/policy/virtual_currency/07.pdf

Fig. 6 Japan's FSA also issued a warning about the risks of ICOs exchange businesses in 2017, with "crypto asset exchange business" being defined broadly to include the act of issuing ICO tokens. As a result, there have been no ICOs in Japan apart from the ones held by the single ICO exchange company in the country. Companies that had been planning an ICO and became unable to hold one are expressing their resentment, but ultimately this de facto regulation of ICOs at a time when the market was roaring and investors were expecting enormous appreciation in the value of their digital assets has been for the greater social good in the sense that it prevented investors from suffering huge losses.

BTC remained strong as a result of the expectation that bitcoins would be the "money of the future" and could be used to make payments at some point (although this is unlikely even in the future). The price of Ethereum rose dramatically as a platform for ICOs. With this strong rise in the price of two types of crypto assets, people began to expect that other cryptocurrencies would also strengthen as the second or third Bitcoin or Ethereum.

As a result, a large number of mostly worthless crypto assets began to see a dramatic surge in their prices starting May 2017. As relatively well-known cryptocurrencies were bought up by investors and appreciated, the associated sentiment was transmitted also to crypto assets that were relatively unknown and were of little worth. This can be thought of as a phenomenon similar to "sector rotation to low-level stocks" when the stock market is on the rise.

And then, the icing on the cake of the 2017 crypto asset market boom was the listing of bitcoin futures on the Chicago Mercantile Exchange (CME) and the Chicago Board Options Exchange (CBOE). With the launch of bitcoin futures, investors began to expect that crypto assets would be officially recognized as financial products and that enormous investment funds would start pouring into them from financial institutions and institutional investors. This expectation was what rocket-launched the price of BTC from USD 10,000 to USD 20,000 within the space of three weeks.

6 Cyber Attacks on Bitcoin Exchanges

From the start of 2018, the crypto asset market entered a correction phase. One reason for the fall in prices was an incident in which NEM tokens with a market value of JPY 58 billion[9] were stolen from Coincheck, a fledgling bitcoin exchange that had not yet completed its registration under the Crypto Assets Act. An unauthorized entry was made into Coincheck's system using the private key of a digital signature managed by the company, and all the NEM tokens in possession of the company were transferred to a different account. All the customer assets in Coincheck's custody were stolen.

How could such a thing happen? For a company to which customers had entrusted their precious crypto assets, Coincheck did not have sufficient safeguards in place. It had put the NEMs deposited by all 260,000 of its customers into a single large wallet. The wallet was connected to the Internet at all times, enabling assets to be

[9] A digital currency, the abbreviation standing for "New Economy Movement."

	Amount (XEM)	Remitting address	Receiving address
2018/1/26 8:26	800,000	NC3BI3DNMR2	NC4C6PSUW5
2018/1/26 4:33	1,000,000	NC3BI3DNMR2	NC4C6PSUW5
2018/1/26 3:35	1,500,000	NC3BI3DNMR2	NC4C6PSUW5
2018/1/26 3:29	92,250,000	NC4C6PSUW5	NA6JSWNF247
2018/1/26 3:28	100,000,000	NC4C6PSUW5	NDDZVF32WB
2018/1/26 3:18	100,000,000	NC4C6PSUW5	NB4OJJCLTZW
2018/1/26 3:14	100,000,000	NC4C6PSUW5	NDZZJBH6IZP
2018/1/26 3:02	750,000	NC4C6PSUW5	NBKLOYXFIVF
2018/1/26 3:00	50,000,000	NC4C6PSUW5	NDODXOWFIZ
2018/1/26 2:58	50,000,000	NC4C6PSUW5	NA7SZ75KF6Z
2018/1/26 2:57	30,000,000	NC4C6PSUW5	NCTWFIOOVIT
2018/1/26 0:21	3,000,000	NC3BI3DNMR2	NC4C6PSUW5
2018/1/26 0:10	20,000,000	NC3BI3DNMR2	NC4C6PSUW5
2018/1/26 0:09	100,000,000	NC3BI3DNMR2	NC4C6PSUW5
2018/1/26 0:08	100,000,000	NC3BI3DNMR2	NC4C6PSUW5
2018/1/26 0:07	100,000,000	NC3BI3DNMR2	NC4C6PSUW5
2018/1/26 0:06	100,000,000	NC3BI3DNMR2	NC4C6PSUW5
2018/1/26 0:04	100,000,000	NC3BI3DNMR2	NC4C6PSUW5
2018/1/26 0:02	10	NC3BI3DNMR2	NC4C6PSUW5

Chart 2 Movement of NEM tokens during the Coincheck incident. *Source* Created by author using NEM blockchain information

deposited or withdrawn at will. The procedure for transferring crypto assets from the wallet was protected by no more than a single cryptographic key, and the safety management of this key appears to have been sloppy, as someone managed to make unauthorized use of it to transfer all the NEM tokens (see Chart 2).

In Chart 2, the "NC3…" address highlighted in gray belonged to Coincheck. NEM tokens worth JPY 58 billion deposited by Coincheck's customers were all stored in this address. Meanwhile, the "NC4…" address highlighted in black was the address the thief had prepared. On January 26, the thief made the first transfer of XEM[10] 10 at 0:02 h. Within 20 min of this, additional transfers worth XEM 5.23 billion had been made. The thief then re-transferred the stolen NEM tokens from the NC4 address to multiple other addresses. There were more illegal transfers from NC3 to NC4 that same day, sometime during the hours of 03:00, 04:00, and 08:00.

Of course, the greatest share of the blame goes to the thief who made these illegal transfers. This person, who then became the sole manager of JPY 58 billion worth of NEM tokens, gradually exchanged them for other currencies over the Internet and, having laundered all the funds, vanished into thin air.

This is not an isolated incident, and the problem is not just Coincheck's. There have been numerous incidents of the hacking of crypto asset exchange companies and the theft of their crypto assets. Exchanges currently operating could also be vulnerable—they may unwittingly be putting the assets their customers have deposited with them at risk. At the current time, there are neither any uniform security standards

[10]ISO code for NEM.

across the crypto asset industry, nor is there any disclosure requirement regarding the management structures, governance, or status of security measures in these companies.

Japan was one of the first countries to enact laws to regulate crypto asset exchange companies, and it has a registration system for such companies. However, the main objectives of existing laws and systems are to prevent money laundering and terrorism financing. Current laws related to crypto assets are not based on an awareness that the exchanges are holding customer assets worth large sums of money and they, therefore, have not created strong user protection mechanisms. Given that the current situation is very different from what had been assumed at the time of these laws' formulation, the laws need to be revised. The crypto asset industry should also utilize systems used by trust banks and insurance companies to autonomously promote initiatives that help limit damage. Further, the authorities must work to dispel user concerns by establishing standards for security measures and enforcing compulsory disclosure. To prevent the recurrence of incidents such as the one discussed above, efforts must also be made to constantly keep relevant systems and regulations up to date.

For most people, one of the strange things about the abovementioned incident is that the NEM funds cannot be restored to the original address even though their transfer to the thief's address can be confirmed. If such a thing had happened with a bank deposit, as soon as it became clear that the stolen funds were in a specific deposit account, that account could be frozen by the authorities, and it could be expected that the stolen funds would eventually be returned to the account they were stolen from.

Right from the time people first began to talk about the Bitcoin, the special concept behind this cryptocurrency has drawn attention. This involves a policy of not being governed by a trusted central bank, which is why the Bitcoin is called "trustless." It is thought that this special characteristic of the Bitcoin is the reason it was able to break through national barriers resulting from differences in governing laws and political systems and become truly international in its usage.

By contrast, the conventional system, which is governed by a trusted central bank, exists in a "trust-based" environment. Because we live in a world that assumes the presence of trusted central authorities such as the government, the central bank, the court system and so on, a trustless world seems extremely special and risky to us. Nevertheless, the existence of the Bitcoin has been acknowledged, and the trust-based and trustless worlds have been coexisting.

For instance, geeks who are directly connected to the Bitcoin network through what are called "nodes," live in a trustless world. On the other hand, amateur users cannot directly connect to a node. They simply have bitcoin deposits with bitcoin exchanges and depend on these exchanges to trade their bitcoins for them. In the case of these amateur users, the bitcoin exchange becomes the "trusted third party," so a trust mechanism exists within this relationship (see Fig. 7).

In the aforementioned incident, the NEM tokens were stolen and laundered in a trustless world. There being no trusted central authority in that world, no entity, including the national government, could arbitrarily rewrite the information to restore

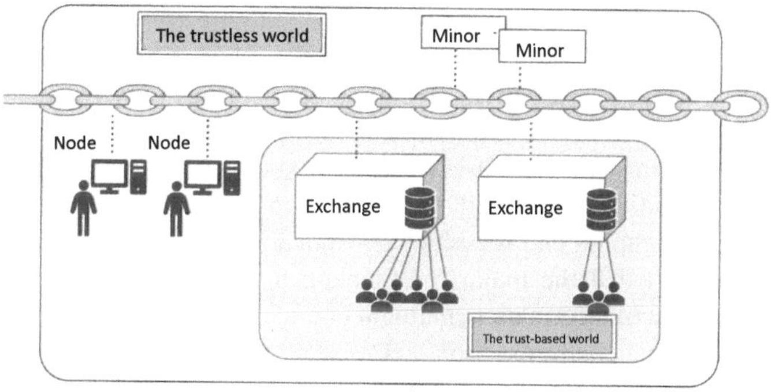

Fig. 7 Challenge of a trust-based world existing within a trustless world

the stolen funds. In light of the NEM theft incident, therefore, trustlessness is a double-edged sword.

Can the government appropriately control this alien concept of cryptocurrencies? In other words, can it make good use of its positive aspects while compensating for/rectifying its negative ones? In order to deal with this novel challenge, those concerned will need to put their heads together and find solutions, including those in the form of international regulation systems.

7 Cashless Society and Central Bank Digital Currencies

(1) Heating Up of the Central Bank Digital Currency Argument—Shock to the System from the Emergence of the Bitcoin

Until around 2012, there were no serious discussions among central bank officials and related persons about the digitization of banknotes (paper money) through the issuance of a central bank digital currency (CBDC). This is probably because of the strong level of confidence in existing settlement systems such as bank note systems, systems provided by the central bank or private banks, and the international settlement system SWIFT (Society for Worldwide Interbank Financial Telecommunication). In a sense, the topic itself was considered taboo. To some extent, people realized that e-money would eventually be used and that the world would become increasingly cashless, but it was thought that this was in the distant future. However, starting around 2013, an increasing number of central-bank officials and others began to bring up the idea of central banks issuing digital currencies. This development was related to the Bitcoin beginning to draw attention on a global scale.

To be sure, the Bitcoin was drawing attention in countries around the world, and its price was soaring, but in the view of financial experts, the currency's utility as a payment method was low, and it was clearly still in its experimental stages. So, imagine the shock waves sent through the financial industry, and especially in the central banks, when the Bitcoin began to be used worldwide via the Internet.

Until then, financial transactions in capital or securities were regulated by each country's financial authorities. Regulatory authorities in each country issued licenses based on domestic laws to businesses facilitating such transactions, permitting them access to the domestic market. With the internationalization of finance, the international exchange of capital and securities expanded among the developed countries, but despite the fact that the majority of financial transactions simply involve an electronic exchange of information, national boundaries have continued to represent major barriers to financial transactions.

However, as mentioned earlier, during the Cyprus financial crisis of March 2013, bitcoins managed to break through this barrier very easily. In principle, anyone can buy and sell bitcoins so long as they are connected to the Internet. In fact, it was widely touted that international transfers could be made very inexpensively using bitcoins compared with regular money transfers, for which hefty transfer charges apply.

The rise in Bitcoin's popularity set many imaginations on fire regarding the future of finance. If existing banknotes and inter-bank networks were difficult to use due to the associated high costs, perhaps they would be replaced by crypto assets, which can be exchanged over the Internet. Perhaps the first central bank to conduct experiments and gain experience in the area would become the de facto standard-bearer of the future. Anticipating such a future, central banks, which have traditionally not competed with their international counterparts, began to compete. As a result, discussing the idea of central banks issuing digital currencies stopped being taboo.

(2) A Diversity of Ideas Related to CBDCs—Three Main Types

Different people and organizations seem to have different ideas about what a CBDC is. Even when it comes to the appellations, apart from the relatively common CBDC, there are terms such as Central Bank Cryptocurrency (CBCC), as often used by the Bank for International Settlements (BIS); Digital Base Money (DBM), as used by the European Central Bank (ECB); and Digital Fiat Currency (DFC), as seen in central-bank discussions in emerging market economics (EMEs).

The technologies used and implementation formats are also diverse. First, there is the concept of central banks issuing e-money similar to Suica. It would not be impossible for an e-currency like Suica to replace banknotes in terms of functionality, but it is predicted that it would be technologically challenging to keep a centrally-managed system like Suica up and running at all times and to maintain its nationwide settlement functions.

Another idea is for central banks to issue digital currencies using blockchain technology similar to that of the Bitcoin. While such a currency would be based on a private blockchain platform like the MUJF coin or SMBC coin and have restricted access, the central bank would fix the value of one unit of the coin at one yen and guarantee this value.

A third and very bold idea is to introduce a currency based on a public blockchain platform, which can be competitively mined by private mining farms and used widely by the public. Those who advocate for this idea are of the view that mining for currencies is an efficient and stable means of operating a digital currency. In addition to the above, there are also a number of proposals for digital currencies based on an amalgamation of one or more of the above formats.

Not all of those proposals can be discussed here, but CBDCs can be divided into the following three types in an effort to understand the direction of the debates.

The first type is inspired by the Bitcoin, and is a form of digital currency currently being researched by central banks in developed countries. Discussions about this type of digital currency, called CBDC or CBCC, are led by the BIS's Committee on Payments and Market Infrastructures (CPMI). There are no examples of actual implementation so far.

The second type of digital currency, called DFC, is being promoted mainly by African nations and EMEs. It is based on the idea of the central bank becoming involved in private-sector platforms (such as M-PESA), the use of which have been promoted toward achieving greater financial inclusion in developing countries in Africa and elsewhere. The discussions have mainly been led by the countries of Africa at the International Telegraph Union Telecommunication Standardization Sector (ITU-T), but other countries—including China, Russia, and India—have also joined.

The third type is a digital currency is being considered by South American central banks, which have been promoting dollarization as a way to combat inflation. One of the characteristics of this type of digital currency, exemplified by such currencies as the Uruguayan e-Peso and the Venezuelan petro, is that it is often extemporaneously launched.

(3) CBDCs in Developed Countries—Research that is Still Far from Implementation

The BOJ's survey titled "Central Bank Digital Currencies—Discussions and Experiments by Overseas Central Banks" (BOJ Review 2016-J-19) summarizes the current status of the study of digital currencies by the central banks of the major advanced nations.

Chart 3 below summarizes the status of the study of digital currencies in key countries as presented by the survey. However, none of these countries has actually issued a CBDC as of the present time. Some of the reasons for this may be that advanced nations have well-developed fund settlement services, the financial system of each country centered around its central bank is a key part of the nation's economic infrastructure, and there is a desire not to impart a needless shock to this system. Therefore, discussions of digital currencies in developed nations are still in the stage of theoretical study.

(4) CBDCs and Financial Inclusion in EMEs and Developing Countries

(i) The Netherlands (De Nederlandsche Bank)

In March 2016, De Nederlandsche Bank (DNB) announced in its annual report that it would develop a prototype of the DNBcoin based on blockchains/distributed ledger technology (DLT). A senior bank official said in a speech later that year in June, that the central bank would conduct its own verification tests on bitcoin software in an effort to more deeply understand the functioning of blockchains. It was also revealed that the DNBcoin had been developed primarily for the purpose of tests to be conducted within the DNB, and that it would not be in wide circulation for public use.

(ii) Canada (The Bank of Canada)

Through a speech delivered by Deputy Governor Carolyn Wilkins on June 17, 2016, the Bank of Canada (BOC) revealed that it would conduct experiments on DLT in partnership with commercial banks and private-sector corporations. BOC staff have explained the overall details of the experiment at various venues, including forums of various kinds. For instance, at the October 2016 Chicago Payments Symposium, the BOC announced its plan to use a pseudo environment replicating interbank transactions to enable private-sector financial institutions participating in the experiment to deposit funds into a BOC special account as security, in return for which the BOC would issue DLT-based central bank debt certificates (deposit securities). The BOC has stated that the objective of this experiment is to comprehend the mechanisms, limits, and possibilities of DLT technology by testing it in an experimental large-scale settlement system environment.

(iii) The United Kingdom (The Bank of England)

In the UK, in February 2016, following discussions with the staff of the Bank of England (BOE), University of London research scholars published a paper proposing a system for the RSCoin, a digital currency to be issued by the central bank. Under this scheme, intermediary entities called "mintettes," which link the central bank and users, would play a specific role in issuing and managing RSCoins. While the central bank would be the issuing entity for RSCoins, multiple mintettes would be commissioned with processing tasks, such as checking and approving the details of transactions and sending the relevant information to the central bank. Further, in order to ensure the appropriate functioning of mintettes, the central bank would regularly check to confirm the consistency of the generated "blocks" (in the blockchain), and if any inappropriate processing were to be detected, the mintette responsible for that process would be excluded.
In a speech given in June 2016, Governor Mark Carney revealed that the BOE was thinking of incorporating the use of DLT in its core operations and studying and analyzing ideas related to the issuance of a CBDC. Further in a public letter of intent to design a new Real-Time Gross Settlement (RTGS) system released in September 2016, the BOE announced that DLT, while not yet mature enough as a technology to guarantee the extremely high standards of stability required in an RTGS system, held the potential to change the way settlements were made, and that the BOE would continue to research this technology in collaboration with academics, fintech companies, and central banks in other countries.

(iv) Russia (The Bank of Russia)

The Bank of Russia announced in October 2016 that it had developed a prototype of a DLT-based financial information communication tool called Masterchain in collaboration with market participants. Deputy Governor Olga Skorobogatova said that the prototype would continue to be studied by the FinTech consortium, including the possibility of its future incorporation within the country's next-generation financial infrastructure.

(v) China (The People's Bank of China)

As of date, the People's Bank of China (PBOC) has not officially announced having conducted experiments related to blockchains or DLT. On the other hand, it has revealed to external sources that it already has the systems in place to start issuing its own digital currency in the medium term. Specifically, the PBOC held an investigative committee meeting on January 20, 2016, at which views on digital currencies were exchanged with experts. Additionally, the investigative committee has asked the PBOC's study group to not just incorporate the results of digital currency-related research from both within and outside China, but also to further clarify the Bank's strategic goals with regard to digital currencies and work toward enabling the Bank to announce the issue of a digital currency as early as possible.
In a Bloomberg article dated September 16, 2016, Deputy Governor Fan Yifei wrote about the format of digital currency being considered by the PBOC. He said that the Bank was leaning toward an indirect approach, where a digital currency would first be issued by the central bank to private banks, and the latter would then offer deposit and withdrawal services related to the currency to the general public. As for the reasons why such an approach was preferred, Mr. Fan noted that utilizing the existing banknote circulation framework would make it easy to gradually replace banknotes with the digital currency, and that the participation of private banks in managing the digital currency issued by the central bank would disperse the risks as well as promote innovation, thereby contributing to the real economy and helping respond to the needs of the people.

Chart 3 Digital currency consideration status in major countries. *Source* BOJ Review 2016-J-19

As recently as 2010, about half the world's population did not have a bank account. However, that number has declined dramatically in recent years, owing to rapid progress in IT-based financial inclusion initiatives in EMEs and developing nations. The M-PESA initiative that was begun in Kenya is a representative example (details in the next section). China's progress toward realizing a cashless society has also been remarkable.

Taking such changes into account, EMEs and other developing economies have begun contemplating the idea of positioning such new means of settlement as "digital fiat currency." I will dedicate a separate section to discussing the actual status of developments toward realizing cashless societies.

What is important to note here is the move to call these new payment methods "digital fiat currency." ITU-T is one of the sectors of the International Telecommunication Union and is in charge of formulating international standards in the field of telecommunications. In 2017, the Focus Group on Digital Currency including Digital Fiat Currency (FG DFC) was set up as a subsidiary body of the ITU-T. The focus group is chaired by representatives from African nations as well as China, Russia and India. Their first meeting was held in October 2017 in Beijing. At the workshop that was also held as part of this meeting, the head of the PBOC's Digital Currency Organization attracted widespread attention by announcing that the PBOC had already completed technological experiments necessary for issuing digital currency.

(5) Central Bank Digital Currency Implementation in South America

Unlike the developed nations, which are still pondering the issue, many central banks in South America have already issued digital currencies. In countries like Ecuador, Uruguay, and Venezuela, a national digital currency is the reality, not a research topic. This has to do with the fact that such countries have long struggled with inflation. Given that their domestic currency systems have never been sufficiently functional, and going by their previous experiences with dollarization policies, they were able to go ahead and issue experimental digital currencies without worrying much about its impact on their existing currency systems.

Of the three countries mentioned above, Venezuela is the one that has drawn the most attention. In January 2018, Venezuelan President Nicolás Maduro ordered the issuance of the first 100 million petros, the CBDC of Venezuela backed by its petroleum reserves. According to Maduro, the price of one petro is equivalent to the price of one barrel of Venezuelan oil. He further explained that shares in oil reserves and in diamond and gold mines would be sold to prop up the currency.

The petro was issued and circulated using blockchain technology, similar to the Bitcoin. It takes the form of an ERC-20 token. In other words, it was issued by an ICO implemented by a country. It is said that Venezuela managed to raise USD 5 billion through the issue of this currency.

Maduro took over as president of Venezuela after the death of former president Hugo Chávez, long known as a high-profile foe of the United States. As is widely known, Maduro's government was subjected to U.S. sanctions that have undermined the nation's economy and resulted in astronomical inflation rates. Maduro was able to implement an executive order creating the petro despite opposition from the country's National Assembly (in which the opposition party is in the majority), which characterized the presidential order as unconstitutional. Under normal circumstances, a country like Venezuela would be unlikely to raise even a single dollar attempting to procure funds in the normal way in the international financial market. Many media reports have expressed serious misgivings about the fact that Venezuela was able to issue a CBDC that was effectively like a magic wand that could make many of its problems go away.

8 Cashlessness and the Future of Currencies

(1) Trends Toward Cashlessness Around the World

When considering the various possible forms of cash settlement systems, one is likely to begin by looking back at the historical stages of the evolution of cash settlement systems. For instance, many human societies progressed from gold coins to paper money, and from paper money to banking system-based electronic payments. One might further consider how the banking system has progressed to allow us to make payments 24/7. One can also think of the progress from bank tellers to ATMs to mobile payment systems. These are the various stages of progress in financial settlements seen in the developed parts of the world.

However, not all the world's countries have gone through the same payment system evolution stages. In the case of telephones, for instance, the developed world had landline phones before the advent of mobile phones. Mobile phones then became increasingly small, and at some point, began to include Internet functions, eventually evolving into today's smartphones. However, in EMEs and developing countries, the smartphone is the first type of phone used by a growing number of people who never had the chance to see or use a landline phone.

The functioning of a bank branch requires electricity, water, phones, and other infrastructure. However, there are many places in the world that do not have such infrastructure. It is in these kinds of places that the digitization of settlements is now spreading rapidly.

For instance, one of the payment methods used widely in Africa is M-PESA. Based on software developed by a Kenyan student in April 2007, M-PESA began as a new settlement/money-transfer service offered by mobile network operator Safaricom using the SMS feature of smartphones. This money transfer service is cheaper than other similar services, and the fee structure is designed to facilitate frequent transfers of small sums.

Of course there are banks, bank branches, as well as banknotes in Kenya, where this new system of payment emerged, but it is only in the capital Nairobi and its suburbs that banknotes can be used for all the usual purposes. Because of the lack of bank branches in the Savanna regions, people living there have no choice but to keep wads of banknotes with them. This, however, puts them at risk of being robbed. When they want to save money, people put it into bottles and bury the bottles in the ground, but this puts the money at the risk of being swept away by floodwaters. Money transfers are entrusted to long-distance bus drivers, but there is no guarantee that such bus drivers will be conscientiously honest. This was the situation in rural Kenya through 2006 (see Chart 4).

It was into this world that M-PESA arrived in around 2007. M-PESA agencies spread rapidly throughout Kenya, enabling people to make money transfers simply by entering the number advertised by the agency into their mobile phones. M-PESA soon became the most widely used method of money transfer (over 90% of those who responded to the survey said that they used it). The legal currency of Kenya is the Kenyan shilling, and M-PESA payments are essentially made in the legal currency.

It appears that the Central Bank of Kenya (CBK) has also become involved in the M-PESA initiative, which is now being promoted as a national project. The initiative, in the same format, is also spreading to other countries, including Tanzania, South Africa, and India.

Meanwhile, Alipay, WeChat Pay, and other QR code payments have become quite common in China. For instance, there are no longer any booths selling entry tickets

(%)

Year	2006	2009	2013
Family/Friends	57.2	35.7	32.7
Buses/matatus (minibuses used as public transport)	26.7	4.0	5.4
Money transfer services	5.3	0.4	1.9
Checks	3.8	1.2	1.3
Direct bank transfers	9.6	3.2	4.3
Post offices	24.2	3.4	1.3
Mobile money	0.0	60.0	91.5

Chart 4 Usage rates of various domestic money transfer channels in Kenya (comparing figures for 2006, 2009, and 2013). *Source* FinAccess National Survey 2013 (since two or more options can be chosen, the total does not add up to a 100)

to the Palace Museum, a world heritage site in Beijing. Instead, there is a large board bearing a magnified QR code that those wishing to gain admission can scan using their smartphones to make an electronic payment. This has eliminated long lines at the entrance and greatly reduced waiting times. It has also eliminated the problem of ticket snatchers, and is likely to have significantly reduced operational expenses related to manning ticket booths and cash management.

It is the inconvenience endured by those without access to the banking system that is propelling the trend toward cashlessness in China and the African countries. As of 2010, half the global population had no access to banks and could not use banks for savings or money transfers (see Fig. 8).

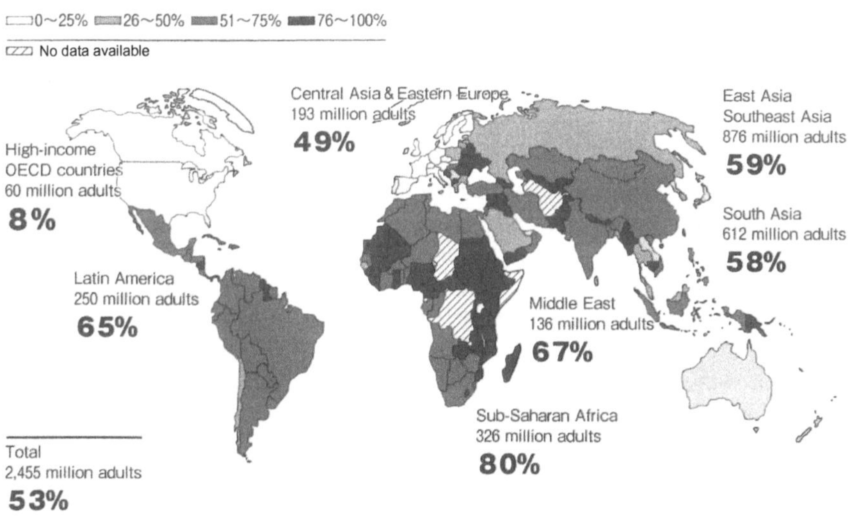

Fig. 8 Ratio of the population without access to banks as of 2010. *Source* World Bank

Of these people, those who were able to obtain smartphones were quite eager to use systems like M-PESA, Alipay, and WeChat Pay, resulting in the rapid spread of such systems. Once something like this happens, business establishments have to hop on board by offering QR-code-based payment methods or risk being left behind. Once most businesses are on board, people stop carrying wallets and small change. Unmanned convenience stores crop up, and society becomes increasingly cashless. It is said that, in China, people seeking donations or begging for money are now forced to print QR codes on their donation boxes or begging baskets.

There are also increasingly cashless societies among the developed nations—Sweden and other Scandinavian countries are some examples. The Scandinavian countries were keen to promote electronic settlements as national projects beginning from the 1990s. Given their small populations, it was important for them as nations to make efficient use of their human resources, and promoting electronic payments was a strategically important means of doing so.

It is a fact that most stores in Sweden either do not or cannot accept cash. It is only tourists who bring in krona notes without realizing this, putting store clerks on the spot, as they are unable to give the customer any change.

Cashlessness directly promotes a more efficient society. Once cash is no longer used, there is no need to spend resources managing, transporting, or guarding it. Once payments are made electronic, theft by store clerks is no longer an issue, and training employees to manage the cash register—which traditionally involves handling cash, coupons, and a variety of cards—becomes a much simpler process.

(2) Trend Toward Cashlessness in Japan

In Japan, however, there is an extremely large amount of cash in circulation, equivalent to 20% of the country's GDP (see Fig. 9). Japan is a relatively safe country and has a large network of ATMs, making it easy for anyone to make large payments with cash. Reflecting this, many people choose to use cash.

For instance, the Kyoto branch of the BOJ sees strong demand for unwrinkled banknotes that is rare even for Japan. Unwrinkled banknotes have traditionally been used in various kinds of celebrations as well as to pay for singing or dancing lessons, and this tradition remains alive even today in the city of Kyoto. It will probably be difficult to relinquish old systems and traditions with a long history.

A country like Japan does not have a blank slate from which to take on the challenge of cashlessness. It has a history of gradually evolving settlement methods. Because of this, Japanese people have a great deal of trust in banks and banknotes. This trust, developed during a long history of experience, is in some ways an obstacle to the spread of cashlessness and, thereby, to society's overall rationalization.

The Growth Strategy Council—Investing for the Future (Headquarters for Japan's Economic Revitalization) decided upon an extremely half-baked target for cashlessness by raising the target rate of cashless payments from 20% at present to 40% in 10 years. If the idea is to increase society's efficiency, the target should be to realize a fully cashless society.

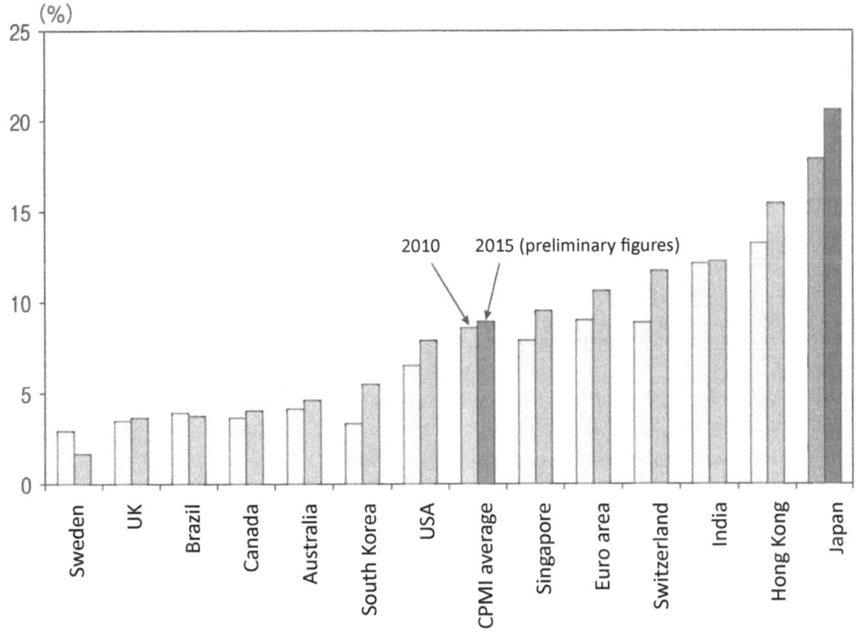

Fig. 9 Outstanding cash in circulation as a percentage of GDP among the world's major economies (2010 → 2015). *Source* BIS Committee on Payments and Market Infrastructures

If such a goal were to be realized, the improvement in efficiency achieved for Japanese society as a whole would be immeasurable. This is particularly true in light of Japan's prospective population decline, which will make it increasingly difficult to find the necessary supermarket or convenience store staff to account for and manage cash, to guard it, transport it, and so on.

Japan can implement cashlessness at a moment's notice if it wants to, because the necessary systems already exist, having been established through the evolutionary stages of its payment methods. Credit cards, prepaid transportation cards, as well as debit cards for instant settlement are all issued and used in Japan today.

However, there are people who do not want to use credit cards because debt is incurred or because of the dangers of overspending. Different generations of Japanese users are most comfortable with different modes of payment, and many in Japan are of the view that accommodating all these different preferences is an important element of customer service.

For instance, bank cards and credit cards with magnetic strips are still used in Japan. Such magnetic-strip-based cards represent a major risk for society, as they have enabled major fake credit card scams. However, a large number of banks are of the view that allowing customers to continue using the cards they have been issued is an essential element of good service that responds to customer needs and increases customer trust.

The credit card business operates based on commissions amounting to more than 3–4% of sales. A great deal of work is involved in processing acquirer-side (member-store) and issuer-side (user) information related to international credit card networks such as Visa and Mastercard, timing the activation of such information accurately, and performing customer management. Many business establishments are unable to afford the fees involved.

By contrast, the cost burden on those making or receiving payments is close to zero in the case of services such as Alipay and WeChat Pay, because the processing is done over the Internet. Of course, Internet-based payment services such as LINE-pay and Mercari also exist in Japan, but they are not widely used.

As society becomes increasingly digitized, cash payments will eventually be replaced by payments using cards and smartphones. Rather than reflecting meticulous and far-sighted planning by the government or the central bank, this transition should be seen as a natural evolution of an economic mechanism playing a key role in the functioning of Japanese society as a whole.

References

Back A (2002) Hashcash-a denial of service counter-measure. http://www.hashcash.org/papers/hashcash.pdf

Bayer D, Haber S, Stornetta WS (1993) Improving the efficiency and reliability of digital time-stamping

Benedetti H, Kostovetsky L (2018) Digital Tulips? returns to investors in initial coin offerings

Chaum D (1982) Blind signatures for untraceable payments. Advances in Cryptology Proceedings of Crypto. 82

Haber S, Stornetta WS (1991) How to time-stamp a digital document. J Cryptol 3(2):99–111

Haber S, Stornetta WS (1997) Secure names for bit-strings. In: Proceedings of the 4th ACM conference

Nakamoto S (2008) Bitcoin: a peer-to-peer electronic cash system. https://bitcoin.org/bitcoin.pdf

Okamoto T, Ohta K (1989) Divertible zero-knowledge interactive proofs and commutative random self-reducibility. Advances in Cryptology—EUROCRYPT'89, LNCS 434, pp 134–149. Springer-Verlag

Chapter 4
Consumer Behavior and Financial Marketing

Tomohiro Senda and Miwa Takemura

Marketing entails gaining an understanding of consumer behavior and leveraging that understanding to establish means of making consumers want to use your products or services. With recent advancements in technology, it has become possible for companies providing services to obtain a large and diverse volume of information on consumer behavior. Therefore, an essential element of contemporary marketing is to use that information to improve understanding of consumer behavior and then use optimal communication methods to provide services that match individual consumers' requirements.

In this chapter, we will use some examples of initiatives undertaken by Mizuho Bank, Ltd. to discuss how banks and their marketing activities will or should change as the technology surrounding financial services evolves.

1 The Role of Banks in Financing

First, let us take a brief look at the role of banks in financing.

What is financing? Financing is the act of an entity with surplus funds lending those funds to another entity with a shortage of funds. There exist many types of lending requirements as well as borrowing requirements, and financial institutions are intermediaries that help optimally match these requirements with each other.

As shown in Fig. 1, there are two types of financing. From the perspective of the lender (individuals, etc.), a typical example of direct financing is equities, while an example of indirect financing is bank deposits. Banks are representative of the type of financial institution that engages in indirect financing.

T. Senda · M. Takemura (✉)
Mizuho Bank Ltd, Tokyo, Japan
e-mail: miwa.takemura@mizuhobk.co.jp

S. Kaji et al. (eds.), *The Economics of Fintech*,
https://doi.org/10.1007/978-981-33-4913-1_4

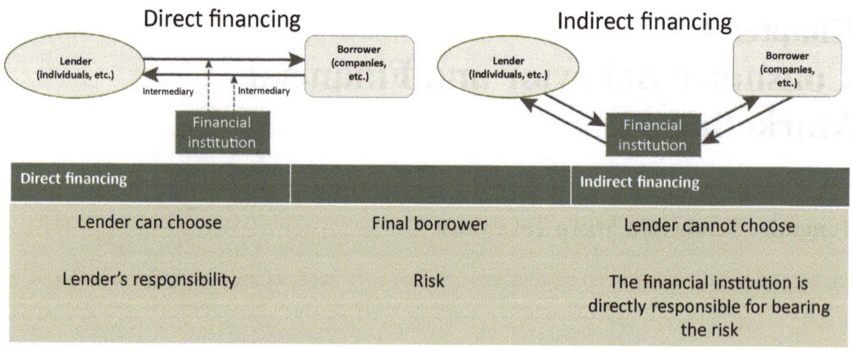

Fig. 1 Methods of financing. *Source* Mizuho Research Institute Ltd

Banks provide a variety of financial services centering on deposits, loans, and exchange, which are their three core business areas.

- Deposits: the business of receiving money deposits from individuals and companies; this is a bank's means of procuring funds
- Loans: the business of lending funds to individuals and companies; this is a bank's means of investing its funds
- Exchange: the business of mediating fund transfers and settlements.

If money were to be compared to blood circulating through society—comprising people, companies, and national and local governments—banks would be like the heart that pumps this blood through a variety of services.

2 Banks and Fintech

It is increasingly clear that fintech—an amalgam of "financing" and "technology"—will greatly change the essential nature of financing. Fintech has led to the emergence of a number of venture firms that provide quick, convenient, and profitable financial services. These firms have begun to consider offering deposit, loan, and exchange services, encroaching on three big business areas that have until now been the exclusive preserve of banks. In other words, it appears that fintech venture firms are a threat to banks.

Online banks that do not have physical branches and conduct their business solely via the Internet, entered the banking industry around the year 2000. Thanks to the convenience of not having to maintain a physical branch, such banks were quickly able to provide highly sophisticated services, causing an increasing number of consumers to use them as their main bank. In this way, even before the spread of fintech, the domestic and international climate surrounding the banking industry had begun to change. It must be acknowledged, therefore, that banks will eventually be driven out of their industry if they continue restricting themselves to their traditional business activities offering conventional services to existing customers.

Going forward, as the applications of fintech continue growing, what is the best way for conventional banks to maintain their raison d'être and effectively compete with fintech venture firms, which are a very real threat to their existence? There are a variety of potential approaches in individual business fields, but Mizuho Bank's view is that it can facilitate innovation in existing service areas through collaboration with fintech venture firms and the adoption of their technologies. In other words, our approach is to adapt to change through synergistic coexistence.

This applies not just to the bank's action plan, but also to marketing activities supporting the action plan. As noted at the start of this chapter, marketing entails gaining an understanding of consumer behavior and leveraging that understanding to establish means of making consumers want to use your products or services. Marketing methods are not something that, once established, are used until no longer functional—they need to be continually upgraded to remain relevant. By adapting to the changes brought about by fintech in the area of marketing, we can get closer to our customers, understand them better, and establish effective methods to make them want to use our services.

3 Marketing and Innovation

Key aspects of running a business include the creation of a client base and market for one's products and services through marketing systems focused on consumer needs, and the use of innovation to generate new kinds of value and customer satisfaction. In this connection, the leading progenitor of modern business management methods, Peter Ferdinand Drucker, wrote the following.[1]

"Because it is the purpose to create a customer, any business enterprise has two—and only two—basic functions: marketing and innovation. These are the entrepreneurial functions."

In the previous section, we mentioned that fintech can be an agency of innovation—that companies can acquire the means to upgrade their marketing activities by adapting to changes generated by the spread of fintech. In this section, I will first explain the roles of marketing and innovation in corporate business activities and then present some examples of innovation realized by Mizuho Bank using marketing and fintech.

(1) What is Marketing?

Let us first take a look at marketing from two perspectives—consumer psychology and behavior, and corporate business activities.

There is a process that goes into making a purchase—the consumer becomes conscious of a latent need, looks for products that could satisfy the need, selects

[1] Drucker (2001).

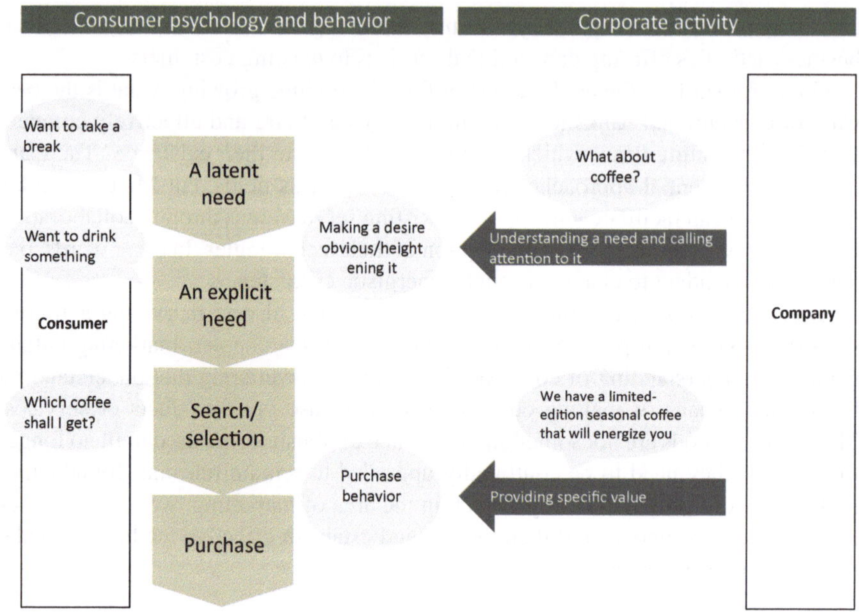

Fig. 2 The perspectives of marketing

the most suitable one, and makes a purchase. Marketing entails understanding the consumer's need and providing value (a product or service) to satisfy that need, and "marketing activities" are the systematization of this process.

Let us assume, for instance, that the consumer becomes conscious of a latent need to "take a break" and "drink something" as illustrated in Fig. 2. By detecting and understanding this latent need, a company can suggest "coffee," thereby heightening the need and enticing the consumer into choosing coffee. By providing value that satisfies the consumer's need in a more specific way at the time of purchase, the company can also provide added value.

(2) What is Innovation?

Innovation can also be understood from the two perspectives of consumer psychology and behavior, and corporate business activities. However, unlike marketing, which simply works on an already-present need, innovation creates new value by suggesting a need the consumer was not aware of in the first place.

For instance, the writers of this chapter do not much like coffee but still enjoy going to Starbucks because it offers a relaxing space where we can drink something and unwind. Starbucks created the concept (the new value) of a third space away from the home or the workplace where one could go to take a break (see Fig. 3). It is the creation of this new value that amounts to innovation.

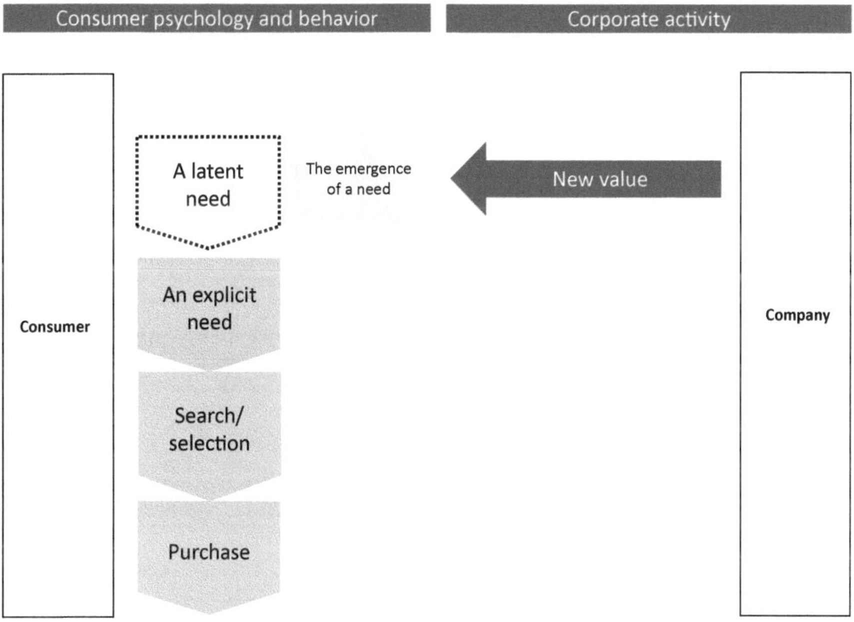

Fig. 3 The perspectives of innovation

(3) Marketing x Innovation—Some Examples

To recap, marketing entails providing value that satisfies an already-present consumer need, while innovation entails creating a new need. Innovation—creating a new need—is a more challenging task than marketing, which simply nudges a consumer toward making a purchase once he/she becomes conscious of a specific need, but innovation without the help of marketing to guide a significant number of consumers toward making a purchase would be futile. It is only by combining these complementary processes that new markets (consumers, business activities) can be created (see Fig. 4).

Example: Softbank x Mizuho (see Fig. 5).

Fintech company J.Score CO., LTD.—a collaborative venture between Mizuho Bank and SoftBank Group Corp.—offers a service called AI Score Lending, which uses big data and artificial intelligence (AI) to provide loans to individual customers that are fully processed online. With the customer's consent, AI Score Lending computes his/her AI Score by consolidating data collected by Mizuho Bank, SoftBank, and Yahoo Japan. Based on this score, the service determines the maximum loan amount and the appropriate interest rate, and the various procedures are speedily completed over the Internet.

Creditworthiness has traditionally been evaluated based on a customer's total assets, annual income and so on, but with AI Score Lending, a customer's future potential and character/lifestyle trajectory can also be taken into account. Specifically,

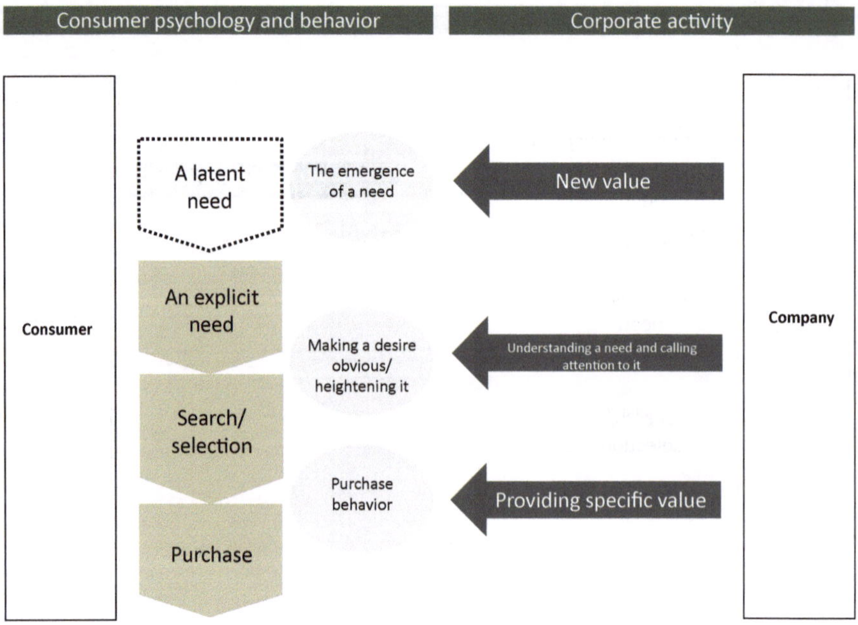

Fig. 4 Creating a new market

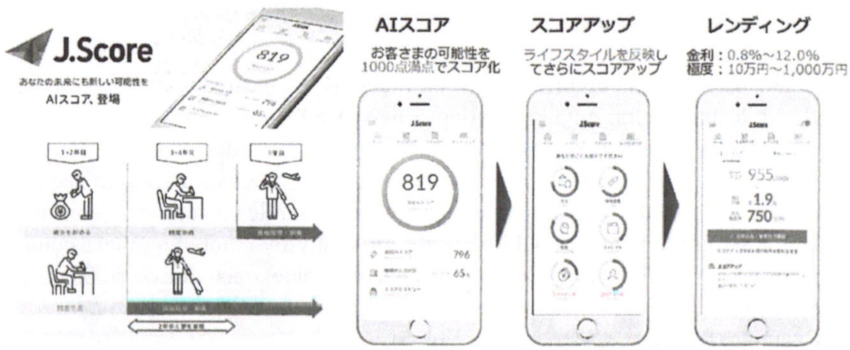

Fig. 5 Service provided by J.Score. *Source* The J.Score website

the service is designed to track customers' day-to-day activities including exercise, study, sleep, and spending habits, and customers who maintain good habits are given high AI Scores.

This service allows Mizuho Bank and SoftBank to provide a new value to consumers, namely "a new way of interacting with money that expands the possibilities of the future (our translation)."

A new service called AI Score Reward was also launched in October 2018, which allows customers to win "rewards" from partner companies based on their AI Score rank, which can be used toward self-actualization or a better lifestyle.

In addition to the above, Mizuho Bank has developed numerous other services, such as a robo-advisor service for asset management (SMART FOLIO) and a smartphone payment app (Mizuho Wallet App) for iPhones, Apple Watches, and Android devices.

4 Consumer Behavior and Marketing—Changes in Consumer Behavior and Methods of Targeting

Setting fintech aside for the moment, let us take a look at the relationship between consumer behavior and marketing from the perspective of consumer data.

As illustrated in Fig. 6, mainstream marketing has conventionally involved a specific set of activities designed to help sell mass-oriented services that were developed by companies based on the limited information available to them. The problem with this is that the needs of consumers are diverse, and mass-oriented services are not equally acceptable to all consumers. In recent years, however, with the evolution of IoT and other technology, it has become possible for companies to acquire large volumes of diverse information on consumer behavior (big data) directly from consumers themselves. This—the point of origin of the information—is the biggest difference between marketing as we have known it so far and marketing in the future.

Practical applications of AI are also becoming increasingly available to help with processing such information, with the result that companies can acquire insights into and analyze the needs of diverse consumers using their large databases of information. This enables them to provide services designed to satisfy the needs of individual consumers. Where, in the past, consumers had no choice but to passively accept mass-oriented solutions, it is now becoming possible for them to actively choose

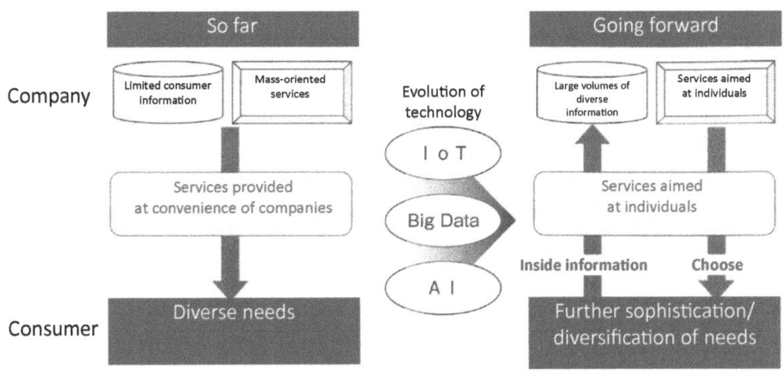

Fig. 6 Changes in marketing activities

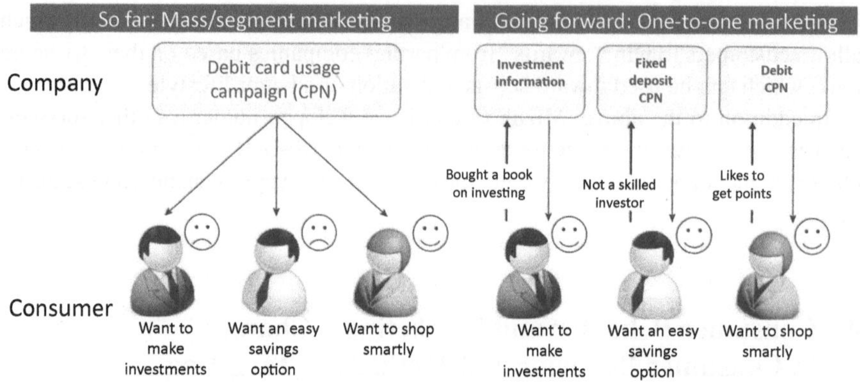

Fig. 7 Targeted marketing

services that match their needs by making their personal information available to companies.

Figure 7 illustrates the difference between conventional and new, targeted methods of marketing. The conventional approach—mass marketing or segment marketing—is uniformly applied to all customers, and it is inefficient because of its inability to cater to the requirements of all consumers alike. The new method, on the other hand, enables each marketing campaign to focus on a specific group of target customers.

This targeted or one-to-one marketing uses an approach called database marketing, which utilizes large volumes of diverse consumer behavior data to comprehend individual consumers' needs more efficiently. The degree of this approach's success depends on how much diverse consumer information a company can obtain and how precisely it can infer the needs of individual consumers using this information.

5 Database Marketing

In database marketing, the large volume of diverse information accumulated in a database regarding a consumer's affiliation, purchase history, and so on is used to infer that consumer's needs and inclinations, and marketing measures designed based on this knowledge are then implemented.

Database marketing uses a database—which is data structured in a way that can be "capitalized"—as the foundation for analyzing consumers and designing, implementing, visualizing the effects of, and refining marketing measures. This process involves implementing a plan-do-check-act (PDCA) cycle as illustrated in Chart 1.

Finding a good balance in terms of the effort put into (1) analyzing customers versus (2) designing marketing measures in the Plan stage of the cycle is key when it comes to sustained implementation of the PDCA cycle in database marketing. The people in charge of (1) and (2) tend to be different, with analysts being in charge

Foundation:	**Capitalizing customer information** Collecting data and putting it into a structure that makes it easy to analyze and use
Plan:	**(1) Analyzing customers** Analyzing customers by diverse criteria with the objective of perceiving/predicting customer needs and formulating marketing measures **(2) Designing marketing measures** Using the data to design marketing measures that are aligned with the company's objectives, to ensure that the measures are feasible
Do:	**Implementing the measures** Implementing the measures by launching them on various communication platforms
Check:	**Visualizing the effect oft he measures** Verifying the effectiveness oft he measures and evaluating them in terms of rules for whether to continue/suspend a measure
Act:	**Refining the measures** Designing and implementing improved measures

Chart 1 PDCA cycle in database marketing

of (1) and business planners being in charge of (2), and in a large organization, even the departments in charge of the two activities may be different. What often happens in such cases is that the analysts view database marketing as an entirely analytical process and maintain an excessively narrow focus that does not take into consideration that the objective of the analysis is to formulate marketing measures. Meanwhile, business planners tend to design measures based on intuition, without taking sufficient account of the data. Such intuitively designed measures often end up going no further than the “Plan” stage. Since they fail to progress to the subsequent Do, Check and Act stages, they are essentially useless.

Of course, it is just as pointless to undertake a business plan that makes it through the Do stage and then runs out of steam. The PDCA cycle is complete only when the effect of the implemented measure has been visualized and evaluated using data, the necessary improvements have been made, and the new measure has been implemented.

(1) Changes in Customer Analysis Methods

Customer analysis, one of the core tasks in database marketing, involves establishing a logic for targeting, i.e., deciding when, where (through what channel), and to whom to propose a certain service in order to promote the use or purchase of that service. The effectiveness of a plan derived from this logic is then estimated, the feasibility of the plan confirmed, and targets set.

Traditionally, it was common to arrive at the aforementioned logic using statistical methods, such as regression analysis and clustering, together with the experience and intuition of the person in charge of the process. However, there are limits to what human experience can do when it comes to understanding or predicting individual consumers’ needs. Thus, in recent years, there have been cases of establishing the logic using AI solely based on data, without taking human experience into consideration.

What is expected from AI in such cases is the formulation of more accurate and more inclusive target lists (including a larger number of targets who will eventually use/purchase the service), and the discovery of new targets who could not have been discovered using human experience, which tends to have a relatively limited scope. Further, services that can automate the establishment of large quantities of logic will make analytical tasks more efficient, enabling the shifting of some analytical resources to design and making it easier to combine the two tasks of analyzing customers and designing measures. In other words, such services will facilitate the shift to one-to-one marketing as well as enhance the functioning of the PDCA cycle.

(2) Database Marketing x Innovation—Some Examples

Let us look at some examples of innovation paired with database marketing. In Fig. 8, the "Targeting method and communication period" segment shows targeting methods along the y-axis, and consumer psychology and behavior along the x-axis. The items from "Occurrence of action/event" to "Behavior" relate to one-to-one marketing approaches. A marketing method based on the occurrence of an action/event involves approaching a potential customer once the need has become apparent. An example would be the proposal of relevant services to a consumer who comes to an asset management consultation meeting. The next item is "Predicting occurrence of action/event," which involves looking for target customers in the same category as targets for whom "Occurrence of action/event" happened. In the sense that it involves prediction, it is more sophisticated, but it is not very innovative as there is no perception of the need arising.

It is difficult to perceive a need arising simply based on data owned by a bank, which only includes customer attributes such as gender and age, information on past transactions, and customer behavior immediately prior to selection of a product. A more accurate prediction can be made by using information related to other services (for instance, credit card usage information), behavior on other companies' websites, and so on. At Mizuho Bank, we have introduced an initiative for perceiving customer needs by utilizing such information with the consent of our customers. Using this method, we can even approach customers in segments that are not usually approached, which allows us to expand the number of customers targeted for a measure, thereby potentially increasing its effectiveness.

The following cooperative venture with a fintech firm is one of Mizuho Bank's initiatives aimed at realizing behavior-based marketing.

Case study: Money Forward for Mizuho (Fig. 9).

Money Forward ME is a personal financial management (PFM) tool offered by Money Forward, Inc., for household budget and asset management. Using this tool, customers can manage all their online finances in one place without having to severally login to all the bank accounts or mileage point services they use.

We mentioned earlier that innovation is the act of creating a need. Using data to perceive customer needs is not as powerful as innovation, which creates a new need where none existed, but the above initiative aims to make interesting innovations possible through intelligent measures (in this particular example, by cooperating in a business venture with a company capable of innovation).

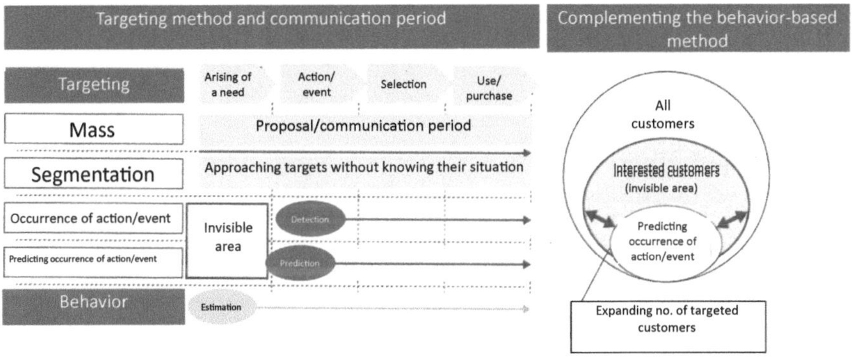

Fig. 8 Innovation paired with database marketing. *Note* Mizuho Bank's definition of behavior-based marketing: a marketing method that aims to expand the number of targeted customers based on their actions/thoughts (behavior), thereby increasing the effectiveness of a measure

Fig. 9 Example of a cooperative venture between a financial institution and a fintech firm. *Source* Mizuho Bank website

6 The Starting Point of Business Activities

As mentioned at the beginning of this chapter, recent advancements in technology have made a large volume of diverse consumer information available to businesses, and it has become essential for businesses to utilize this information to provide services and communication that are in line with consumers' needs. Another important business activity is to create new markets, which involves taking the initiative to create new needs (i.e., innovation) in addition to marketing to consumers based on their existing needs.

At Mizuho Bank, we have discovered that we can innovate by adapting to change through coexistence with fintech firms, but fintech is not the only means by which banks can innovate. The important thing is to continuously think about what it is that consumers (customers) are seeking and choose effective methods for responding to those needs.

Reference

Drucker PF (2001) The essential Drucker: selections from the management works of Peter F. Drucker (Japanese edition), Diamond, Inc

Chapter 5
The Impact of Fintech on Existing Financial Institutions

Kazuhiko Tajimi

1 An Overview of Fintech

Fintech is a colloquial term created by joining together the words "finance" and "technology."[1] It would be appropriate to define fintech as the group of technologies that have been transforming financial services in recent years. In its broad sense, "technology" here refers to information and communication technology or ICT. Financial services themselves have existed for over a century, but the nature of these services has changed dramatically with the rapid evolution of ICT in recent years, as a variety of simultaneously convenient and low-cost services are generated one after another.

This evolution of financial services is being spearheaded by associations or companies called startups. Startups all over the world have been revolutionizing the provision of financial services using new technologies. It would be impossible to provide a comprehensive list of all such new services, but personal financial management (PFM) is a representative example. People use a wide range of financial services including banking, insurance, and investment services. What PFM service providers do is to enable them to check their usage status of each of these services in a single view. Secure password management and web scraping[2] are some of the new technologies used to provide PFM services. Of course, these technologies are no longer all that new, but they were quite experimental when PFM services first became popular.

Startups that are revolutionizing financial services are also called fintech companies, and several of these have now become extremely large companies.[3] The nature

[1] It used to be written FinTech, but has recently become widely established as "fintech."

[2] This is in the process of being replaced by read APIs (Application Programming Interfaces) offered by banks, which will be discussed in detail later.

[3] A unicorn is a startup valued at over JPY 100 billion, which far exceeds the scale of a small or medium-sized enterprise.

K. Tajimi (✉)
Mizuho Financial Group Inc, Tokyo, Japan
e-mail: kazuhiko.tajimi@mizuhofg.co.jp

S. Kaji et al. (eds.), *The Economics of Fintech*,
https://doi.org/10.1007/978-981-33-4913-1_5

of financial services itself has changed significantly. They are no longer limited to the financial sector nor bound by the size of the company, and they have expanded the scope of competition.

2 Technology and the Financial Sector

The financial sector and technology are now so interconnected as to be inseparable. Going back in history, it was the 1960s that core banking was introduced, and since then, technology has always formed the backdrop to the evolution of financial services, be it online systemization to improve operational efficiency, the strengthening of customer information management and other supporting services, or the introduction of internet banking.

As banking services involve money, the falsification of information cannot be allowed, and changes need to be reflected promptly. Information handled by banks is updated daily, and financial institutions ensure correct information handling by investing a lot of money and time in updating their ICT systems. These systems are essentially back-end systems, meaning that customers do not come directly in contact with them. With fintech, however, this is changing in a big way, because fintech companies provide front-end services, a good example being PFM services.

Companies that support financial technology are also evolving rapidly. Systems integrators[4] that have traditionally supported the back end of financial operations tend to be large companies,[5] but most fintech companies leading the evolution of front-end services are small-scale startups.

From famous fintech companies to virtually unknown startups and entrepreneurs who are still in the process of setting up their companies, everybody's sights seem to be set on the financial sector. A large number of business ideas are coming together, being inspired by each other, and creating a virtuous cycle leading to rapid evolution in fintech.

Why does the financial sector attract startups? Probably because the financial sector took a lead in introducing ICT systems, making it easy for startups to deal with financial information, and because of the simultaneous development of all the technologies required for utilizing this information.

Financial information is fundamentally easy to handle. Account balances, transaction histories, dates, and other categories of information are recorded numerically, and banks have been recording and accumulating this information on a daily basis

---

[4]In Japan, they are sometimes called SIers, although this is not standard in English-speaking parts of the world.

[5]It must be mentioned that this is special to Japan. Financial institutions in Japan have tended to outsource system development. In most U.S. and European financial institutions, the system infrastructure may be supplied by external organizations, but customization of the system is done by in-house systems engineers. Japanese banks do have in-house IT staff, but there is a big difference between IT staff and systems engineers capable of systems development.

right from the time core banking was introduced. Traditionally, this kind of information was managed by each financial institution separately, and while customers could access their information, they were unable to interact with it in digital format.

As the Internet become widespread, however, it became possible for customers to see their data in digital format too. The account balances and transaction histories of millions of customers amount to an enormous volume of information, but rapid progress in computing technology has enabled the processing of this volume of information. Meanwhile, the evolution of cloud computing alongside processing capabilities has done away with the need for enormous investments in storage devices for storing all the accumulated data. It is on the strength of historical developments such as these that fintech has been able to make an entry into the market in such a big way.

Since 2010, there has been an explosive increase in the scope of data that can be handled. In addition to transaction histories, financial institutions are now able to obtain information related to customers' internet banking histories and behavior on other websites, including information not directly relevant to financial institutions. To know their customers better, financial institutions even gather customer information from social media and retail store purchase histories. Many companies in the retail sector go to the extent of collecting data through in-store sensors and cameras,[6] though this is rare in the financial sector. As the scope of information spreads, the amount of data accumulated also grows exponentially. In 2016, the amount of data in circulation was to the tune of 98 exabytes[7] per month.

It has also become easy to store data generated on a day-to-day basis. Public cloud services such as Amazon Web Services (AWS) and Google Cloud Platform (GCP) enable large volumes of data to be stored without the need for a server of one's own. Computer performance has also been improving by leaps and bounds to help handle the increasingly diverse types of data generated. In May 1997, a supercomputer called the IBM Deep Blue defeated chess champion Garry Kasparov. Smartphones these days have ten times the computational performance of the IBM Deep Blue.[8] In other words, the hand-held devices we carry around in our pockets are capable of outperforming a chess champion and also functioning as tools to provide financial services. This is the age we are living in.

[6]The use of data from security cameras for non-security purposes violates the Personal Information Protection Law, so companies are required to explain their motives to and get consent from customers in advance.

[7]According to Cisco (2017), the global IP traffic run rate was 1.2 ZB per year (i.e., 96 EB per month).

[8]Computational performance is measured by floating point operations per second (FLOPS), and the Deep Blue was able to achieve 11.38 GFLOPS, but the iPhone 6, which comes with an Apple A8 chip, can achieve 115.2 GFLOPs. According to the well-known Moore's Law, the number of transistors on an integrated circuit (IC) chip doubles every 18 months. Given that an IC chip's sophistication increases with the number of transistors, it is natural that computing power should also increase exponentially. Some point out, however, that the pace of increase in the number of transistors on an IC chip is falling short of Moore's Law.

It is not just our devices that are becoming more powerful. The algorithms they use are also evolving rapidly. As mentioned earlier, the kinds of data that can be handled continue to increase and diversify. A well-known concept is an artificial intelligence (AI) function called deep learning.

Deep learning is based on neural networks,[9] emulating the characteristics of the human brain, and has a long history. The reason it has been drawing attention recently is because its performance has far surpassed that of competing algorithms and reached a level where it can be put to practical use in applications where the algorithm's discernment is even greater than that of humans.[10] However, considerable computing power is required for building mathematical models based on deep learning, and it has to be mentioned that rapid improvement in computational performance is what has enabled the evolution of deep learning.

By 2010, the resolution of cameras built into smartphones had surpassed 10 megapixels, which is higher than what the naked eye can perceive.[11] This means, for instance, that cancers can be detected much more effectively using machines to diagnose images taken by gastroscopes. This is one of the uses of deep learning, and technological advancement was necessary to achieve this.

3 Outlook for Technology

Is absolutely anything possible with a powerful technology like deep learning? The answer to this question as of 2018 is that it is still too early to tell. For instance, there is something called the symbol grounding problem. A three-year-old human child may never have seen a seahorse, but is very likely to be able to guess that it is a "horse of the sea" simply by putting the words "sea" and "horse" together. To a computer, however, the word "seahorse" is no more than a sequence of letters, and it would not be easy for it to match it to an image of a seahorse, because the meaning of the word "seahorse" is not "grounded" in a computer. Researchers are working tirelessly on difficult problems like this and will probably solve them eventually. However, there still remain many types of data processing that do not come easily to machines.

[9] The synapses of the human brain are connected on many layers, and deep learning is what happens when these connections span numerous layers, i.e., go deep down. Neural networks are algorithms that have a vast scope. Countless algorithms have been derived from neural networks for various purposes.

[10] In 2012, University of Toronto Professor Geoffrey Hinton achieved a superior error rate of around 17% for deep learning compared with the much larger error rate of 26% for other methods, winning the ImageNet Large Scale Visual Recognition Challenge (LSVRC). As of 2016, the error rate has dropped below 5% and deep learning algorithms have become mainstream.

[11] When it comes to perceiving things clearly, the human field of vision is 2° or so. Taking into account the processing ability of the brain, this is the equivalent of 7 megapixels in terms of computer resolution.

It is extremely difficult to envisage what kinds of technologies will emerge in the future and when, and how they will change our lives, but an example of precisely such a prediction endeavor is the hype cycle[12] (see Fig. 1).

In the 2018 hype cycle, blockchain technology is plotted on the graph somewhere between Peak of Inflated Expectations and Trough of Disillusionment. Nine years before that, in the 2009 hype cycle, there was no mention of blockchain technology. It was too early for it to be included in the hype cycle at that time, as it was only in 2008 that the Satoshi Nakamoto paper on bitcoins was published and in 2009 that the currency became available for use.

Blockchain technology, which had attracted the attention of nearly no one in 2009, has become indispensable in the context of fintech in 2018. It is a good example of something that did not even exist 10 years ago, is causing a stir today, and is hard to predict the trajectory of over the next 10 years.

4 Status of Existing Financial Institutions

With the rapid emergence of a large number of fintech companies, services offered by banks are also changing. Based on nine job attributes, the University of Oxford estimated which of a list of 702 jobs are likely to be computerized in the next 10 years. According to the estimate, roughly 47% of all U.S. jobs are highly likely to be replaced by computers, including professions such as bank loan officers; bookkeeping, accounting, and auditing clerks; and credit authorizers, checkers, and clerks[13] (see Chart 1).

This is no time for financial institutions to be idle onlookers. They must anticipate the future, five or 10 years down the road, and consider innovative measures without delay.[14]

While the importance of a technology-oriented perspective cannot be denied, a user-oriented perspective is also extremely important. Millennials[15] and Generation Z,[16] who are called "digital natives" because of their familiarity with computers and

---

[12]Gartner, an IT-related research and advisory firm, publishes a graphical presentation of the cycle of emerging technologies for the reference of companies considering IT investments. The graph divides the cycle into five phases, namely, Technology Trigger, Peak of Inflated Expectations, Trough of Disillusionment, Slope of Enlightenment, and Plateau of Productivity.

[13]The study mentions a variety of occupations including sports officials and hotel desk clerks, but only finance-related examples have been cited here in the context of fintech.

[14]Mizuho Financial Group, Inc, has announced plans to cut 19 K jobs, while the Mitsubishi UFJ Financial Group, Inc. and Sumitomo Mitsui Financial Group, Inc. have announced plans to cut 9.5 K and 4 K jobs, respectively. Apart from this, plans to consolidate and reorganize bank branches have also been announced.

[15]Also called Generation Y, the Millennials are people who were born between 1980 and 1990, but some definitions include people born between the mid-1970s and mid-1990s.

[16]Members of Generation Z, which is the generation after Generation Y.

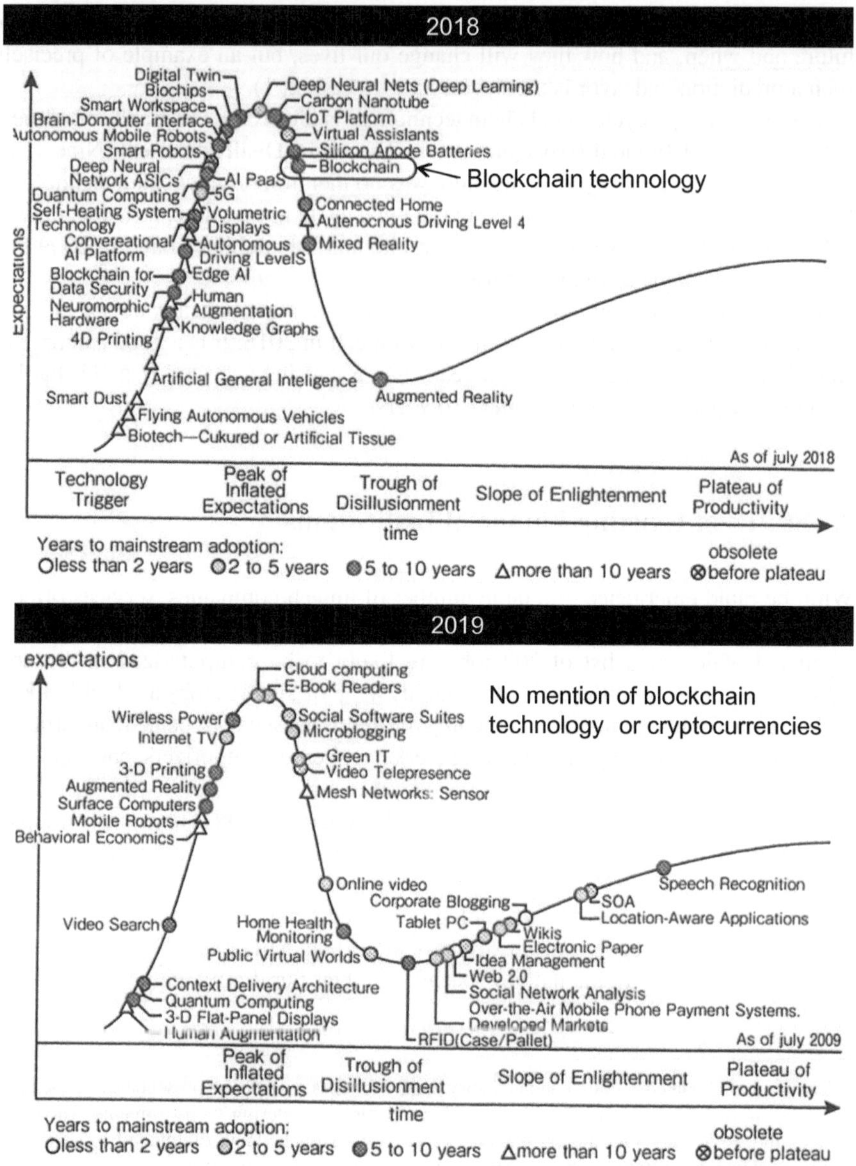

Fig. 1 The hype cycle. *Source* Gartner

the Internet from a very early age, are the future users of financial products, and financial institutions have to develop services that they will be able to appreciate.

Loan Officers	Bill and Account Collectors	Inspectors, Testers, Sorters and Samplers
Umpires, Referees, and Other Sports Officials	Paralegals and Legal Assistants	Motion Picture Projectionists
Real Estate Brokers	Hotel, Motel, and Resort Desk Clerks	Camera and Photographic Equipment Repairers
Hosts and Hostesses, Restaurant	Telemarketers	Financial Examiners
Insurance Appraisers	Sewers, Hand	Opticians
Animal Breeders	Watch Repairers	Pesticide Handlers, Sprayers
Telephone Operators	Tax Preparers	Dental Laboratory Technicians
Compensation and Benefits Managers	Library Assistants	Surveying and Mapping Technicians
Cashiers	Data Entry Keyers	Landscaping and Groundskeeping Workers
Ushers, Lobby Attendants, and Ticket Takers	Etchers and Engravers	Operating Engineers and Other Construction Equipment Operators
Gaming Dealers	Customer Service Representatives	Door-to-Door Sales Workers, News and Street Vendors, and Related Workers
Manicurists and Pedicurists	Bookkeeping, Accounting, and Auditing Clerks	Helpers–Painters, Paperhangers, Plasterers, and Stucco Masons
Credit Authorizers, Checkers, and Clerks		

Chart 1 Occupations and professions highly likely to be computerized in the future

A survey of Generation Z[17] and Millennials showed that 53% considered all products and services offered by banks to be similar, 71% would rather visit the dentist than listen to something a bank employee had to tell them, 33% expected banks to disappear in the future, and 73% would like to see financial services offered by companies like Google, Amazon, and Apple.

Under such circumstances, financial institutions have, unfortunately, been put on the back foot. This was probably one of the reasons for the collapse of Lehman Brothers in the global financial crisis of 2008. In the wake of the crisis, many financial institutions around the world suffered considerable asset valuation losses even if they were not driven to bankruptcy, shaking the world's confidence in finance. The root of the problem was that highly risky financial products were being traded as though they were low-risk products. However, the financial market has become a globally connected market, so a problem in one part of that market can easily spread worldwide. This was what happened in 2008, prompting financial authorities throughout the world to tighten financial regulations[18] to prevent another such crisis.

Japanese financial institutions also had to write off their losses and formulate measures to prevent the reoccurrence of such a crisis. Meanwhile, technologies such as cloud computing, blockchains, and deep learning were advancing in the fintech industry. For financial institutions, the global financial crisis of 2008 was indeed the

---

[17] Viacom Scratch (2013).

[18] To prevent another financial crisis, various regulatory frameworks have been agreed on or brought into effect since the collapse of Lehman Brothers, including Basel III, a regulatory framework on bank capital adequacy (September 2010), an increase in capital requirements of global systemically important banks' (G-SIBs; November 2011), and the Volcker Rule, which regulates the investment activities of U.S. banks (July 2010).

consequence of their own actions, but it was also a lost opportunity to adopt these new technologies.

5 Startups and Fintech Companies Entering the Field of Financial Services

Even as financial institutions were put on the defensive, startups began to offer a range of financial services. Rather than jump right into the provision of large-scale services, they began small, specializing in one particular product or service, unlike traditional banks that offer a comprehensive range of financial services. There were startups offering only housing loans, startups specializing in SME financing, and startups offering credit scoring models. Some users began to make use of these services. True, these companies did not offer the full range of services, but the services they did offer were appreciated by the "early adopters," i.e., customers who are among the first to start using a new service.

This phenomenon is called unbundling, because it involves the unbundling of financial services packages and the separate selling of each service. The next step from this is to bundle the various services offered by startups into a comprehensive package of services. This is called rebundling. Many financial institutions have already introduced personal financial management (PFM) services, which is a good example of rebundling.

The information advantage of financial institutions must be mentioned here. Ordinarily, financial institutions examine the financial situation of companies seeking loans, and loans are only approved for companies judged capable of repaying them. This used to be a task only financial institutions, which employed loan officers, were capable of undertaking. These days, however, there are numerous sources for acquiring information about companies. Financial information is amassed by accounting software used by companies, a company's reputation can be discovered via social media, and the amount of business a company is doing can be inferred from satellite pictures of its parking lot (how full or empty it is). In this way, financial institutions are losing their information advantage, and fintech companies have begun to develop credit extension businesses of their own.[19]

The same is true of personal loans. These days, a fairly good estimation of an individual's creditworthiness can be made using information obtained from social media or PFM services, so financial institutions are gradually losing the information

[19]Though not a fintech company, e-commerce company Amazon has begun its own credit business, Amazon Lending, using sales information as a criterion for assessing creditworthiness. The Japanese e-commerce company Rakuten has started providing a similar service of its own. If a company does all of its business through e-commerce, companies like Amazon or Rakuten are in a better position than traditional financial institutions to understand its performance.

edge they used to have in conducting credit businesses. To put it another way, individuals and SMEs now have a better chance of procuring funds on good terms if they are willing to disclose relevant information about themselves.

There are numerous new sources of information relevant to the credit business, and different fintech companies might focus on different sources. As described above new businesses can easily be started thanks to the availability of digital information and cloud computing, which requires a low level of initial investment.

6 What Should Existing Financial Institutions Do?

Conventional financial institutions are falling behind fintech companies. Unfortunately, the first thing they must do to catch up and continue providing services to their existing customer base is to digitize their handwritten documents.

Specific measures being adopted differ from one financial institution to another. Some are acquiring or partnering with fintech companies that are already providing their own set of services, while others are setting up internal departments for new business creation (see Fig. 2). In Japan, three megabanks and some regional financial institutions have already set up specialized departments for this purpose. The Mizuho Financial Group has established Blue Lab, a company for open innovation, in partnership with Silicon-Valley-based venture capital firm World Innovation Lab and others. The Mitsubishi UFJ Financial Group has also established Japan Digital Design, Inc. for new business creation. Apart from these, there are many other initiatives financial institutions are undertaking, such as promoting accelerator programs, providing space for these programs, and sharing laboratories with fintech companies.

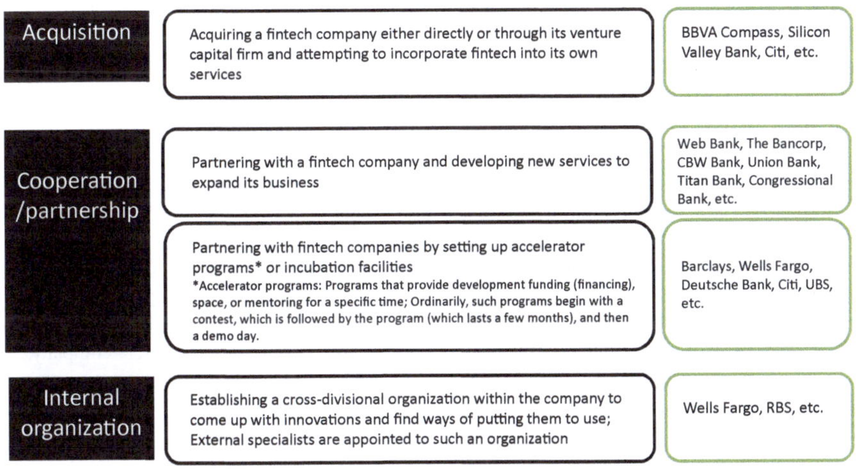

Fig. 2 Fintech initiatives taken by overseas financial institutions. *Source* Mizuho Research Institute Ltd

In addition to fintech companies, IT giants and companies like Amazon are also gradually entering the banking business. Banks, on the other hand, are prevented by the Banking Act from entering other business areas. Although the June 2018 revision of the Banking Act relaxed some of the regulations, banks or bank holding companies still essentially need the advance permission of the Prime Minister[20] to acquire or possess anything over the standard percentage of voting rights (5% for banks, 15% for bank holding companies) in a finance-related IT or other company.[21] In brief, the hurdles are high and many conditions are attached to banks entering other business areas, and conventional investment-related restrictions make it difficult for banks to gain dominant positions in these areas.

Of course the hurdles for companies in other industries attempting to enter the banking industry are also high, as they need to obtain a banking license first. However, as in the case of Amazon's entry into the lending business,[22] it is easy for such companies to enter the business from a position of strength, because they can consolidate the data they have accumulated through their other businesses[23] to provide better services.

In the Japanese market, there are now many banks that have been established by retail companies. Examples include Rakuten Bank, Ltd. (2000), Seven Bank, Ltd. (2001), AEON Bank, Ltd. (2006), and Lawson Bank, Inc. (2016). All these banks are in possession of customers' purchase histories in the retail sector, which gives them an edge when it comes to operating their banking businesses. Of course, the use of information has to be in accordance with the Personal Information Protection Law, and there are likely to be other issues as well, but the fact that they have customer contact points at their respective e-commerce sites or stores is an advantage for these retail-origin banks.

Banks should also be able to find ways to enter the retail and other industries. The barriers for companies from other industries entering the banking industry have become lower with a narrowing of the information advantage gap, but meanwhile, banks are lacking in many kinds of expertise possessed by companies in other industries. In such a situation, banks need to not just work on getting the Banking Act revised in order to make it more difficult for other industries to enter the

[20] Permission is given on condition that said permission will or is likely to contribute to an improvement of the services offered by the bank or bank holding company.

[21] The negative phrasing notwithstanding, this is a major relaxation of the rules for banks. Other regulations, apart from matters related to investment in IT firms, were also simultaneously relaxed, such as the uniform 50% rule for income dependence related to associated businesses, which means that at least 50% of the income of a subsidiary company must come from the parent company.

[22] In Japan, this business is conducted by AMAZON CAPITAL SERVICE LIMITED LIABILITY CO.

[23] Despite this advantage, companies are not allowed to use customers' personal information for any purpose not authorized by the customer. Information that is not classified as personal information falls outside the scope of the Personal Information Protection Law, but moves to expand the usage scope of such information are proceeding cautiously and can only be implemented after obtaining customers' understanding and consent.

banking industry, they must also supplement their own capabilities by strengthening partnerships with companies in other industries.[24]

7 API as a Means of Partnering with Other Industries

In 2017, the Banking Act was revised to relax regulations regarding the investment ratio of banks and bank holding companies in other companies. In 2018, another revision was made to the Banking Act with regard to open APIs.

An API itself is not a new technology. It is merely an interface that connects several software programs. The APIs referred to here are web APIs, which help transfer information from one program to another over the Internet. A cleverly designed API can make it easy for multiple programs to work together, creating an environment conducive to new business creation. This concept is called the API economy.

The "open" in open API indicates "externally disclosed," in the sense that banks, which provide financial services, develop APIs that can access their data and deliver it to the appropriate fintech companies.[25]

The advancement of technology is what prompted the Banking Act to take APIs into consideration. The PFM services mentioned earlier take the user IDs and passwords of individual users and use them to aggregate information from financial institutions and other websites using a method called web scraping (or screen scraping). Web scraping has been in use for a long time, but there were a few problems with it. Not only were users reluctant to hand over their passwords, there were also security concerns regarding the accessing of financial institutions' data resources via methods/routes not directly controlled by those institutions. Switching to APIs enables secure management of IDs and passwords as well as more-efficient information transfer.

8 Approach to New Business Creation

What kind of new businesses can APIs create? One example is Uber, the ride sharing application provided by U.S.-based Uber Technologies, Inc. In the Uber app, the user's current location is indicated on the map, and the desired destination is input by the user. The app uses these two pieces of information to select the appropriate cab and dispatch it to the user's current location. Payments are made through a credit card already registered with the app, and the receipt is sent electronically via email. After the ride, the user and the driver both get to rate each other, and this information

[24]In November 2018, LINE and Mizuho Bank announced their intent to set up the LINE Bank. From Mizuho Bank's perspective, this was a step aimed at benefitting from LINE's customer contact points.

[25]These fintech companies are called electronic payment agents.

is used to improve services. There is nothing groundbreaking about the technology used by Uber. What is important about it[26] is that it has found a way to provide a service in response to an existing need at a low cost.

Another thing banks can learn from innovative new services is how to win customers. No innovative new service has ever started off with a large number of users from the get go. Take the example of Apple's iPod. Music was always distributed through physical media, even though the media evolved over time from records to cassettes to CDs. With the arrival of CDs, musical data had already been digitized, so that even before the arrival of the iPod, music could be sent or received in the form of digital data. Of course, sharing such data without the right permissions has always been illegal, but there have been users who did so nevertheless.

The iPod legally liberated people from having to use physical media for the distribution of music. In the beginning, many people clung to physical media like CDs because the intangibility of digital data made them insecure, but the convenience of the latter soon won over many users, expanding the iPod's user base.

Attention must be paid to early iPod users. There were probably some users who enjoyed music through digital data even before the iPod was launched, and others who may have wanted to experience a new service like that offered by the iPod without fully understanding it. Even if only one in a hundred used the service, they could have encouraged their friends and acquaintances to try it, potentially expanding the user base to ten in a hundred. With a few people in each demographic already roped in, it became easy to eventually win over the remainder.

Focusing on capturing early adopters is a viable strategy. Compared with the general population, a larger percentage of early adopters tend to be technologically adept, which puts them in a unique position to vet new services.[27] It is also easier to troubleshoot or smooth out problems in the early stages, when the service has only a few users. Because a large number of early adopters tend to be technology geeks (enthusiasts), they are valuable sources of feedback. Not all start-up businesses succeed. Many fintech companies are constantly refining their ideas to eliminate users' pain points by focusing on early adopters. A small percentage of them go on to become unicorns like Uber Technologies.

If banks and financial institutions want to come up with new business ideas so as not to lose out to fintech companies, there are many things they can learn from the approach used by fintech companies, particularly with respect to speed. Conventionally, companies have spent a lot of time refining a new business model before putting it to the test, but now it has become necessary to courageously test run multiple business models concurrently without waiting to refine them. This is a similar approach to that which venture capital firms take when they invest concurrently in a diverse

[26]To quote Tsukuba University Associate Professor Yoichi Ochiai, "Telling ourselves that there is nothing impressive about the technology is a recipe for perennial defeat. (…) I want to emphasize "low cost" and "clever"." (The Securities Analysts Association of Japan [2018], our translation.).

[27]If a new service does not have potential, finding out sooner rather than later helps the company cut its losses and get out while the damage is still small. This is an ideal approach for startups, which cannot afford to make enormous investments.

range of startups. The most important thing is for banks and financial institutions to provide users with prototypes at an early stage and learn from them.

9 Organizations for New Business Creation

So far, this chapter has offered many suggestions for promoting new business creation. It is becoming increasingly important for financial institutions to acquire technologies already used widely by fintech companies, such as deep learning and other machine learning technologies, distributed ledger/blockchain technologies, cloud computing technologies, and API technologies. As mentioned above, it is important to establish direct interfaces with users, and incorporating a design thinking approach is likely to facilitate the creation of such direct interfaces. Another effective strategy may be to dispatch staff to Silicon Valley, where a large number of new businesses are born.

The above, however, are largely tips related to technologies and methodologies, and efforts to leverage those technologies and methodologies will not in of themselves guarantee the ability to easily generate new businesses. As suggested by the old saying "seeing is believing," the best way to gain a good understanding of a new technology or business method is to actually utilize the technology or method in question. Even when new business ideas are imported to Japan from Silicon Valley, they often fail to find acceptance here.[28]

The best ways to address new business creation often differ from the methods a company might ordinarily use to expand or rationalize its existing businesses, and Japan's current corporate cultures are often unsuited for effectively undertaking new business creation.[29] It is therefore important for Japanese companies to promote the establishment of a corporate culture suitable for new business creation.

There may be ways to do this while avoiding clashes with the existing culture. For instance, financial institutions and other companies often promote new business creation by establishing laboratories and R&D centers as separate organizational units—aiming to compartmentalize the creative work and minimize the impact of the parent company's corporate culture.

However, changing a corporate culture probably should be considered as entailing "transformation" rather than mere "innovation" or "new business creation." Just as "digital transformation" describes a switch from analog to digital systems and

[28]This is called the "pitcher-catcher problem." Employees dispatched to Silicon Valley are "pitchers," the information they send back to Japan is the "ball," and the people responsible for interpreting this information back in Japan are "catchers." The problem is that the catchers are incapable of catching the ball (interpreting the information) without an understanding of what is happening in Silicon Valley.

[29]To avoid financial crises, financial institutions have become required to comply with numerous regulations in conducting their business. Consequently, rigorous regulatory compliance has now become a core part of financial institutions' culture, which is very different from the culture of fintech companies, which accept risk-taking as a natural part of doing business.

processes, "corporate digital transformation" can be seen as an effort to totally revamp a company through the introduction of digital technologies and the adaptation of corporate culture to harmonize with those technologies.[30]

Along with corporate culture, corporate management methods also need to be adapted, and organization theory suggests some ways that this might be done. There is no single correct solution, but Moore[31] (2017) asserts that companies should manage their investments by dividing them into four zones.

- Innovation: Create a new business; recover investment in 3–5 years
- Transformation: Expand the new business; recover investment in 2–3 years
- Performance: Achieve growth in existing business; recover investment in 1 year
- Productivity: Increase productivity; recover investment in 1 year.

The gist of Moore's argument is that a company's operations in each zone should be managed separately based on whether the company in question is on the offense (by creating disruptive innovations) or on the defense (because of its competitors' disruptive innovations).

With fintech companies creating disruptive new services one after the other, financial institutions have either been forced into defensive positions or are attempting to gain the upper hand through innovations of their own. In such a situation, Geoffrey Moore's approach may come in handy.

References

Cisco (2017) The Zettabyte era trends and analysis. Cisco (PDF)
Viacom Scratch (2013) Millennial disruption index. Viacom Media Network

[30]METI has established a website for digital transformation called METIDX: http://www.meti.go.jp/policy/digital_transformation/index.html.
[31]Geoffrey Moore.

Chapter 6
Fintech Entrepreneurship

Masahiro Fukuhara

1 The Economic Significance of Entrepreneurship

(1) Malfunctioning of Capitalism

As Joseph Schumpeter pointed out, capitalism is a system that inherently leads to the creation of large bureaucratic organizations that impede innovation, resulting in a gradual rise in debt and unemployment. To break out of this stagnation, we need "creative destruction" through innovation-driving entrepreneurship.

Why does capitalism malfunction? As companies grow in size, they acquire "relationship capital" and "brand capital" through doing business with customers over the longer term. These provide stability to a business. Unfortunately, as many studies show, human beings tend to become complacent when placed in stable environments, which slowly saps their ability to acquire new knowledge and develop new technologies. This eventually leads to shortages of knowledge capital and human capital.

It takes time to accumulate knowledge capital and human capital, which, once spent, are difficult to recover. However, knowledge capital and human capital are what drive productivity. Economic growth can be explained as "labor times capital times productivity." If the engine driving productivity malfunctions, supply constraints emerge, and the economy stagnates. Japan faces a clear shortage of labor as society ages and birthrates decline, but the country's immigration policies have not caught up to this reality. This will pose a challenge to the country's economic growth going forward.

M. Fukuhara (✉)
Institution for a Global Society Corporation, and Faculty of Economics, Keio University, Tokyo, Japan
e-mail: m.fukuhara@i-globalsociety.com

S. Kaji et al. (eds.), *The Economics of Fintech*,
https://doi.org/10.1007/978-981-33-4913-1_6

(2) Innovator's Dilemma

The Innovator's Dilemma by Clayton Christensen clearly outlines the timeline and mechanism by which a big company falls into dysfunction from both the supply and demand sides of an economy.

From the demand side, there is no incentive for a company to introduce a new product to replace an existing product that enjoys success thanks to the company's relationship capital and brand capital (because of the cannibalization effect). For customers, too, the cost of switching to a new product can be quite high. As a result, the company's existing relationships with major existing customers stay intact simply due to inertia.

From the supply side, except in the case of products or services that have no substitutes due to, say, patent protections, competition intensifies with time, and profit margins slowly shrink. As profits decline, the scope for new product development diminishes.

Then abruptly, when a major technological or business model innovation takes place, startups or companies entering the market from a different industry claim the market share of the well-established big company.

The above process of innovation, which is taking place in most parts of the world, is beneficial because it maintains employment levels and economic activity in the long run. Japan, however, is still saddled with large corporations that are unable to change. In other words, even as a large number of Japanese companies grapple with the innovator's dilemma, their strongholds are beginning to be threatened by the technological innovations of businesses from Silicon Valley and other parts of the U.S., where a large number of companies are driving change, and from China, where companies are growing rapidly. Moreover, Japanese economic stagnation is expected to become more pronounced as the country's labor population shrinks amid a decline in birthrates and the aging of society.

(3) Encouraging Entrepreneurship

It is clear what Japan must do. It must encourage entrepreneurship. It must foster an entrepreneurial spirit and establish a system for promoting the establishment of businesses that can lead to innovation. The ongoing fintech revolution offers a wealth of opportunities for aspiring entrepreneurs in Japan, especially given that innovation has so far been held in check due to stringent regulations governing the Japanese financial industry.

2 Fintech Entrepreneurship in Japan and Elsewhere

(1) Japan's Lack of Entrepreneurial Spirit

According to a 2017 survey by Accenture, global investment in fintech ventures amounted to USD 27,445 million. Of this, Japan accounted for only USD 105 million.

Even taking into account the difference in economic scale and the strictness of financial regulation in Japan, the gap is too large. Why are so few new businesses being set up in Japan?

In a December 2017 survey of people likely to be interested in entrepreneurship conducted by the Japan Finance Corporation, respondents' positive impressions regarding entrepreneurship included "high income levels (77.5%)," "a great deal of freedom (75.8%)," and "the ability to capitalize on one's strengths (90.2%)." On the other hand, their biggest concern was "income instability (81.6%)." The highly risk averse nature of Japanese people may be psychologically preventing them from starting their own businesses.

The main reason those who wanted to start their own businesses had not yet done so was "insufficient funds on hand (56.5%)." However, most respondents who had successfully started a business said that they had "managed to procure the required funds (74.1%)," so it would appear that funding is not necessarily the key hurdle.

(2) Mental Barriers to Entrepreneurship

Taking such facts into account, the main requirement for effectively promoting entrepreneurship in Japan may be psychological counseling. Looking deeper into the psychology of aspiring entrepreneurs in Japan, it becomes clear that nearly half of those who are nervous about starting their own business do not know much about what it takes to start a business or how to write a business plan, and this lack of knowledge may be the biggest factor standing in their way. The following sections offer a handy prescription for solving the problem.

3 Guide to Fintech Entrepreneurship

(1) Acquiring the Right Information

As mentioned above, a large number of people are nervous about starting their own business, but are the risks associated with starting a business really that great? Many articles on the Internet stoke fear by stating, for instance, that the success rate of new businesses is 6%. However, according to the 2011 White Paper on Small and Medium Enterprises in Japan, 70% of newly created companies were still in business 10 years after their establishment. This is definitely not a low survival rate. So long as one undertakes sufficient market analysis and other preparations and formulates a strategy that takes into account one's technological capabilities and other special strengths, entrepreneurship does not have to be all that risky.

(2) Importance of Design Thinking

Nowadays, many events are organized to provide support to aspiring entrepreneurs, and there is no dearth of ideas that an aspiring entrepreneur could successfully commercialize. However, the potential value of those ideas can only be effectively realized when the ideas are shared and discussed with potential customers.

In many cases, aspiring entrepreneurs with brilliant ideas keep those ideas under wraps. This prevents those ideas from finding supporters, and they end up being nothing more than pie in the sky. Ideas have no value unless they can be converted into actual products and services that customers will appreciate and pay good money for.

Entrepreneurs who have previously worked for big companies tend to develop products and services based on ideas and launch them while simultaneously attempting to promote their brand among potential customers. Although this approach is reasonable for a big company with a solid financial foundation, it can be suicide for a startup with limited funds, because those funds often run out during the initial test-marketing stage. The initial product or service is often somewhat different from what customers were hoping for and, while making the requisite adjustments, the fledgling company runs out of funds earlier than anticipated even in the worst-case scenario of its business plan.

The risk of being unable to implement the business plan can be significantly lowered by starting a dialog with potential users at the initial concept stage, commoditizing the product or service only after the prospective customer base is assured, and then maintaining communication with customers to further improve the product or service.

This entails gaining an understanding of potential users' needs, discovering solutions to problems that may not be evident to them, and offering product and service solutions they can truly appreciate. This approach, called "design thinking," has proven quite effective and can be summarized as follows: (1) fully empathize with target customers and question them repeatedly to bring to light real challenges they may be facing without being aware of it, (2) develop a prototype and receive feedback on it through frequent communication with target customers, and (3) maintain regular dialog with customers even after the product or service has been launched to enable further improvement of the product or service.

It is important to realize here that, although many customers are not fully aware of all the challenges they face and may not be interested in buying new products or services, they will certainly be interested in buying solutions to the problems they face.

A good example of the use of this needs-focused approach is seen in the case of Apple's former CEO, the late Steve Jobs, who was an afficionado of Japanese consumer electronics products. However, he noted that such products were accompanied by thick user manuals and were more technology-focused than user friendly. In light of that situation, Jobs came up with the idea of developing a more user-friendly (people-friendly) product to replace the Japanese products, and that idea was the seed from which Apple's smartphone grew.

Apple products typically do not come with user manuals. The thinking behind them is that, if a user cannot pick up a product and start using it right away, it is not user friendly. This focus on what is called User eXperience (UX) is a result of the design thinking approach. Japanese companies tend to focus on their existing customers. Having created a product, Japanese companies make minute refinements to it based on the requirements of existing customers, which makes it difficult for that product to reach a wider audience. One could say that such companies truly suffer from the innovator's dilemma.

(3) Steps to Setting up a Business

This section explains the elements of design thinking and the steps to establishing a business.

Step 1—Solve a problem

A business should begin not with an idea but with a problem. One must first empathize with target consumers and gain a thorough understanding of a problem they may be facing, then find and offer a solution to that problem. Products or services must not be based on ideas conceived in a vacuum.

Step 2—Gather business partners

A company is a gathering of people, so people are the most important asset when it comes to setting up and growing a company. In *Good to Great*, a global bestseller on corporate strategy and management by Jim Collins, the author says that the secret to success is to ask "first who, then what"—first get the right people on the bus, then decide where the bus is going. In fact, most startups change track several times after they have launched their first product, going on to address societal needs through products or services quite different from the original ones. In other words, having discovered a problem, found its solution, and set up a business, the most important next step is to find the people with whom to run the business. It is essential to gather a diverse workforce with various competencies and skills that can synergistically complement each other. According to IDEO, the company most popularly associated with the design thinking approach, only an organization with a diverse staff is capable of understanding the real problems consumers face and providing real solutions to those problems—this is based on IDEO's own experience.

Step 3—Formulate a capital policy

An important question to consider when preparing to set up a business is whether to self-finance or not, and if not, how to procure the funds—whether through a bank loan or through venture capital (including angel investors). Self-financing is the best option if it is possible, but most aspiring entrepreneurs do not have sufficient funds of their own to start a business. Further, most financial institutions do not extend loans to venture businesses (although it is possible to obtain funding from the Japan Finance Corporation if one has technology patents or sophisticated technological capabilities). As a result, entrepreneurs have to rely on venture capital if their own funds are not sufficient for the task.

Before deciding to make use of venture capital, it is important to formulate a long-term capital policy. Most entrepreneurs are not initially knowledgeable about capital policy and do not have a clear, long-term capital policy. This is something they eventually come to regret. It is essential to formulate a long-term capital policy alongside a long-term business plan, and utmost care must be taken in doing so, because the capital policy cannot be revised at will later. Once the founder's equity has been diluted as the result of venture capital or other equity investment, there is no going back.

A common mistake many companies make is to issue a large number of stock options at the start. Since not much cash is available in the early stages, lawyers, advisors, and others who may provide help are issued stock options instead. This becomes a problem when the company decides to make an initial public offering (IPO), because it stands in the way of meeting one of the conditions of an IPO, namely that the number of stock options cannot be over 10% of the total shares issued. An IPO is the process by which founders and investors "exit," i.e. cash out to recover their invested funds by listing the company on the stock market. The subsequent inability to meet the IPO criteria caused by the initial issuance of a large number of stock options may make it difficult to procure venture capital.

In formulating a capital policy, it is important to create a roadmap starting with the original round of funding from angel investors when the company is set up, through Series A funding during the early stage, when product and service prototypes are created, Series B funding during the intermediate stage, when the company rapidly expands its client base, Series C funding, when the company manages to capture a good share of the market, and on, to the exit. It is important to forecast in advance how the equity ratios of the founders and other investors will change during these stages. Chart 1 is an example of a capital policy format for one stage, but such a chart must be prepared for each of the stages in advance.

The ideal founder-equity ratio depends on the specifics of each case, but founders must take note of the different kinds of ratios possible and what their implications are. How would you evaluate the capital status outlined in Chart 1 based on these implications?

Scenario 1: The founder retains two-thirds or more of the voting rights

In this scenario, the founder retains absolute management control. Investors have neither the right to sell the company nor to nominate directors, which gives the founder a great deal of freedom when it comes to managing the company.

Scenario 2: The founder retains half to less than two-thirds of the voting rights

The founder can freely nominate executive directors and get ordinary resolutions passed at a general meeting of shareholders and has considerable freedom in managing the company. However, since investors have veto rights, their approval will be necessary when it comes to decisions that require a special resolution, such as those related to new rounds of funding or the company's sale.

Scenario 3: The founder retains one-third to less than half of the voting rights

The founder has veto rights and can prevent investors from changing the name of the company, undertaking a new round of funding, or selling the company against

Shareholder composition	Equity	Ownership ratio	Including dilutive shares (stock options, etc.)	Ownership ratio
Founder A	1,000	15.3%	(2,000)	23.1%
Founder B	800	6.1%	(800)	9.3%
Management/Total	1,800	29.5%	(2,800)	32.4%
Employees	100	1.2%	(2,800)	4.6%
Employee stock ownership	0	0.0%		0.0%
Employee stock ownership/Total	100	1.6%	(400)	4.6%
Company stakeholders/Total	1,900	31.1%	(0)	37.0%
Acquaintances, advisors, and other supporters	300	3.6%	(400)	7.3%
Acquaintances, advisors, and other supporters/Total	300	4.9%	(3,200)	7.3%
Business partner A	500	8.9%	(300)	6.7%
Business partner B	200	3.1%		2.3%
Business partner C	200	3.1%		2.3%
Candidate partner companies/Total	900	14.8%	(300)	11.3%
VC A	1,000	20.4%	(1,000)	15.4%
VC B	1,000	15.3%	(1,000)	11.6%
VC C	500	11.5%	(500)	8.7%
VC D	500	11.5%	(500)	8.7%
VC and other investment companies/Total	900	49.2%	(3,000)	44.3%
General shareholder: Founder's profit General shareholder: Secondary offering General shareholder: Public offering Qualified institutional investors				
General shareholder ratio	0	(0)	(0)	(0)
Grand total	6,100	100%	7,400	100%
Dilutive share ratio				13.5%

Chart 1 Example capital policy format. *Source* Created by Author

the founder's wishes. However, everything else is in the hands of investors, who can easily get their resolutions passed in a general meeting of shareholders.

Obviously, it is vital to carefully consider such issues as how venture capital would add to the company's value, whether external capital is really necessary, and whether it would be possible to use one's own funds supplemented by loans from family and friends.

As shown in *The Social Network*, a film portraying the founding of Facebook, companies with multiple co-founders are liable to run into capital policy problems over time. The initial capital policy must outline how each co-founder's rights can be protected in a scenario where the co-founders cannot agree on the direction in which they want to take the company.

Step 4—Formulate a venture capital policy and sign contracts

Below is the process by which a startup can receive venture capital, with the entire process taking anywhere from 6 months to a year. It is important to set up a system to ensure that the funds never dry up.

1. Successfully compete in a startup competition or other venues to attract the interest of venture capital firms (VC firms)
2. Sign a non-disclosure agreement (NDA) with a VC firm
3. Establish the basic terms of the investment contract
4. Perform due diligence

5. Sign the investment contract
6. Receive funding

As mentioned above, an exit strategy is a prerequisite for startups seeking funding from VC firms, which attach overriding importance to the exit strategy and are therefore intent on promoting their own exit strategy-related interests in various ways when negotiating investment contracts with startups. Startup founders must duly protect their own interests by making sure they clearly understand all the ramifications of a given investment contract proposal. Increasingly, VC firms participating in startup funding expect to receive preferred stock. Preferred stocks are more advantageous for the investor, so founders must understand the different (preferential) rights conferred on the investor by preferred stocks compared with common stocks as described below, and accordingly be firm in their negotiations.

Shareholders have three key rights—(1) the right to receive a share of the company's profits in the form of dividends, (2) the right to receive a share of the company's residual assets, and (3) the right to vote at a general meeting of shareholders. The difference between preferred stockholders and common stockholders is that the former get preferential rights with regard to (1) and (2) over the latter. Many VC firms force founders to include clauses in the investment contract that will give the them preferential rights over the founders (who own common stocks) when it comes to receiving dividends or a share of the residual assets.

It is not difficult to understand why a VC firm investing in a startup would insist on being given preferential rights to residual assets. After all, startups have almost no finances of their own, and they would have very limited residual assets if they were to go bankrupt. VC firms also insist on having a say in the sale of a startup. This is because founders, who own shares at book value, could be tempted to sell the company cheaply if there is a buyout offer, and this would prevent the VC firm from recovering its investment.

However, provisions can be made for weaker or stronger voting rights for preferred stock compared with common stock, and it is important for founders to use this to establish a strong framework for protecting their own rights. Because of their funding requirements over the medium term, founders tend to give VC firms the upper hand in negotiations. However, care must be taken not to make the wrong move at this stage as it could have serious consequences for subsequent fund procurement.

Another thing to be careful about is the drag-along rights provision. A drag-along rights provision, which is activated when investors want an exit despite opposition from the founders, compels minority shareholders to sell their shares in the company on the same terms as the other sellers. For instance, if a company offers to buy a 100% stake in a startup, this could be profitable for investors. The founders may want to continue running the company they built, but the drag-along rights provision could be activated to force investors with limited voting rights to sell their shares. This is obviously something founders need to be aware of.

On the other hand, because preferred stocks have (the previously described) preferential rights over common stocks during a given investment period, setting a different (higher) share price for preferred stocks in comparison to common stocks would increase the entrepreneur's autonomy.

Step 5—Formulate a financial regulation compliance policy

The financial industry is heavily regulated. There are measures to protect the rights of depositors, countermeasures against money laundering, credit quality audits by the financial authorities, and other strict regulations. However, there are many gray zones when it comes to laws and regulations governing fintech, resulting in numerous cases of fintech firms making use of loopholes to enter the field without adequate legal compliance. If a firm wins strong customer support, the regulatory environment is accordingly relaxed to become more permissive of the relevant loopholes. If a firm that has won consumer support goes on to betray the confidence of its customers and disadvantage them, however, the relevant regulations may be tightened. The commotion surrounding cryptocurrencies in 2018 is a typical example of this pattern of events.

Thorough regulatory compliance requires the establishment of complex systems and a large staff to run these systems. Compliance imposes a heavy cost on existing financial institutions by eating into their revenues. Similar regulations imposed in the field of fintech are bound to discourage new developments in this field. Since national borders are easily transcended in the financial industry, a country that imposes strict regulations risks stifling financial innovation. Innovations flourish in countries with more relaxed regulatory environments, helping their companies grow rapidly. In light of this, the tightly regulated country may then relax its own regulations, but domestic companies entering the market at a late stage may still easily be dominated by stronger companies from overseas.

The UK has established special zones called sandboxes, where financial regulations are more relaxed, and has been skillfully promoting fintech entrepreneurship and innovation in these strategic zones. Japan, on the other hand, is behind the curve in this regard, and the country's financial industry is being left behind as a result. This situation also encourages regulatory arbitrage, whereby entrepreneurs simply move to countries with more relaxed regulations instead of attempting to set up their financial business in Japan.

(4) Write a business plan and an elevator pitch

A survey of aspiring entrepreneurs revealed that the biggest challenge faced by entrepreneurs was writing business plans attractive to VC firms. Writing an attractive business plan is not difficult so long as the following points are covered.

- The problem to be solved
- The proposed solution to the aforementioned problem
- A network of personal connections that can be relied on to support the prospective company
- The potential that can be tapped into in the target market
- The technologies to be used
- The competitors

- The proposed market strategies (price leadership/high value-addition)
- The sales, cost, and profit outlook, and the rationale behind that outlook
- The other members who will run the business
- The proposed cashing-out (exit) strategy for investors and founders

Aspiring entrepreneurs should write up business plans encapsulating their ideas, enter startup competitions, and revise their plans as they go along as part of the process of setting up a company.

Having written a business plan, it is important to craft a brief story that will captivate investors. This is what is called the "elevator pitch." It is a short description of a business plan that can be told to a potential investor in an elevator. The point of an elevator pitch is that it can be told within the space of a minute or so, while the elevator ride lasts, and arouse the interest of the listener in that short time. VC firms receive presentations from a large number of aspiring entrepreneurs. They are usually short on time and uninterested in most of the ideas they hear. This is what gave rise to the concept of an elevator pitch—a story that can concisely convey the attractiveness of a business idea in the space of a minute.

A good elevator pitch is less about what is said and more about how it is said. It is a story crafted using words that appeal to the emotions rather than merely to logic. Whether a story can move someone (investor) or not depends not just on what is said but how it is said, and, therefore, by extension, on the attributes of the person telling the story. The art lies in communicating to the investor what kind of person one is and why one is the right person to set up this particular business. Preparation and experience are both very important when it comes to making an elevator pitch, and it can easily take several attempts to get it right.

4 Preparing for Entrepreneurship

Entrepreneurship is the driving force of innovation and one of the key engines that keep capitalism going. Unfortunately, the rate of entrepreneurship in Japan is lower than in the rest of the world. A big reason for this is a lack of knowledge, which erects mental barriers to entrepreneurship.

Many Japanese university students participate in startup competitions while they are students, but then go on to work for big companies. During their lives as salaried employees, they acquire a narrow range of knowledge capital applicable to their own company and jobs. However, their multifarious and innovative knowledge capital diminishes along with their market value as human capital. Meanwhile, in other parts of the world, numerous students in top universities have conspicuously gone on to become entrepreneurs and make noteworthy contributions to societal progress. The entrepreneurial path is not an easy one, but the experience gained on the path is remarkable, and the potential sense of achievement and financial rewards available to entrepreneurs who successfully solve problems can make it well worth the associated risks and efforts.

In their old age, most people wish they had tried and failed rather than not having tried at all. Successful entrepreneurship entails mastering a broad range of management skills and artistry. It is certainly not easy, but giving it a try is a good experience in itself and, even in the event of failure, it may well lead to other kinds of rewarding career opportunities. Our hope is that more students will learn about and acquire practical experience in entrepreneurship, thereby adding one more thing to their list of career options after graduation.

Chapter 7
Fintech's Impact on International Capital Markets

Spyridon Mentzas

1 Why Fintech Companies Are Growing Rapidly

(1) Robust Investment in Fintech Companies

The fintech industry began to develop amid investment into U.S.-based startups at an astonishing rate starting around 2010, and, influenced by overseas trends, the word "fintech" began to gain popularity in Japan from around 2015.

In terms of cumulative investment in fintech between January 2010 and June 2015, the U.S. is head and shoulders above other regions at USD 31.6 billion, followed by the UK and the rest of Europe at USD 9.8 billion, then China, India, Canada, and Israel in that order (Fig. 1).

Analyzing the trend further by year shows that fintech investments in 2014 amounted to USD 6.7 billion in the U.S., USD 1.1 billion in Europe, USD 900 million in Asia,[1] and USD 54 million in Japan. The following year (2015), U.S. investments nearly doubled, to USD 13.8 billion; Europe saw a 40% increase, hitting USD 1.5 billion; and investments in Asia increased five-fold, to USD 4.5 billion. Meanwhile, investments in Japan increased only slightly, to USD 65 million.

The trend changed dramatically in 2016. U.S. investments fell by around 30%, to USD 9.2 billion, while European investments doubled, to USD 2.4 billion, and Asian investments rose so dramatically as to surpass U.S. investments, hitting USD 11 billion. Meanwhile, Japanese investments finally broke through the USD 100 million barrier to reach USD 150 million.

S. Mentzas (✉)
HoJoJo Partners Inc, Washington, USA
e-mail: mentzas@hijojo.com

[1]For the purposes of this chapter, Asia excludes Japan.

S. Kaji et al. (eds.), *The Economics of Fintech*,
https://doi.org/10.1007/978-981-33-4913-1_7

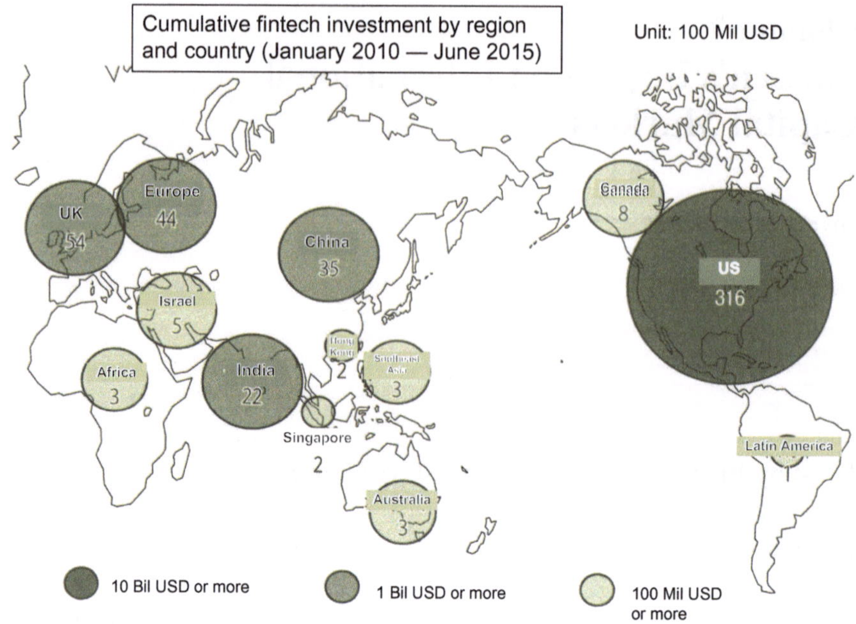

Fig. 1 Cumulative fintech investment by region and country. *Source* Prepared by HiJoJo Partners using materials from Business Insider UK

There were several reasons for the major trend shift in 2016. For instance, LendingClub,[2] one of the biggest U.S.-based fintech companies, was embroiled in a fraud scandal and underwent a leadership change. As a result, the company's market value temporarily fell by 50%, and share prices have still not fully recovered to date. The scandal increased investors' concerns regarding the still relatively new fintech industry as a whole.

In Asia, meanwhile, fintech investments were gathering steam with a series of major investment projects. China-based Alibaba Group invested around USD 700 million in India-based Paytm from 2015 through 2016, while Ant Financial,[3] a major Alibaba shareholder, attracted USD 4.5 billion in investments. Following fintech investment trends in different countries serves, unfortunately, to highlight the scantiness of Japanese investments in this area.

(2) Background to Rise of Fintech

The main factor behind the rise of fintech in the U.S. and Europe was probably the emerging trend of "disruption" (disruption of existing systems and mechanisms). For

[2]LendingClub's business model is based on credit scoring individuals and small and medium-sized enterprises (SMEs) seeking loans and helping them find loans at interest rates calculated based on loan loss risks.

[3]Parent company of payment platform Alipay, which Japanese consumers are also familiar with.

instance, access to financial services had always been restricted for some low-income groups and SMEs in these regions. Adding to this were the lack of transparency in fee structures, high fees charged for financial services by some financial institutions, complex procedures, and mass-oriented services not tailored to individual needs. All this contributed to user dissatisfaction with the existing financial services. It was in this climate that fintech companies emerged to disrupt the existing structure of financial services with their new services.

The trend caught speed with support from the Millennials, defined as the generation of people born in the 1980s through 2000—people who are currently in their 20s or 30s. The Millennials, also described as the "smartphone generation," did not like the idea of waiting at bank counters in this digital age. They preferred cheap services over services offered face-to-face, so their desires were in concert with fintech companies that skillfully used technology to provide convenient services. In other words, fintech in the U.S. and Europe emerged in response to a new business opportunity created by the outdated ways of existing financial institutions.

The background to the rise of fintech in Asia, however, was very different. Here, there were no well-established financial systems that could be targeted for disruption in the first place. Despite this, the fintech industry in Asia has attracted investment surpassing that in the West. Why? The answer is financial inclusion (making financial services available to a larger number of people). In Asia, especially in its developing countries, there are very few bank branches or ATMs outside the urban centers, and a large number of people are so poor as to be unable to even open a bank account. This gave rise to initiatives aimed at promoting financial inclusion. Specifically, the sharp rise in the use of smartphones or other smart devices among young people combined with support from the government and other organizations to encourage the rapid growth of fintech in an effort to reduce financial exclusion.

In Asia, where social infrastructure is lacking in many areas, it is cheaper to distribute smartphones than to lay phone lines for fixed-line phones. It therefore makes sense for governments to adopt the former as policy.[4] Meanwhile, youngsters, who tend to be heavy users of smartphones, find that these are not just phones but devices that, when connected to the Internet, can provide access to a wide variety of services. Smartphone penetration rates by country are 64% for Japan, 92% for South Korea, 83% for China, 81% for Taiwan, 88% for Malaysia, 72% for Vietnam, 83% for Hong Kong, and 91% for Singapore,[5] showing a close correlation between the penetration of smartphones and fintech services.

In Asia, in particular, government initiatives are behind the spread of fintech. Let us take a look at a system called the "regulatory sandbox," for instance. Just as a sandbox is a sand-filled pit for children to play in safely, a regulatory sandbox is a safe environment created by the government for selected companies or services in designated financial areas by restricting their users and relaxing the regulations.

[4] A strategy that bypasses stages of the path taken by developed countries to directly incorporate the latest infrastructural system is called leapfrogging.

[5] From a 2018 press release by AUN Consulting, Inc.

Regulatory sandboxes are used for testing new services or technologies in a deregulated environment. If a sandbox trial succeeds, actual financial regulations are relaxed and the service is made available to society at large.

Trials such as the above have to be implemented because of the difficulty of relaxing regulations at a stroke in the financial sector, which tends to be one of the most heavily regulated sectors in any country. Singapore, Malaysia, Thailand, Hong Kong, Taiwan, India, and Bahrain are some Asian countries that have introduced the sandbox system and seem poised to create new trends through public-private partnership.

The previous section mentioned that Asia had invested USD 4.5 billion in fintech in 2015. Two-thirds of this investment was in the areas of payments (40%) and lending (24%), with payments mainly indicating smartphone payments (e.g., Alipay, Samsung Pay, and Apple Pay). Compared with the West, much fewer people in Asia have easy access to credit cards as means of acquiring credit, and stores are also less capable of investing in card readers or paying a commission to card agencies, so electronic payments have been growing at a rapid pace as an alternative to credit cards. Electronic payments are receiving a further boost from stores because they save stores the effort of distinguishing between real and counterfeit money.

When it comes to lending, the fact that there are so few financial institutions in Asia has meant that loans have not been available to all sections of the population. Only the lowest-risk borrowers, i.e., those with houses or cars to pledge as security, have traditionally been eligible for loans.

In recent years, average incomes have steadily been rising, and people have progressed from being barely able to put food on the table to aspiring to greater affluence, but many still do not possess anything of worth that can be pledged as security toward a loan from legitimate financial institutions, which give loans at legal rates of interest. Such people have, therefore, had to resort to borrowing from loan sharks at annualized interest rates of 50% or 100% if, say, they wanted to buy a refrigerator, cooler, or some other household appliance and lacked sufficient savings of their own.

In an effort to solve this problem, one fintech company operating primarily in Vietnam has entered partnerships with employers (companies) to obtain employee attendance management data with the consent of the employees. Using the data obtained, it has created a system for selling refrigerators and other household appliances to employees with long employment histories and good performance records on credit, to be paid back in installments deducted from their salaries. The interest rate on said credit is 0%.

The fintech company in question makes a profit even without charging interest on loans because it bulk-buys appliances such as refrigerators and coolers of specific kinds from manufacturers at highly discounted prices of 15% or so. Employer companies also benefit from such an arrangement, because it encourages their employees to work hard and lowers employee turnover. Thus, the fintech company has created a business model that benefits all the parties concerned—the employees, their employers, and the fintech company itself.

(3) Distribution of Notable Companies by Region and Sector

Fintech100 is an annual report of top-ranking fintech companies published by KPMG International Cooperative and H2 Ventures. It includes a list of 50 leading fintech companies (the Leading50) and 50 emerging ones (the Emerging50). The companies are selected based on several criteria including total capital raised, rate of fundraising, geographic and sectoral diversity, ability to attract consumers and lead the market, and the X-factor, which is defined as the degree of product, service, and business model innovation (Fig. 2).

The 2017 Fintech100 included 19 U.S.-based companies, 10 Australian companies, nine Chinese companies, eight UK-based companies, and only one Japanese company. The box in Fig. 2 names all the Asian companies included in the 2017 Fintech100. The number of Asian companies included in the list has been increasing steadily and comprised a majority in 2017. In particular, the growth of Chinese fintech companies is remarkable, with the top three companies all being from China—Ant Financial (payments) at No. 1, ZhongAn (insurance) at No. 2, and Qudian (lending) at No. 3. The list has also included several Indian and Singaporean fintech companies, but Japan made it on the list for the first time in 2017, with a single company.

Moving on, let us take a look at the specific sectors within Fintech that are drawing attention and the extent of funding they have received. In terms of investment amount, lending (32 companies) is the top sector, followed by payments (21 companies). The

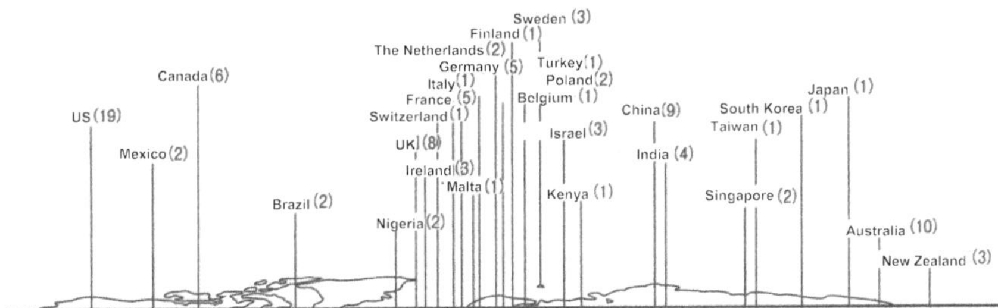

16 leading companies (China 9, Oceania 5, India 1, South Korea 1)
(1) Ant Financial [Payments]—China, (2) ZhongAn [Insurance]—China (3) Qudian [Lending]—China, (6) Lufax [Capital]—China, (7) JD Finance [Lending]—China, (16) Xero [Accounting]—New Zealand, (24) Prospal [Lending]—Australia, (27) 51 Xinyongka [Lending]—China, (31) Dianrong [Lending—China, (33) LendingKart [Lending]—India, (35) VivaRepublica [Payment]—South Korea, (36) WeLab [Lending]—China, (37) zipMoney [Payments]—Australia, (38) Rong360 [Lending]—China, (42) Pushpay [Payments]—New Zealand, (44) AfterPay Touch [Payments]—Australia

15 emerging companies (Oceania 8, Singapore 2, India 3, Japan 1, Taiwan 1)
Ain/vallex [ForEx]—Australia, Banqer [EdTech]—New Zealand, Capital Float [Lending]—India, TapPay [Payments]—Taiwan, CoverGenius [Insurance]—Australia, HyperAnna [Analytics]—Australia, KredX [Factoring]—India, Macrovue [Wealth]—Australia, MoneyMe [Lending]—Australia, MoneyTree [Wealth]—Japan, Silent8[Cyber Security]—Singapore, SoCash [Banking]—Singapore, Tic:Toc [Home Loan]—Australia, Valiant [Lending]—Australia, NeoGrowth [Lending]—India

Fig. 2 Regional distribution of notable fintech companies based on the 2017 Fintech100. *Source* Prepared by HiJoJo Partners based on materials from Fintech100, H2Ventures, and KPMG lending and payments sectors combined receive over half of all fintech investments. In Japan, the word fintech conjures up the image of bitcoins and other cryptocurrencies, blockchain technology, or AI and big data, but the focus overseas is on other sectors. Incidentally, the Fintech100 ranking includes four blockchain technology and cryptocurrency-related companies and three data analytics (AI, big data) companies.

Of course, companies that have achieved success in lending and payments businesses place great emphasis on obtaining and utilizing data. For instance, SoFi (Social Finance Inc.), the ninth company on the list, offers student loan refinancing to American students (or graduates) compelled to take out student loans thanks to skyrocketing school fees. Unlike public-sector financial institutions, which target a broad category of customers, SoFi mainly targets elite young workers of the Millennial generation.[6]

Unlike traditional financial institutions, which offer loans to all students at the same rate of interest, SoFi uses AI to evaluate customers' creditworthiness—based on customers' abilities and work history, as well as the school they are affiliated with, their MBA or other postgraduate program, and their career path—and offers student loan refinancing on different terms based on each customer's credit score. By limiting its target customers to students or graduates with good academic records, who have a good chance of becoming wealthy in the future and are unlikely to default on their loans, the company is able to offer much lower interest rates than its competition. Compared with the standard 6–8% interest rate for student loans, SoFi is able to offer refinancing to selected students at a 4–6% interest rate, which allows it to make a good profit on funds procured at a 1–3% interest rate. SoFi's business model, which began with student loan refinancing, has now expanded to include housing loans, asset management, and deposits.

Of the Leading50 companies on the Fintech100 list, only eight are listed. The remaining 42 are still unlisted. The total funding received by the Leading50 companies in 2016 amounted to USD 4.8 billion or so, but these companies' cumulative funding as of 2016 was roughly USD 27 billion (approximately JPY 3 trillion), giving a glimpse into the scale of fintech investment in recent years.

Meanwhile, the Emerging50 group of companies received around USD 600 million (JPY 65 billion or so) in 2016, and their cumulative investment that year was around USD 1 billion (approx. JPY 110 billion). In other words, in a single year (2016), the Emerging50 companies received more than half of the JPY 110 billion funding they have received through their lifetimes. Dividing the total funding received by the Emerging50 companies in 2016 by 50 gives an average of just JPY 1.3 billion per company, but the fact remains that investment in fintech companies overall is quite robust.

Some of the main investors in Fintech100 companies are venture capital (VC) firms, including Sequoia Capital, Index Ventures, Founders Fund, and Y Combinator. Sequoia Capital is a famous American VC firm, known for investing in companies such as Apple, Google, Cisco, LinkedIn, Oracle, and PayPal, and it currently has

[6] SoFi calls them HENRY (High Earners Not Rich Yet).

branches in China, India, and Israel. Founders Fund is known for series A funding of companies such as Facebook, Google, and SpaceX. One of the partners of Founders Fund is Peter Thiel, who cofounded PayPal with Elon Musk, who later founded Tesla and SpaceX. Y Combinator functions as an incubator for startups right from their founding by being involved in and providing coaching on various things including management, marketing, and business models. This VC firm is known for having invested right from the early stage in Airbnb, a vacation rental company that is attracting an increasing number of users even in Japan.

Another major class of investors in startups are strategic investors, which include credit card companies, such as Mastercard Incorporated and the American Express Company, as well as investment banks, such as the Goldman Sachs Group, Inc. Strategic investors invest not just with a view to profiting from an increase in a startup's market value or share price, but also in anticipation of synergies that may be generated by partnering with it. For instance, credit card companies could anticipate a decline in their own users with the rise of fintech companies in the area of payments. By financing the startups, these card companies can diversify their business and ensure that they are positioned to ride the new wave. Another benefit for strategic investors, in addition to being able to observe new ideas at work from close quarters, is that, depending on the level of business partnership with a startup, M&A options become available to them ahead of their competition.

(4) Fintech Business Conditions in Japan

In the West, new fintech companies have begun to take over the space originally occupied by traditional financial institutions in the service sector. In Asia, where traditional financial institutions were lacking, fintech companies have emerged to occupy the empty space. Meanwhile, in Japan, investment in the fintech industry is quite scant. Why is this so?

Among companies entering the fintech sector, some had already been providing financial services, while others were not originally involved in finance. Some attempt to incorporate fintech into their existing business framework, while others establish entirely new businesses. In the case of Japan, existing financial institutions including banks, securities companies, and insurance companies are expanding into fintech. This is in contrast to the U.S., where in addition to newly established startups, IT or e-commerce companies such as Apple and Amazon are expanding into fintech. Apple has introduced its new payment service, Apple Pay, and Amazon has begun a new initiative of offering loans to companies that sell on Amazon based on their sales information on the platform. Having information about the sales performance of sellers on its platform gives Amazon the ability to determine how much it can lend to a seller and how much it can expect to recover. This is a business model existing financial institutions cannot hope to replicate.

In sharp contrast to Japan, startups in Asia are rapidly developing financial service businesses that did not exist before. When existing financial institutions expand into new businesses, it is very difficult for them to engage in "disruption" in the American manner, because they want to avoid the cannibalization of their core businesses. It is not easy for a business to destroy its own functions and operations, so it inevitably sets its sights on near-sighted and short-term targets, such as improving business efficiency or cost reduction. It is also difficult for Japan to build something up from the start as in the case of Asia, because Japan already has a well-established financial infrastructure and because, from the perspective of established financial companies, there is no service that is so important or essential as to warrant the creation of a new company that might disrupt the *status quo*. Moreover, the financial industry in Japan is very heavily regulated, which makes it difficult for startups to obtain licenses to operate in this industry.

However, there is one change that is taking place in Japan's fintech industry, and that is a gradual increase in investment in fintech startups.. Moreover, this investment is coming not just from institutional investors such as VC firms, but also from other businesses. Existing financial institutions are also entering partnerships with startups and providing them support in the form of accelerator programs, thereby sowing the seeds for the definitive rise of a fintech industry. Carefully nurturing these new businesses is sure to breathe fresh air into the stale environment consumers had become resigned to.

In the field of investment, for instance, a new type of business called social trading is emerging, driven by a startup from Israel. In social trading, registered users make their entire portfolio (equity, bonds, FX, and bitcoins and other cryptocurrencies) public, and all users are ranked based on the performance of their respective investments. This allows investors to observe the portfolios of their peers and learn from them or copy the investment strategies of specific users. This is called copy trading. The business model is based on allowing investors who lack confidence in their investment strategies to ride on the coattails of more expert investors. Users being followed receive a contingent fee when their investments prove profitable, resulting in a profitable situation for both leaders and followers and a matching of goals.

The above is just one example of a startup based on novel concept or service that nobody had thought of before. If such startups emerge and prove successful in Japan, it will give rise to a wave of entrepreneurship in this country too. One can only hope that this will be enabled by a cultural change whereby those who stand out from the crowd are not punished for it.

2 Why Japan Does not Produce Unicorns like the U.S

(1) Breakdown of Venture Capital Investment by Country and Stage

The previous section discussed the fintech industry, which has been drawing attention for the robust investment in startups. This section will take one step back and focus on the differences between capital markets, especially in the U.S. and Japan.

Looking at investment trends in unlisted companies as per the VEC YEARBOOK (also known as the Annual Report on Japanese Startup Businesses) by country, investments the U.S., which were around JPY 3.6 trillion in 2011, expanded significantly in 2015, to over JPY 7 trillion (Chart 1). Investments have remained around JPY 500 billion a year in the EU, but have been growing rapidly in China, which saw JPY 2.5 trillion worth of investments in 2015. Investments in Japan, meanwhile, have been languishing at just over JPY 100 billion, which is a fiftieth of investments in the U.S.

While it is natural that the absolute amount of investments would be greater in the U.S., another big difference is in the amount of investment in each stage (growth phase) of a startup. The growth of a startup is divided into four main stages—the seed stage, the early stage, the expansion (or growth) stage, and the late stage.

The seed stage is the founding stage of a startup, when the commercial side of the business is not yet fully established, and the company is engaged mainly in R&D and product development. Ordinarily, startups are funded during this stage by family and friends, or a limited number of investors called "angel investors," so this first round of investment is also called the "angel round."

In the early stage, startups are engaged in product development, preliminary marketing, manufacturing, and sales activities. At this stage, the company's products and services become more tangible, which tends to attract VC firms and other professional investors.

During the expansion (growth) stage, a company is already posting sales, but compared with the first two stages, it needs significantly more funding in this stage in order to accelerate its marketing efforts to catch up with or get ahead of the competition. During this stage, in addition to major VC firms, strategic investors also invest in the company with the aim of entering business partnerships.

By the late stage, a company not just has a sustainable cash flow, it is also usually making a profit, has gained recognition in the wider market, and is almost ready for listing on the stock market.

Figure 3 shows investment trends in the U.S. for each stage. In recent years, investment in expansion-stage or late-stage startups has grown exponentially, while the percentage of seed funding within overall investment remains tiny. The overwhelming share of seed round investments can be considered high-risk-high-return

Region	2011		2012		2013		2014		2015	
	No. of cases	Amount	No. of cases	Amount	No. of cases	Amount	No. of cases	Amount	No. of cases	Amount
US	4,050	36,191	3,991	33,469	4,295	36,663	4,442	61,516	4,380	71,475
Europe	3,186	5,305	3,132	4,552	3,206	4,606	3,408	4,848	3,006	5,359
China	1,505	15,927	1,071	8,924	1,148	7,779	1,917	20,137	3,445	25,084
Japan	1,017	1,240	824	1,026	1,000	1,818	969	1,171	1,162	1,302

Chart 1 Annual investment in unlisted stocks by country (in JPY). *Notes* (1) Conversion rates: USD/JPY = 121.0, EUR/JPY = 134.3, CNY/JPY = 194 (amounts for each year were converted using the average exchange rates for calendar year 2015). (2) The data for the EU uses the number of companies instead of the number of cases. (3) In the case of Japan, the figures are based on fiscal years (April through following March). *Source* Prepared by HiJoJo Partners based on the VEC YEARBOOK 2016

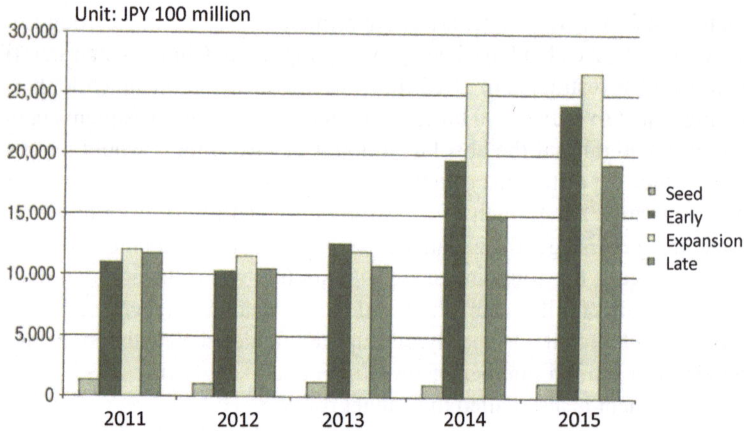

Fig. 3 Investment trends in the U.S. by stage. *Source* Prepared by HiJoJo Partners based on VEC YEARBOOK 2016

investments, because the startup company's business direction is not yet clear, its battle with rival companies to win market share is not transparent, and it has no clear outlook for securing the necessary workforce, so it stands to reason that the level of investment companies in this stage would be low.

In the late stage, most startups have already established their business and are preparing to make an initial public offering (IPO; stock offering). To that extent, risks are limited and the returns are also limited. When it comes to investing in startups, the risks are considered to be lowest during the late stage. Late stage investments doubled between 2013 and 2015 in the U.S., which has produced over 100 unicorns, which are defined as startups with market values of over JPY 100 billion. The fact that there are so many startups to choose from could be playing a role in attracting investment. As for whether U.S.-based investors prefer to invest in startups with no clear future outlook or startups such as Airbnb, which have a certain presence in the industry and are already profitable, Fig. 3 provides a clear answer at a glance.

Similar data is not available regarding Japanese investment in startups, but according to the VEC YEARBOOK 2016, when the executives of around 300 startups were asked which stage they thought their company was in, 55% responded that they were either in the seed or early stages, with less than 5% considering their company to be in the late stage.

There are several reasons why so few Japanese startups are in the late stage. While most Japanese VC firms invest anywhere from JPY 50–200 million per startup, the fact is that there are not as many investors in Japan as there are in the U.S., so most startups choose the option of listing on the stock exchange if they want to procure significant funds. In cases where they seek investment from strategic investors, the due diligence process takes time, and unless information is exchanged from a significantly early stage, the startup risks running out of funds in the meantime. In recent years, however, strategic investors have been setting up internal corporate venture capital (or CVC) funds with a view to speeding up investment decisions, so we may see robust investment using CVC funds going forward.

Some examples of Japanese startups in the late stage are LINE and Mercari, which are only a year or two away from IPOs. Unfortunately, there is no well-established system for ordinary investors to invest in a company during the late stage. Such investors have no choice but to wait for the company to go public. By contrast, ordinary investors can invest during the high-risk-high-return seed round if they go through a crowd-funding website. In the U.S., in addition to being able to invest during the seed round through crowd funding websites, ordinary investors are also able to invest alongside institutional investors during the late stage, and this could be what is encouraging the creation of unicorn startups. If late stage investments by ordinary investors became possible in Japan, it would reduce the incidence of almost daily limit-ups from the public offering price following a company's IPO. In other words, the price of the stock can be adjusted in one go during the late stage to narrow the gap between supply and demand.

In Japan, because very few startups can expect funding during the late stage, they choose the option of raising funds through an IPO. The 66 companies that were listed on the Tokyo Stock Exchange (TSE) Market of the high-growth and emerging stocks (Mothers) from January 2017 through May 2018 were able to raise an average amount of JPY 800 million by issuing new shares or selling existing shares. Of these companies, 50 were able to raise less than JPY 1 billion. In the U.S., early-stage startups can usually raise around JPY 800 million. Startups in the expansion stage can raise anywhere from JPY 2–5 billion, while late-stage startups often raise anywhere from JPY 10 billion to several trillions of JPY. It is true that listing a company makes it easier not just to procure funds, but also to recruit staff and receive funding from financial institutions as the company's level of recognition goes up. However, there are also downsides to listing a company too early, before it begins posting sufficient sales and profits, or before its business model has been fully established.

There are also costs associated with listing a company. One-time costs including fees paid to brokerage lead managers to help with listing the company, IPO screening charges, costs associated with preparing prospectuses, and fees paid to accounting and auditing companies can add up to over JPY 100 million. Additionally, there are running costs associated with strengthening governance and compliance and employing investor relations (IR) staff to be the public face of the company. Of the 66 startups listed on the TSE Mothers, over half (34) had current profits less than JPY 100 million at the time of listing, with the average profit for the current term being JPY 120 million. Following their IPO, such companies face uphill battles to meet their one-time IPO costs as well as their running costs after the IPO. However, Japanese startups that are slowly expanding in scale often have no other choice, because their only realistic option for raising funds is to make an IPO. If they were able to raise substantial funds before making an IPO like their counterparts in the U.S., they would have the option of strengthening their foundations before making an IPO when the time is ripe.

(2) IPO Returns of Startups in the U.S.

For U.S.-based startups, a major trend change has been observed regarding market value growth (1) from founding to IPO and (2) from IPO to the present (2017). During the 1990 s and first half of the 2000 s, enterprise values increased phenomenally after a company became listed, but in recent years, the enterprise value of startups has tended to increase substantially in the period before listing, while returns following IPO have been limited. In Fig. 4, the light-colored bars represent "private multiples," i.e., the multiples by which a company's market value grew from its first round of funding to the time of its IPO. The dark-colored bars represent "public multiples," i.e., the multiples by which the company's market value grew from the time of its IPO to 2017. Amazon, for instance, went public in 1997. The company's market value grew by only 10X from its early-stage fund raising to the time of its IPO. Since going public, however, Amazon has become a major corporation, having so far achieved a 1000X growth in market value since its IPO.

In the past, U.S.-based companies also followed a growth path similar to that of Japanese companies, going public while still small and then achieving significant growth subsequently. However, starting around 2004, with companies such as Google, there was a major reversal of the trend. Companies such as Facebook and Alibaba achieved a growth in market value close to 10,000X before listing, but subsequently achieved smaller multiples of growth because of their already considerable heft at the time of the IPO (JPY 10 trillion and JPY 15 trillion, respectively, for Facebook and Alibaba).

From the perspective of startup founders, not rushing to go public is better for retaining agility, focusing on running the company, and making the best choices for

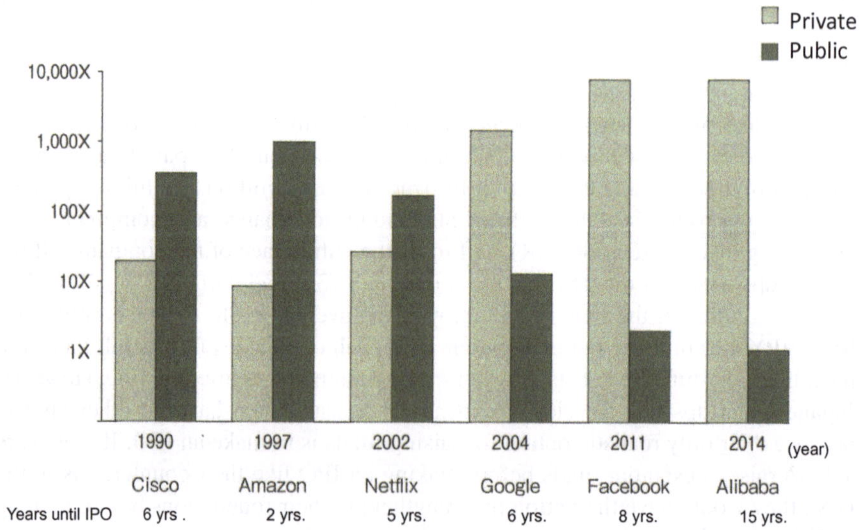

Fig. 4 IPO returns of U.S.-based startups. *Source* Prepared by HiJoJo Partners based on Equidate

expanding the business, compared with going public and having to expend a lot of energy rushing to prepare quarterly financial statements and being criticized harshly for their management choices by securities company analysts and investors. Even in the U.S., until the 1990s, the only way for startups to raise money was to go public, but now, with an increase in expansion-stage and late-stage investors, companies can afford to carefully consider the right time to go public. Meanwhile, renowned institutional investors such as Fidelity Investments, Wellington Management, and Baillie Gifford, which traditionally invested only in listed stocks, are finding that this strategy no longer delivers a satisfactory performance. They have therefore been proactively expanding their portfolio to include expansion-stage and late-stage investments too.

What kind of late-stage startups do they invest in and what are the returns on such investments? Between January 2016 and April 9, 2018, there were 71 U.S.-based and foreign companies that (1) listed on U.S. stock exchanges, (2) had a market value of USD 500 million or more at the time of listing, and (3) had issued shares to raise funds even before listing. Comparing the market value of these companies before and after listing (keeping the number of shares already issued constant), 77.5% (55 companies) were found to have posted an increase, while 22.5% (6 companies) were found to have posted a decrease, so it can be said that the probability of an increase in returns is quite high even for companies that receive late-stage funding. The rate of increase in market value was also remarkable, with the average rate of increase for all 71 companies being 545% (89.5% weighted average, taking market value into account). For companies that posted a decline in market value after listing, the average rate of decrease was 20.3% (19.3% weighted average, taking market value into account). In other words, the returns for investors have been quite sumptuous. Strong performances of this kind are playing a role in further attracting investors to late-stage investments.

(3) Mature Late-Stage Market in the U.S.

How are opportunities for late-stage investment made available in the U.S.? While the availability of expansion- or late-stage funding allows startups the luxury of not having to rush into an IPO, the situation also has its downsides for seed- and early-stage investors, founding members, and employees, because they have to wait longer to profit from their investment when the company goes public. In 2010, the average time from founding to IPO in the U.S. was around eight years, but this period had lengthened to an average of 10.7 years as of 2017. Of course, many of these startups see a steady increase in market value during the pre-IPO period, but since investors cannot convert this rise in book value into cash in the form of realized profits, the money is effectively dormant.

The holding period for investments in VC firms averages 10 years. Say a VC firm invests in a newly founded startup four years into the establishment of a particular fund. Unless the startup goes public or is acquired by another company before the fund is due to mature, the VC firm will be unable to repay customers who have invested in the fund in question. Meanwhile, founding members have to accept lower salaries and bonuses in the years before a company goes public, but this could coincide with an increase in their financial burdens as their families expand and their children grow up and need to be put through school. In the past, challenges of the above nature would sometimes force startups to go public early on in their growth.

In this context, "secondaries" (secondary market transactions), which give ordinary investors the opportunity to invest in late stage startups, have come to the rescue. Secondaries allow investors to buy existing shares in a company from current shareholders without the company having to issue new shares. In Japan, securities companies are forbidden from proactively soliciting shares of unlisted companies, but in the U.S., there are securities companies that specialize in handling unlisted stocks. There are also what are called single name special purpose vehicles (SPVs), which allow a large number of investors to form a fund to finance a single startup, as an alternative to the direct sale of stock. However, as in the case of Japan, most unlisted companies in the U.S. restrict the right to transfer shares, which means that third parties cannot buy the shares of current shareholders without the consent of the company or its major shareholders, who have the right to restrict the transfer of shares. Moreover, no matter how stellar the performance of a late-stage startup, unlisted stocks are considered more risky than listed stocks, so there are systems to restrict their purchase by all but wealthy investors (called "accredited investors" in the U.S.).

Ride-sharing service Uber and vacation-rental service Airbnb are famous U.S. unicorn startups that ordinary investors would not usually have access to, but a large number of investors have invested in them using schemes such as the above. According to an estimate by HiJoJo Partners,[7] the company I am affiliated with, secondary transactions in the U.S. amounted to around JPY 300 billion in 2016, and almost JPY 1 trillion in 2017. These are enormous sums, especially when one considers that the total investment in unlisted stocks (all stages) in Japan amounts to just over JPY 100 billion.

Secondary transactions in the U.S. are thought to have begun with the founding of a startup called SecondMarket in 2004, which began to sell the shares owned by Facebook employees on the secondary market around a year before Facebook went public. The shares sold for such high prices as to cause Facebook's market value to soar to a few trillion JPY, making the headlines. In 2014, the American stock exchange Nasdaq acquired SecondMarket and rebranded it as NASDAQ Private Market, which is now operated as a subsidiary of Nasdaq. In 2017, trading in unlisted stocks tripled from the previous year's volume to around USD 3.2 billion (JPY 350 billion or so), with 73% of sellers being startup founders or employees.

[7]"Hijojo" in the company name "HiJoJo Partners" means "unlisted" in Japanese, and one of the missions of the company is to encourage and support unlisted companies and help them go public when they are ready for it. The company's aim is to establish systems to help unlisted companies raise funds and enable late-stage investments, thereby contributing to the creation of a large number of unicorns in Japan like in the U.S.

(4) Japanese Business Climate not Conducive to Rise of Unicorns

In the U.S., the number of unicorns (unlisted companies with a market value of over JPY 100 billion) has been rising consistently. There are currently 130 unicorns, four times the number there were five years ago. The number of unicorns in Japan, however, can be counted on one hand. A company has to attain a market value of JPY 100 billion or more before it can become a unicorn. This means that, if a regular round of fundraising involves increasing the number of outstanding shares by 10–25%, at least JPY 10–25 billion would have to be raised in that round. However, Japan lacks big players who can invest on that scale, and this may be the main reason the country cannot produce unicorns. Of course, if unicorns became a more common phenomenon, investors may become more interested in investing in them, but this is no more than a chicken-and-egg conundrum.

Staying with the chicken and egg theme, a large number of Japanese startups are forced into premature IPOs, somewhat like an egg that hatches before the chick has fully developed. "Going public" is seen as a goal, but the fact is that a large number of startups subsequently end up floundering if they go public before they are ready.

Nurturing unicorns requires an ecosystem that can support budding companies. In this context, the fact that new crowd-funding legislation in Japan has made it possible to invest risk money during the seed stage of a company is a welcome development. However, under the current law, there is an upper limit on the amount of funds that can be raised (JPY 100 million per year per company), which is not sufficient for expansion-stage or late-stage funding. For investors, the seed and early rounds are the most high-risk-high-return rounds, but since the average Japanese startup does not have a very high market value at the time of listing, the returns are limited relative to the risks.

In the U.S., financial institutions help ordinary investors invest safely in late-stage startups using the single name SPV instrument, negotiating with startups to remove share transfer restrictions, and scanning the hundreds of pages of contract documents on behalf of investors. Meanwhile, angel investors who invested during the seed round or VC firms that invested in the early stage of a startup can sell a portion of their shares in the late stage, thereby realizing profits and freeing up funds to invest in newer ventures. In this way, there is a healthy circulation of risk money.

In recent years startups' market values have been increasing with every round of fundraising from the seed stage to the late stage. In 2009, 7% of funds raised pertained to rounds when a startup's market value had declined, but this figure had fallen to 2.8% by 2018. This allows investors to feel safe participating in the latest round of fundraising. Fintech companies have begun taking advantage of the business opportunity associated with the decreasing level of risk as a startup progresses into the expansion and late stages, with companies such as SecondMarket providing ordinary investors the opportunity to invest in expansion- and late-stage companies over the Internet.

In Japan, founders or founding members who sell their own company's shares tend to be seen as betraying the company, and companies limit the ability of executives to sell their stock, especially if the company has received VC and other funding.

By contrast, the U.S. has a system for relieving the financial uncertainties or family-related financial burdens company executives may face. In Silicon Valley, in fact, VC firms not only recommend that executives sell around JPY 300–500 million worth of their equity in the secondary market, they even proactively help them find buyers. The thinking behind this approach is that it will restrain equity owners' desire to take the company public as early as possible in order to cash in on their investments. In other words, the entire system is geared toward nurturing startups to become unicorns. As for the rationale behind the JPY 300–500 million figure, the idea may be to give company executives enough money to buy a home, set aside school and university fees for their children, and employ home helpers to relieve the burden of household chores on their wives. Allowing executives to sell equity worth JPY 2 billion, on the other hand, would not only encourage wasteful spending, it would also lower their incentive to grow the company.

Chapter 8
Architecture and Legislation Brought by Cryptoassets

Masakazu Masujima

In cyberspace, an architecture (to be described later) composed of program codes (hereinafter "codes" refers to program codes) is increasingly disciplining people by circumventing laws and contracts. Such phenomenon is currently mainly discussed on online platforms (digital platforms), and as methods to facilitate transactions on digital platforms through machine learning and deep learning based on massive data processing become more prevalent, the role of codes as the instruction format for transaction processing is increasingly significant in transactions. Consequently, Japan is also taking measures to increase the transparency and fairness of transactions related to digital platforms through disciplining the operators of digital platforms.

In this chapter, we will focus on cryptoassets, which are expected to have more significant impact on the trading society, and discuss the current situation where the phenomenon in which code architectures circumvent laws and contracts to regulate people is infiltrating the trading society through block chain technology or distributed ledger technology (DLT)[1] which does not require digital platformers.

1 Discipline in Cyberspace

In considering discipline in cyberspace, it is necessary to understand the concept of a code-based application architecture.

There is no established definition of the term "architecture" in the legal world. For the time being, we would like to advance discussions with the definition of "physical

[1] The ranges of the technology indicated by the terms block chain technology and distributed ledger technology seem to be different in various discussions, but in the context of this article, the term distributed ledger technology (DLT) is used.

M. Masujima (✉)
Mori Hamada & Matsumoto, Singapore, Singapore
e-mail: masakazu.masujima@mhm-global.com

S. Kaji et al. (eds.), *The Economics of Fintech*,
https://doi.org/10.1007/978-981-33-4913-1_8

and technical structure that restricts or enables the activities of any entity" proposed by Associate Professor Satoshi Narihara of Kyushu University, a researcher in this field.

Buildings, which are the "architecture" of physical spaces in which we are living, function as physical structures that restrict people's behavior. For example, airports are designed to prevent people from illegally entering the country or importing or exporting prohibited goods. It is often said that the method of replacing regulations by buildings is also used politically. For example, by crossing large highways between neighboring wealthy and poor areas, politicians can restrict the flow of people between the two areas without the need to enact laws and fix the gap.

Now, what about cyberspace, in which economic value will be derived from our integrated operations with physical space? Cyberspace consists of multiple layers, and users mainly connect to the application layer to benefit from the services provided by various providers. Each provider that offers services through an application writes codes and deploys them to embody the service.

As services in cyberspace are implemented by codes and are provided digitally only in accordance with the codes, users cannot, in the first place, take any action beyond what is specified by the codes. For example, even if a seller wishes to add special conditions to an item in C to C auction service, he or she cannot attach special conditions if the dashboard of the auction service does not permit such special conditions to be described; even if there are no rules to prohibit the addition of special conditions, the seller cannot do that.

In this way, service providers can impose discipline on users through codes, rather than by rules, in cyberspace. Users can only act "in predetermined ways". The point here is that in cyberspace, the architectural constraints that correspond to the physical structure constraints in physical space can be imposed by code at a lower cost, more flexible, and with greater discretion than in physical space.

Currently, architectural private regulations imposed by digital platformers in particular are uncertain in that they are implemented by codes that are not directly recognized by users. Therefore, there is a growing need to address this issue from a consumer protection perspective, and many raise a question whether such digital platforms are a hotbed of unfair trade practices for small and medium businesses that provide information and services to users on platforms. In cyberspace, where data is the source of value, the digital platformer is essential. In the future, however, architectural private regulations by digital platformers, who will dramatically increase data processing capacity with high-performance hardware and artificial intelligence in the future, may function as powerful regulations that go beyond national discipline by laws and regulations. State power itself has finally come to realize this.

This chapter is based on the question of whether events with the same structure as those on digital platforms with dramatically enhanced capabilities with artificial intelligence are taking place in blockchain technology through the spread of cryptoassets as digital native assets (asset classes that exist only electronically, not "digitizing" something that exists in a non-digital form by computers). The DLT used to implement cryptoassets may not be able to adopt the same regulatory approach to digital platformers because it does not necessarily require current digital platforms and operators assumed by the current concept of regulations. The scope of the issue here includes how the system can introduce discipline into transactions of cryptoassets that may adopt an architecture without intermediaries such as platformers.

2 What Are Cryptoassets?

(1) Understanding in the International Financial Context

According to the report[2] issued in the U.K., the birthplace of fintech and the second largest number of start-ups after the U.S., cryptoassets are, in a word, "one application of distributed ledger technology" to the representation of property value. From a functional perspective, cryptoassets are used as a generic term to refer to "a cryptographically secured digital representation of value or contractual rights that uses some type of DLT and can be transferred, stored or traded electronically."

In the context of international financial supervision, the Financial Stability Board (FSB), in its report to the G20 countries, defines crypto-assets as "a type of private asset that depends primarily on cryptography and distributed ledger or similar technology as part of their perceived or inherent value."

Whereas the FSB examines and monitors the impact of cryptoassets on international finance mainly from a macroprudential perspective, the Financial Action Task Force (FATF) has long focused on the deployment of viral currencies from the viewpoint of money laundering and the prevention of terrorist financing.

In the 2015 guidance (Guidance for a Risk-Based Approach to Virtual Currencies[3]), the FATF defined virtual currency as "a digital representation of value that can be digitally traded and functions as (1) a medium of exchange; and/or (2) a unit of account; and/or (3) a store of value, but does not have legal tender status," indicating the direction that countries should incorporate virtual currencies into the framework of the anti-money laundering and terrorist financing regulations through a risk-based approach." The term "kaso tsuka" in the Payment Services Act in Japan is a Japanese translation of the term "virtual currency" in this guidance, and the definition of the term in this guidance is said to be incorporated into the Japanese legislation.[4]

In October 2018, the FATF revised its Recommendations in response to the subsequent development of virtual currency-related businesses, particularly the emergence of a new form of use of digital tokens (token sales) for the purpose of financing. The revised FATF Recommendations change the term "virtual currency" used in the 2015 Guidance to "virtual assets" and redefines it as s as "a digital representation of value that can be digitally traded or transferred and can be used for payment or investment purposes. Virtual assets do not include digital representations of fiat currencies,

---

[2]https://www.gov.uk/government/publications/cryptoassets-taskforce.

[3]http://www.fsb.org/wp-content/uploads/P101018.pdfAnnex2-Glossary.

[4]http://www.fatf-gafi.org/publications/fatfgeneral/documents/guidance-rba-virtual-currencies.html.

securities, and other financial assets that are already covered elsewhere in the FATF Recommendations."

(2) Understanding in Japan

In December 2018, the Study Group on Virtual Currency Exchange, etc. (hereinafter referred to as the "Study Group"), in which the FSA serves as the secretariat, published a report on comprehensive regulation of virtual currency-related businesses (hereinafter referred to as the "Report"). In view of international trends, the Report proposes that "virtual currencies" be referred to as "cryptoassets." However, as is evident from the above history of the FATF and the definition of crypto-assets in the FSB, the use of cryptoassets in the context of international financial supervision is not merely a paraphrase of the vital currencies defined by the FATF at the time of 2015, but rather an expansion of the scope of the application of digital tokens using DLT, thereby expanding or more generalizing the scope of the discussion.[5]

In the following sections, the term "cryptoassets" in this chapter refers to assets that the international financial regulatory community is trying to capture through the terms "crypto-assets" or "virtual assets" in the context of international financial supervision, rather than "cryptoassets" that merely change the name of a virtual currency in the Payment Services Act.

3 Impact of DLT in Financial Services

In order to understand the nature of the impact on current laws and regulations by code-based architecture, which may be provided by cryptoassets, it is necessary to organize the relationship between the financial products already subject to regulation and DLT. To do this, we should first understand what the potential of DLT is recognized in the context of financial services.

Briefly explaining them, although DLT is only one of the ledger implementation technologies, it is a technology that enables uniform ledger management through an architecture different from the architecture of centralized management of ledgers by traditional central administrators, such as relational databases. Such difference is considered to provide the value that conventional databases do not provide for financial transactions.

The following is a detailed explanation.

(1) Significance of DLT

There are various types of DLT, and there is no internationally agreed definition of what is called DLT.

[5]It is close to the understanding of the virtual assets created by the FATF. However, depending on the range of the stable token whose value is linked to the statutory currency, it is possible to think that the understanding of cryptoassets in Japan is classified differently.

However, in the context of international finance, DLT is considered to combine the following four functional characteristics.

(i) Data Distribution: Many participants can share the same ledger and access the data.
(ii) Decentralization: Ledger updates are carried out by many participants through agreed processes and rules.
(iii) Cryptographic techniques: Authentication of participants, verification of recorded data, and consensus building are performed using cryptographic techniques.
(iv) Programmability: The terms and conditions of the contract are automatically executed by the coded computer program.

In addition, DLT has two types of techniques: a permissionless method, in which everyone can participate in consensus building on ledger updates, though the cost of consensus building is high; and a permissioned method, in which participants who can participate in ledger updates are limited to improve the cost efficiency of the network as a whole. According to its design concept, a variety of variations exist with regard to "who can access what data" and "who can be involved in updating the ledger."

(2) Impact of DLT

Bearing in mind that DLT has the four functional characteristics mentioned above, the international financial regulatory community has conducted a variety of studies on the impact of DLT on financial services. As a result, it has been concluded that DLT may provide benefits to financial institutions and users in the following respects:

(i) System resilience

By sharing ledgers with a large number of participants, the ledger system can be operated successfully even if a particular participant loses data due to an accident. The ledger system can also have a high cyber resistance because system attackers cannot bring down the system unless they attack a large number of participants. In short, the use of DLT provides the benefit of increasing system resilience by eliminating single points of failure, which are vulnerabilities in the centralized system.

As a matter of course, financial institutions have incurred enormous costs in enhancing the resilience of their systems, as failure-induced system down is not particularly permissible. DLT has the potential to significantly reduce these costs.

(ii) Efficient Settlement Process

The direct access of large numbers of participants to the ledger provides the benefit of eliminating the cumbersome matching process that has been unavoidable in the payment system.

Needless to say, the essence of financial services lies in precise operations in accordance with predetermined rules.

A settlement system based on the premise that each business operator has a different book requires a matching process to maintain consistency among the books of each business operator. However, this is very costly and can be regarded as a structure that induces operational errors. Elimination of these problems through the use of a single book provides tremendous benefit to financial services.

(iii) Efficient Reporting, Auditing and Monitoring

A distributed ledger model that allows many participants to access a common book reduces information asymmetry within a financial institution or between multiple financial institutions, between financial institutions and customers, and between financial institutions and regulators. Real-time access to a common book by players in different circumstances reduces the need for manual reporting from one to the other. This is because those who need to know the situation can access and check the ledgers themselves.

One of the benefits of this feature becomes evident when financial products are implemented using DLT. Considering, for example, the management of a partnership fund using DLT, an investor can adopt an implementation in which the manager's activities can be confirmed in real time. Increased transparency, for example, can help raise the question of whether the rule that the operator must report the fund to the investor on a quarterly basis is reasonable.

The second benefit is related to the resolution of information asymmetries between financial institutions and regulators. If a regulator has direct access to the ledgers, it is not necessary to seek a report from a financial institution. The use of appropriate analytical tools by regulators can also enhance the stability of the financial system by enabling the early detection of macroprudential problems that adversely affect the financial system.

(iv) Automatic Execution of Transactions

The programmability of DLT can realize automatic execution of various financial transactions. Typically, a particular asset represented by a distributed ledger may be locked and automatically delivered to the other party when certain conditions are met. Because the entry ("satisfying a particular condition") may be from outside the distributed ledger system (this is called oracle, etc.), this feature allows various contracts to be executed automatically on the system. The term "smart contract" is used to refer to the technical characteristics of such a distributed ledger system.

In ordinary contracts, what content the parties agree on and whether the other party will execute the contract in accordance with the agreement are considered to be different matter. Therefore, based on the trust that state power, more specifically, judicial authority, can ultimately enforce the performance of the contract, the parties conclude the contract with the expectation that the agreement will be complied with by the other party. In other words, it has been assumed that the contract mechanism inevitably accompanies the risk of uncertainty in the counterparty's fulfilment of the contract. The functional characteristic of the automated execution of transactions using DLT is considered to be a major convenience in financial transactions with value transfer, because it reduces the various costs associated with the uncertainty of the counterparty's fulfilment of the contract.

(v) Digital Tokenization of Traditional Assets

Since DLT is basically a technology for unified ledger management, various assets previously managed in a centralized database can be managed using DLT.

DLT has the technical characteristics that allow each participant to share the ledger balance, and the ledger updating can be done by a non-centralized, specific consensus algorithm and automatically according to the program. Accordingly, if it is legally or technically ensured that the record of the ledger balance represents the amount of specific assets held by each participant, the update of the record of the ledger balance can be treated as "transferred by the owner of the asset." This is sometimes referred to as asset tokenization because it is generally felt as if the asset were digitized.

If an asset is tokenized under DLT, it is possible to benefit from the technical characteristics of the distributed ledgers listed in (i) to (iv) above with respect to asset transactions. Especially when automated execution is ensured, asset transactions can be highly efficient and deliver substantial benefits.

4 "Tokenization" of Traditional Assets

Of the impacts of DLT on financial services presented in Sect. 3, (v) Digital Tokenization of Traditional Assets is closely related to the topic of this chapter. The cryptoassets discussed in this section include those that are not covered as financial assets under existing financial legislation such as statutory currencies and financial instruments in the context of international financial regulation. Therefore, the relationship between what is called traditional asset tokenization and cryptoassets should be summarized.

As suggested earlier, the traditional asset tokenization is, in fact, an update of the record of the ledger balance of the management ledger of the traditional asset rights holder. In order for such "tokenization" to take place, it is necessary to assume that the rights holder of the underlying asset is changed by updating the record of the ledger balance. In order to do so, it must be legally ensured that the updating of the ledger balance record leads to a legal change of the rights holder of the underlying asset; in other words, a "change of the record of the ledger balance" equals a "change of the ownership of the underlying asset."

With regard to traditional assets, we will consider, with specific examples by type, how the transfer of the rights holder *erga omnes* by updating records of ledger balances is legally secured.

(i) The type in which the law ensures that the asset is transferred *erga omnes* by updating the ledgers

The Act on Book-Entry Transfer of Corporate Bonds and Shares (hereinafter referred to as the "Book-Entry Transfer Act") stipulates that the transfer of securities, such as corporate bonds, public bonds, and stocks, which are handled by book-entry institutions shall legally become effective by updating the records of the holders in the book-entry transfer account register. In addition, the Electronically Recorded Monetary Claims Act stipulates that the assignment record of the electronically recorded monetary claims by the electronically recorded monetary claim recording institution shall have the effect of legally assigning the electronically recorded monetary claims.

In these cases, it can be said that the individual law ensures that the asset rights holder of subject to the record transfers by updating the record of the ledger balance.

(ii) The type in which legal interpretation or structuring allows the asset to be considered to be transferred *erga omnes* by updating the ledgers.

The transfer of ownership of movables will effective only by the manifestation of intention of the parties, but the transfers of real rights concerning movables may not be asserted against third party, unless the movables are delivered (Articles 176 and 178 of the Civil Code). Delivery of possessed thing may be effected by transfer of possession by instruction without actual delivery (Article 184 of the Civil Code). By using the method of transfer of possession under this instruction, the updating of the ledgers may be treated as the transfer of movables legally.

For example, Owner A of gold shall deposit the gold with the book manager and the book manager shall record the owner of the gold. A will, after agreeing with B that the Gold shall be assigned to B and that the delivery thereof shall be effected by means of the transfer of possession by instruction, instruct the book manager to retain the gold thereafter together with the rewriting of the books for the Assignee B. The updating of the ledgers may then be treated as the transfer of ownership of the gold in a way that it may be asserted against a third party.

(iii) The Type in which assets will not be considered to be transferred *erga omnes* solely by updating ledgers

For example, with respect to real estate, the transfer of ownership may be effected by mutual agreement between the parties, but unless this is recorded in the real estate registry, the transfer of ownership may not be asserted against a third party (Article 177 of the Civil Code). The real estate registry is a ledger managed by the Legal Affairs Bureau and is updated only through procedures in accordance with the Real Estate Registration Act. Even if a private business operator prepares a ledger for the management of real estate and manages the transfer of ownership on its ledgers, it is impossible to determine the transfer of real estate as long as the contents of the ledger are not reflected in the real estate registry.

Some of these assets can be converted into types (i) and (ii) by structuring. For example, if real estate is transferred to a trust and the beneficial interest is converted into a beneficial interest, it can be subject to the Book-Entry Transfer Act, and the same argument as (i) can be applied.

As described above, for traditional assets, for example, as seen in (i) above, since the updating of ledgers ensures the legal transfer of rights for electronic claims by the Electronic Monetary Claims Recording Act, if the electronic monetary claim recording institution maintains ledgers through a distributed ledger and refers the records of ledger balances as "tokens," these electronic claims can be "tokenized" by DLT.[6] In light of the above 2, if the custodian of the movables has the proxy possessor node and notifies the movables custodian node to change the name of the movables owner recorded in the ledgers from A to B, based on the agreement on the transfer of the movables between A (wallet holder) and B, the movables may be treated as tokenized.

As mentioned earlier, if assets are tokenized under DLT, it is theoretically possible to benefit from the four functional characteristics of the distributed ledger detailed in Sect. 3 (1) with respect to asset transactions.

For example, if the automated execution of a transaction is secured for an asset managed in a distributed ledger, it is possible to enjoy the benefit of extremely efficient asset transactions.

In particular, if the asset is not legally determined for the unit of transaction, the tokenization by DLT allows assets to be traded in small pieces. The idea of trading in small holdings of assets is the same concept of securitization. From an information engineering perspective, the traditional asset tokenization attempts mean the application of DLT to existing asset management ledgers. From a financial engineering perspective, however, they do not differ from securitization technology in many cases.

5 Extension of Encryption Assets

As can be seen from the above, in order to tokenize a traditional asset, it is necessary to organize and manipulate methods and technology for matching the rights holder on a distributed ledger that implements a token with the rights holder of the asset. In short, traditional assets are an asset class that is recognized as assets under the current law. This means that laws concerning the ownership and transfer of the rights to the asset have been established. Thus, in order to assume that the rights holder of the underlying asset has been legally changed by a change in the balance on the digital book, there must be a law on the ownership and transfer of rights (typically private law), and the occurrence and transfer of tokens will be governed by a system of private law that is governed by the law of any country.[7]

In contrast, the assets that we must consider under the name of the cryptoassets are those for which the basis of these private laws is not clear. This includes just digital records on a distributed ledger, such as Bitcoins, that do not have any underlying real assets or cash flows. What needs to be considered here are virtual currencies such

[6]See the report by the Study Group on Legal Issues Concerning the Use of Distributed Ledger Technology in Securities Transactions (Bank of Japan Institute for Monetary and Economic Studies, November 2017) for details on the issue of using DLT under the Book-Entry Transfer Act.

[7]Since tokens are easily transferred across borders via the Internet, the question of which country's law should be governed by should be resolved. However, this is a problem covered by international private law and is not new in quality.

as Bitcoins and Ether, and in some cases, some types of cryptoassets that collect revenue by smart contract and allocates it to the holders of cryptoassets with a token digitized using DLT (called a stable coin or stable token) as a currency unit.

The following cryptoassets are assumed for consideration using specific examples.

The Cryptoasset T is an asset developed as the only means of payment for transactions between users and access to other services deployed on a distributed Network N that operates without the developer's involvement using DLT. In accessing Network N, the user must pay 0.0001 T per access fee to Network N, and 0.0001% of the cryptoassets T that the user has received as a fee when he or she deals with or provides services to other users on Network N.

These fees are not received by someone on the network. They are automatically and directly sent to Wallet W that no one manages on the network by a smart contract. The incentive design for the maintenance and expansion of Network N automatically allocates the Cryptoasset T accumulated in Wallet W to the address of the holder of Cryptoasset T according to a predetermined formula at UTC 0:00 on the last day of January, April, July, and October of each year. This allocation is conducted according to the amount of the Cryptoasset T held.

In order for such cryptoassets to function, it is important to consider how to design a consensus algorithm for changes in books, and how to design a compensation structure for such changes. However, the focus here is not on that, but rather on a private legal framework behind the above mechanism.

The Cryptoasset T is coded in such a way that the access right to the distributed Network N is architecturally secured by codes, and that users who possess the Cryptoasset T can receive the profit earned by the ecosystem formed by the distributed Network N. Thus, at least theoretically, those who want access to distributed Network N, who want to provide services thereon, and investors who are not interested in these but believe that the ecosystem formed by distributed Network N is profitable,[8] may become consumers of Cryptoasset T. If there is a consumer, then there will be a service provider in the distributed Network N who tries to provide services to other users to acquire the Cryptoasset T, and there will also be a supplier who tries to earn profits by selling the acquired Cryptoasset T. In some cases, there may be a company who tries to match demand with supply by intermediating transactions.

The question of how to manage these algorithms in a decentralized manner so that the ecosystem can sustainably distribute the supply and demand of these cryptoassets T is a major issue, but if this will be possible,[9] we must think about how this kind of discipline will be enforced in the future.

[8]In some cases, this includes speculators who anticipate that other investors will think so and who think that they will be able to gain trading gains from this.

[9]And we are in an environment where we cannot deny the argument that such management, given adequate data, can be done better by deep-learning machines which are capable of changing algorithms than by humans who are subject to biases due to greed or other cognitive systems.

6 Discipline on Cryptoassets

(1) Identification of the problem

How are the Network N and the Cryptoasset T, described in the example above, developed in practice? First, there must be a Network N developer, but the developer need not be a corporate organization, but just a community of developers. Engineers from all over the world interact with each other using Skype and other peer-to-peer communication system to develop a network on GitHub (a cloud developer community), and release it in a way that everyone can set up a node.[10] Rewards to developers can be anything; for example, they may receive a certain amount of cryptoassets T, depending on their contribution.

Once released to the public, Network N and Cryptoasset T will operate without any administrators. This means that there is no entity equivalent to the service provider in the terms of use. Even if an entity equivalent to an administrator can be found in Network N or Cryptoasset T, the attribution and transfer of Cryptoasset T is decentralized by DLT, and the collection of access fees and transaction fees to Network N is automatically carried out by coding in the distributed ledger itself. In addition, the wallet W to which fees are collected is a wallet not under the control of anyone and not accessible by the developer. Even if there is an entity that drafts a terms of use, it is not reasonable to create a relationship of rights and obligations in which the entity itself would bear responsibility for such a code-based automatic behavior.

It is not an exclusive matter of law to regulate an entity and its behavior. Discipline by architectures, which are physical and technical structures, may be possible, and non-legal social norms and markets may bear such function. The problem here is how these will be regulated by law when considering the network implemented by DLT and the cryptoassets used thereon.

(2) Discipline under the Business Law

Business law is a disciplinary method that ensures the appropriateness of an entity and its behavior by directly disciplining an entity. As for cryptoassets, if there is an entity that manages the generation of the cryptoassets, the person may be the subject of discipline, but it may be possible to introduce discipline by having the broker of the cryptoasset transaction or the trustee of the cryptoassets management be the subject.

In the case of a network, if there is a network administrator, the person may be the subject of discipline. However, as the network administrator is not involved in individual transactions, it may be difficult to regulate the network administrator with respect to transactions.

---

[10]When releasing to the public, they will be carefully tested in a closed state to allow them to function autonomously and gradually expand their access to the network, creating a situation in which everyone can eventually set up a node.

In the case of networks and cryptoassets implemented by DLT, it may be difficult to identify the administrator who may be justified to imposing discipline as a responsible entity (in the case where it is not possible to place responsibility on an entity due to the degree of involvement in the network or cryptoassets, or where it is impossible for regulators to regulate the entity because it is not so involved in the network as to observe the responsibility). It is therefore necessary to examine the establishment of regulatory targets and the content of specific regulations.

For example, the Cryptoasset T mentioned above do not fall under any of the securities listed in the current Financial Instruments and Exchange Law. Since the Cryptoasset T is used as a means of payment for services, it can be regarded as a virtual currency as defined in the Payment Services Act. Therefore, the subject of regulation is a business operator who engages in the sale and purchase of the Cryptoasset T, its proxy and brokerage.

If the developer attempts to raise funds to develop the Network N by selling the Cryptoasset T to unspecified parties, the developer is regulated as a virtual currency exchange service provider for its sales activity, but if it does not engage in such sales activity, it is not immediately subject to the regulation.

In addition, the report of the above-mentioned study group proposed that the Financial Instruments and Exchange Act be applied to the purchased tokens as falling under Paragraph (1) Securities if a certain profit distribution is expected. Therefore, if this is enacted, it is necessary to submit a securities registration statement for the sale of the Cryptoasset T to a large number of persons, and if the sale is entrusted, it is necessary to entrust the sale to a Type I Financial Instruments Business Operator.[11] In addition, the secondary market for the Cryptoasset T and its transactions are subject to the regulation of unfair trade[12] under the Financial Instruments and Exchange Act, as well as the self-regulation issued by the self-regulating body for financial instruments exchanges and a Type I Financial Instruments Business Operator. In this case, it is unclear whether or not discipline of the virtual currency legislation under the Payment Services Act will be imposed on the Cryptoasset T, but if it is imposed, the consistency of discipline between the two will be sharply questioned.

Although the content of discipline may differ in each country, it does not seem that the private law discipline described below will be filled by approaches to business law regulation.

(3) Discipline under Private Law

As for digital platforms, especially the typical multifaceted, market-oriented digital platforms, there are terms of use issued by platformers to multiple categories of users. Platformers often assume that they are not involved in individual transactions between uses of different categories within the platform, so the details of the terms and conditions of transactions between users may be vague. In particular, on a CtoC

[11] It has been proposed that the issuer should be a financial instruments business operator in order to balance the regulation on self-offering of Paragraph (2) Securities.

[12] In relation to the appropriate allocation of administrative resources, certain reservations have been made to regulate insider trading.

platform where the service provider is not a business operator, the terms and conditions of transactions may not be explicitly clear, partly because there is no business law applicable to service providers.

The platformer (designer and operator of the market) regulates the user through the implementation of codes that make the market work, making it impossible for the user to choose any action other than a specific action, or by using the default settings that the user will take specific action if the user does not choose any action. This discipline is not, in principle, the basis of contractual responsibility for the platformer, since they are governed by a code-based architecture that does not take the form of terms of use.[13]

While it is known that by using code-based architectural discipline platformers can circumvent legal and contractual responsibilities to users to a certain extent, similar structures can be seen for distributed networks and cryptoassets.

Rather, from the perspective of private law discipline, it would be more difficult to enforce effective discipline for distributed networks and cryptoassets than for existing platforms, as follows.

Firstly, even if there is an entity regarded as an administrator on a distributed network, many authorities are executed in a decentralized manner, so it is considered that the terms of use would be minimal. Of course, by decentralizing the authority, it is possible to assume that there is no administrator, and in that case, the terms of use may not be issued.[14]

Secondly, whether it is installed on the side of the cryptoasset or on the network side, payment and distribution matters can be automatically executed by the code side. Therefore, there is no room to interact with the notion of a consensus of effect among parties. In addition, there may be no person equivalent to the platformer (counterparty to the transaction), so it is possible that no observations can be made. If there is a platformer, when the code automatically purchases goods in e-commerce and charges the purchase price, the user may take some form of counteraction by claiming that the transaction is invalid to the platformer or by stopping the payment so that the payment is not charged.

On the other hand, in the case of a service that uses cryptoassets as a settlement means, as in the example of the Cryptoasset T mentioned earlier, a real-time charge is made by code only, whether it is an access fee or a service fee, and no one manages the billing destination Wallet W (i.e., there is no private key holder).

Even if a contractual relationship under private law has not been established, it is technically possible to charge a fee without anyone to whom a user can raise an objection.

---

[13] Of course, if the content of the code prevents the realization of the rights guaranteed to the user by the terms of use, it will cause the problem of default by the platformers. In addition, if the restrictions imposed by the code would seriously harm the reasonable expectations of the user who entered into the business relationship, the platformer may assume responsibility based on the doctrine of good faith and fair dealing.

[14] For example, Ethereum's terms of use, which are oriented towards a distributed world computer, contain only a risk presentation and indemnification clause and a dispute resolution clause associated with its use.

A relief would be that if such a cryptoasset or network exists, their codes would basically be reviewable by anyone.

Thus, by reviewing the code, it is possible to confirm what the terms of the transaction embedded in the codes are.

Although there may be a limited number of people who can actually review the code, it is possible that trusted individuals will disclose the results of the review to ensure the reliability of the system.

If information is disclosed and transparency is ensured, other forms of discipline—the power of market forces and reputational norms—will provide incentives for their developers to make the architecture of decentralized systems appropriate.

At present, DLT is still in the early stages of development. So as far as I know, there are not many applications that adopt a truly distributed architecture as theoretically assumed in a distributed system, and many projects are conceived to design services by combining it with a centralized system.

In this case, the system administrator will be the starting point, and the system administrator will create a reasonable relationship of rights and obligations between the system administrator and the user or between the users, centering on the terms of use issued by the administrator, by making full use of general principles such as the default rules of private law, the doctrine of good faith and morals, and public order and morals.

7 Building an Integrated System Design

We have examined how the circumvention of laws and contracts by codes, which is currently a topic of intense discussion in platform regulation, will be manifested in cryptographic assets, and how the tools of laws and contracts can be approached against them, taking into account the tokenization derived from the technical characteristics of distributed ledgers and the differences between cryptoassets and traditional assets.

DLT is still in the early stages of development. In particular, with regard to the permissionless-type distributed ledgers (generally called "public block chains"), there are a number of issues that need to be overcome from the viewpoint of compliance with existing laws and regulations, such as data protection, as well as many technical issues. Thus, current projects mainly adopt an architecture that enables the identification of the responsible entities in some way. Starting with those entities, it is believed that issues above can be addressed by applying discipline currently emerging for platformers.

Networks are said to be distributed and concentrated in the course of their development. While DLT may be positioned as a solution to the adverse effects of excessive concentration of platforms on the online network, it should also be remembered that distributed architectures may make it difficult to identify responsible entities, thus making it difficult to regulate by law. From the viewpoint of efficiently controlling the negative externalities of networks, institutional designers need to consider an integrated approach that includes activities to establish technical standards for architectures, rather than sticking to laws and regulations alone.

Chapter 9
Fintech: Toward a New Era of Finance

Jumpei Miwa and Yusaku Matsui

1 What We See in Fintech as a Regulator?—Laying Out the "Finance Digitalization Strategy"

In several years, we often see the term "FinTech" in major economic newspapers and magazines, and it is now widely conceived to the general public at large. While "FinTech" is generally used as a term coined from the fusion of "finance" and "technology", the term also implies a wider motivation of coherent service promotions to create innovative financial services through the combination of the two concepts, rather than a simple fusion of them. It is also observed that the term is often used to describe technology-driven innovative initiatives in financial services as a whole.[1]

Why, then, do we draw much attentions to the "FinTech"? While regulators, policymakers, businesses, and users may have different angle of views to the financial innovation made by FinTech, but intuitively, the common view seems that they feel it quite different nature from the conventional IT adoptions to financial services they have experienced so far.

In the history of banking services in Japan, the efforts toward IT adoption by banks has been undergoing since the 1970s, following the launch of standardized bank-wire system, namely the Zengin System (Zengin Net[2]) in 1973. Thus, IT adoptions in financial services have been made along with the stage of developments in information and communication technology. And almost all banks including cooperatives

[1] Some people refer to it as "TechFin" in the sense that technology changes financial services.

[2] See the National Bankers Association website (https://www.zenginkyo.or.jp), etc.

Jumpei Miwa—Director, Fintech and Innovation Office, Financial Services Agency; Yusaku Matsui—Deputy Director of Banking, Payment and Insurance Regulations Office, Financial Services Agency. It should be noted that the part of the text that covers the opinions of the author is the author's personal opinion.

J. Miwa (✉) · Y. Matsui
Financial Services Agency, The Government of Japan, Tokyo, Japan

S. Kaji et al. (eds.), *The Economics of Fintech*,
https://doi.org/10.1007/978-981-33-4913-1_9

attain smooth bank settlements and fund transfer services using this infrastructure. Based on this, banks have built robust mainframes and customized high-performance and useful ATM systems that fit Japanese service-oriented sense. By means of the robust mainframes, Japanese banking sector has collectively sustained a high level of security in centralized maintenance and operation.

We, as a financial and regulatory authority, have taken policy measures in line with these IT vogues. Especially since the latter half of the 1990s, the emerging Internet-only banks, currently called as the "traditional challengers," has gradually transformed conventional physical banking services into those carried out through an open network. Relevant guidelines and standards concerning the IT security have been arranged through cooperative efforts made among industry and government. These developments are still in progress in line with the incremental cyber risks.

Furthermore, with the advent of businesses of electronic money (e-money), funds transfer services and settlement services are becoming more diverse than ever. Corresponding to it, additional regulatory efforts have been made to enable the companies without bank license to operate money transfer transactions in the form of registry licensing of "funds transfer business"[3] through the enforcement of the formulated "Payment Services Act."[4]

The financial transactions has been transformed as technologies develops for the past several decades, but the most material financial digital transformation in recent times have been set out around global financial crisis in 2008. The virtual currencies, which are now collectively called as "crypto-assets", have been deployed by the launch of Bitcoin, and it is becoming the main driver of financial transformation that leads to the new concepts of digital currencies and ICOs in later years. At the same time, the advent of new devices, such as smartphones launched in 2007 by Apple's iPhone, has more than impacted to the financial transactions to retail services, which enables people to facilitate their accesses to financial services they had never experienced before. The usability by such services has also improved over time in the name of enhanced user experiences and interfaces. In tandem with the use of smartphones, the 4th generation mobile communication system (4G) has improved the communication speed and the quantity of data transmission that enables connections from smartphones to the Internet environment without stress.

These changes has given rise to opportunities to unleash online services through Internet using banking services. In addition, applications of personal financial management (PFM) services, which effectively aggregate financial account information, are generally provided by firms other than banks. It is becoming more popular in Japan that companies offer the convenient PFM services with apps of "personal bookkeeping" which integrate data on bank account balances and credit card payment history by usage of smartphones. There is also a value shift on data or

[3]Payment Services Act (Act No. 59 of 2009).

[4]A person other than a bank, etc. who engages in exchange transactions of not more than the amount equivalent to one million yen in the course of trade. In order to engage in the funds transfer service, he/she shall obtain registration from the Prime Minister in advance pursuant to Payment Services Act.

digitized information obtained from customers through such services. Using personal data in finance, people can be affordable to wider financial services to the area of settlements, remittances, credit, and use of investments by handy smartphones.

Even in non-banking services, new businesses are also extending to use wearable devices to gather detailed health data and then insurers are able to provide services tailored to the individual's needs. Digitized data has catered the possibility of creating new added value and services based on smartphones or other useful handy devices.

As the digitized data is, among others, becoming more valuable than ever, the service provision in financial services is also changing. Customer's digitized data itself represents the customer's needs to build a customer-oriented business model based on the needs they provided. This implies a new rise of personal empowerments in financial services. Asset management services that were previously offered only to certain layers, such as the mass-affluent or more, can be provided to many people. These trends can be said to be a major transformation in the history of financial services, and a sign of the advent of the new era of finance.

Mori (2017)[5] hypothetically interpreted this FinTech trends above, noting that "the digitalization revolution caused by the combination of the internet and mobile technologies resulted in increased customer initiatives and turned past recipients into providers of information."

Due to the reform of financial services by FinTech, we assume that the financial system may eventually result in the transactions dominated by P2P and C2C without any economic intermediaries where existing financial institutions currently operate. However, as such a landscape is not realistic at this stage, it is precise to assume that now is in the phase of transition towards the sight where no banks may exist. At this time we, as a financial regulator, should monitor how the relationship between existing financial institutions and customers will change with the progress of FinTech.

Based on this perspective, the current phenomenon will prepare the shift from the conventional model of providing typical one-size-fits-all products based on a supply-side logic to a C2B type of direction based on customer information which seeks to identify more shared values. It should be noted that the term C2B does not mean that customers sell products directly to businesses, but that initiatives are shifting to the customer side. The term C2B is used to describe such a direction (Fig. 1).

At current juncture, most of incumbent financial institutions can only accumulate customer information through required KYC data and obtain information such as deposit or withdrawal records through bank deposits. However, as banks and other entities become more collaborative with customer data held by other companies such as FinTech companies, it will be possible to add new digitized information and conduct in-depth analysis using extended data sets. This will also enable the provision of bespoke financial services, the acquisition of new customers and understanding of their financial needs.

[5]Nobuchika Mori (2017) "Will fintech create shared values?" Speech at Annual Tokyo Conference of the Center on Japanese Economy and Business, Columbia Business School on May 25, 2017 (provisional translation). For details, please refer to the FSA website.

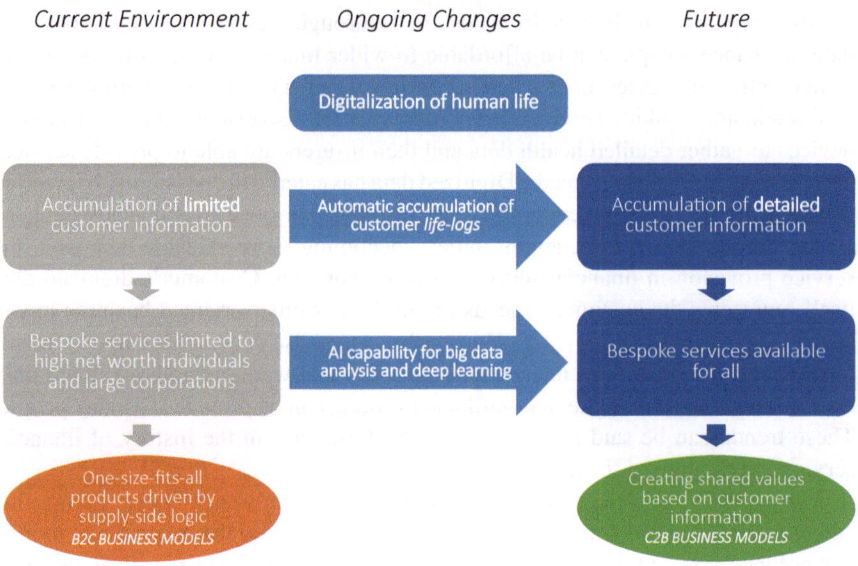

Fig. 1 Nature of ongoing changes

As data becomes more digitized, the cumulative customer information combined with technologies such as artificial intelligence (AI) can change information that was asymmetric between customers and service providers. This is also applicable to the issue of data sharing through the API between financial institutions and third parties. Thus, the new wave of data sharing begins to change the financial landscape significantly.

*API stands for "Application Programming Interface" which means a specification or mechanism whereby functions of an application and related data are called from other applications and connected. This will be addressed in later Section.

In response to changes of circumstance, JFSA has released the policy package titled "Financial Services Policy: Assessments and Strategic Priorities 2018" in September, 2018. We have also formulated the "Finance Digitalization Strategy (FDS)", envisaging the current circumstances of fast-paced digitalization in financial services. Figure 2(1) and (2) provide an overview of 11 priorities stated in the FDS. In particular, in light of the opportunity of innovative changes in the financial business, the FDS highlights the agenda concerning improving data sharing, modernization of financial payments and open engineering by APIs, and the renovation of regulatory frameworks in more function-based and cross-sectoral manner for facilitating data use in financial services.

With the provision of new services by FinTech, we also observe that the incumbent functions of financial institutions are being unbundled along with the entrance of new players, and the functions are being re-bundled with non-financial services in a manner that meets customer needs. What we are seeing in FinTech is the coherent or

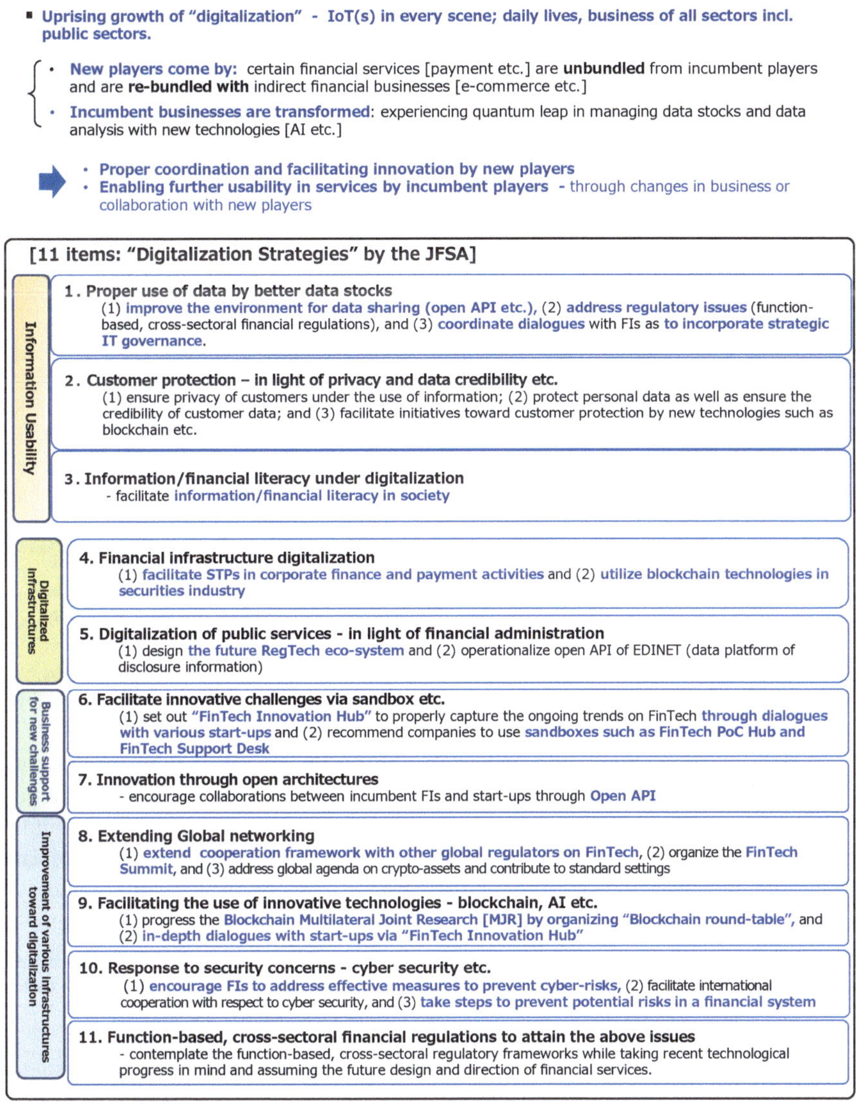

Fig. 2 (1) Policy response to the accelerating digitalization (1)—Finance digitalization strategy—(Released on September 26, 2018)

incoherent changes made by unbundling and re-bundling for transforming financial businesses by emerging financial players.

Traditionally, it is generally conceived that the sources of power in current financial institutions have been attributed from wide branch networks and capital-intensive full-line-up businesses, sustained by massive IT systems and balance sheets. In the new wave of FinTech world, such sources of power are most likely to be replaced

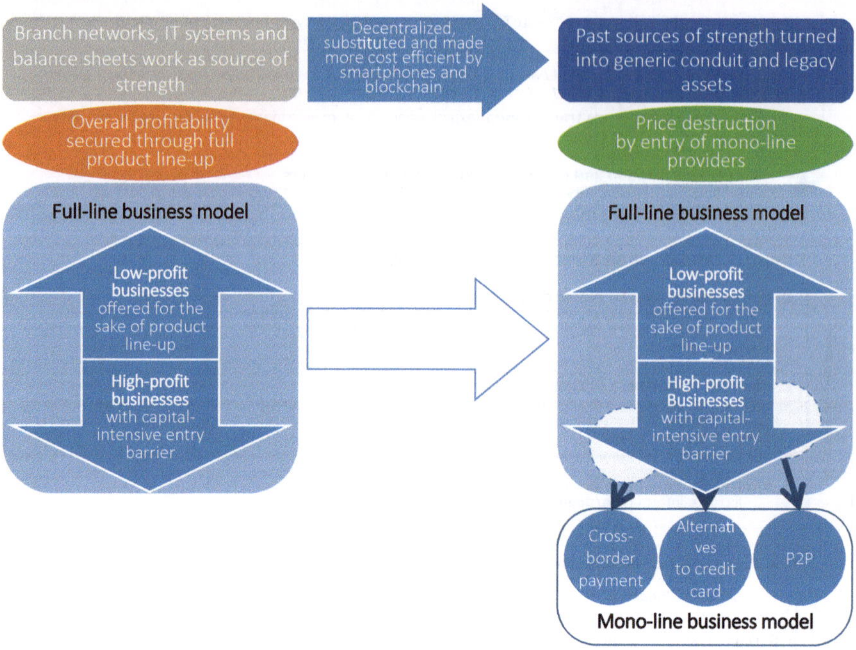

Fig. 3 Key players—Would infrastructure continue to protect incumbents? *Source* Mori (2017)

by businesses of accumulating and analyzing customer information by big data, making major improvements in customer relationships by new marketing methods, and providing a bespoke lineup tailored to customer needs. It is also likely that the traditional source of strengths become "legacy" in incumbent financial services and only profitable operations are "unbundled" by FinTech companies (Figs. 3 and 4).

There is an another possibility that the regulatory system based on current silo-type perimeters categorized by banks, security firms and insurers etc., will not fit with the actual situation in the midst of technological innovation and the modernization of financial services.

The FDS aims to heretically review financial regulatory frameworks into a more function-based and cross-sectoral one that fits the current changes. This is a series of considerations aimed to transform the current regulatory framework. In other jurisdictions, it is often referred to as "function-based" or "activity-based" regulatory framework. Concerted discussions are currently being held by the Financial System Study Group of the Financial System Council at JFSA. Details are described in Sect. 3 below.

There is a possibility of a transition to be more decentralized and autonomous financial system in which there are no human interventions, as typified by the public blockchain deployed in the current Bitcoin etc.

As shown in Fig. 5, JFSA should anticipate medium- to long-term shifts for the change of the financial system, and consider the future required policy responses

Potential new success factors		Prospective key players and their roles?
Capital	Branches, IT systems and balance sheets	Incumbents' current source of strength but may turn into generic conduit and legacy assets.
Knowledge	Customer information	Distributers accumulate information on detailed life activities. Banks know only about total monthly payment amounts.
	Technology	Incumbents are experimenting with in-house development, acquisition of ventures and alliance with tech companies
Customer convenience	Access with customers	Banks have more customer access points than FinTech ventures, but less than distributors.
	Product range	No single group currently covers all of the financial and non-financial services needed to realize the full potential of FinTech
Trust	Customer confidence in service providers	Be it a financial institution or other entity, the one with a customer-oriented business model, strong relationship with customers and strong professional competence will gain customer confidence

- **What will be the key factor for becoming the leader in new forms of financial services? Which entities will play the central roles?**
- **Will the financial institutions merely provide infrastructure, or become the core of value creation by collaborating with other entities?**

Fig. 4 Key players—Who will command the new success factors?

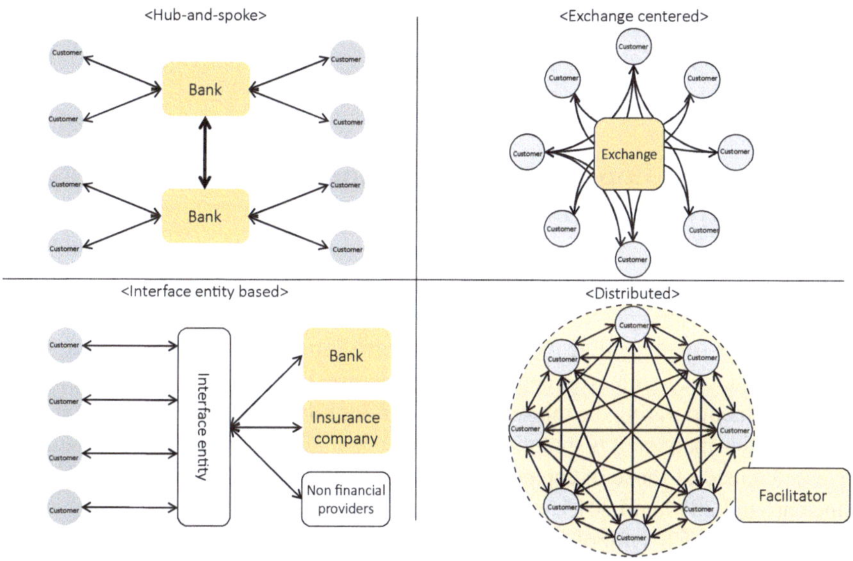

Fig. 5 Future shape of financial network?

in a forward-looking manner, as to whether we, regulators, are able to sustain the existing regulatory frameworks or not in the future. In particular, with regard to the decentralized financial system, comprised by the "crypto-assets", the further deployments other than crypto-assets are gaining global attention.

Indeed, the statement at the July 2018 meeting of G20 Finance Ministers and Central Bank Governors[6] has highlighted that "technological innovations, including those underlying crypto-assets, can deliver significant benefits to the financial system and the broader economy. Crypto-assets do, however, raise issues with respect to consumer and investor protection, market integrity, tax evasion, money laundering and terrorist financing. Crypto-assets lack the key attributes of sovereign currencies. While crypto-assets do not at this point pose a global financial stability risk, we remain vigilant."

In the statement issued at the meeting[7] in March 2017, only one year ago, it was further stressed that "to ensure that we will reap the benefits and opportunities that digital innovation offers, while potential risks are appropriately managed, we encourage all countries to closely monitor developments in digital finance, including consideration of cross-border issues, both in their own jurisdictions and in cooperation with the FSB and other international organizations and standard setting bodies." Comparing these two statements, it is acknowledged that the global attention for financial innovation, such as blockchain-based financial systems (e.g. crypto-assets) has been enhancing. The necessity of policy responses and initiatives based on such global attention will be addressed in Sect. 4 below in light of the emerging issue of decentralized financial system.

2 Proactively Improve to the Environments Where Innovative Financial Services Are Created

(1) Seeing the FinTech as an "opportunity"

It is observed for several years that financial institutions in Europe and the U.S. are capturing the recent environmental changes caused by FinTech as a new "opportunity," and incorporating the innovation as a material source of their corporate strategy in a proactive manner. It is sometimes indicated that their motivations have been reactive and ahead of those of Japanese financial institutions. This has become evident since around 2014 and 2015.

Jamie Demon's symbolic remark at the Euroeconomy conference in May 2014 in Riyadh, Saudi Arabia, made us perceived regarding a next threat for financial institutions. He stated that "we're going to go to have competition from Google and

[6]See G20 Finance Ministers and Central Bank Governors Statement (provisional translation) (July 21–22, 2018: Buenos Aires, Argentina) (see the Ministry of Finance website).

[7]The G20 Finance Ministers and Central Bank Governors Statement (provisional translation) (March 17–18, 2017, Baden-Baden, Germany) (see the Ministry of Finance website).

Facebook and somebody else."[8] This indicates that incumbent players should take a strategic shift in response to the big shade of potential competitors.

Against this backdrop, incumbent financial players has begun to acknowledge that they should remove the self-IT-customization developed by themselves, as their inflexible technological deployments are inferior to emerging technology companies under agile strategies. For recent half of the decade, there has been a growing strategic changes among financial institutions, especially US and Europe financial institutions, to acquire start-ups in Fintech-related fields to incorporate both technologies and new services into their source of management, or to collaborate with them in the form of alliance for further interactions with them.

In the first FinTech wave around 2015, incumbent financial institutions drew attention to the so-called "FinTech disrupters" as a new threat. However, most FinTech related start-ups have not taken such attitudes, rather they have inclined to form collaborative relations or consortium networks to gain the knowledge. It may be wise to say that, while maintaining a certain level of competitive environment, financial institutions and FinTech companies are balancing both elements of competition and cooperation.

In contrast, concerning the situation in Japan, the banks have been providing functional ATMs by renovating it for about 40 years and ensuring a high level of safety. It is generally perceived by Japanese people that ATMs have been used not only for simple deposit and withdrawal services, but also for direct bank-to-bank transfers, tax payments, depository bookkeeping, term deposits including foreign currency deposits etc. In fact, we do not see such functional ATM services in foreign financial institutions.

As noted, internet-only banks has also increased since late 1990's. In fiscal 2017, the outstanding balance of deposits possessed by them has reached to around 17 trillion yen.[9] In the amount of prepaid cards and e-money services, recent data in fiscal 2017 indicated that the transaction volume (transaction volume) by the fund transfer business exceeds one trillion yen.[10]

On the other hand, in terms of the strategic nature of IT investment, U.S. banks positively invest in the purpose of next change and proactive IT adaption, while Japanese banks are relying on more conservative investments in light of maintenance of existing mainframes. In terms of the number of engineers at financial institutions, IT engineers in the U.S. institutions is much higher (Fig. 6).

[8]See, e.g., JPMorgan's Demon Sees Facebook to Google Challenging Bank, (Bloomberg May 7, 2014) (https://www.bloomberg.com/news/articles/2014-05-06/jpmorgan-s-dimon-ses-sees-faciebook-to-gogiccalling-bank-online).

[9]Aggregated value based on data published on the websites of Aeon Bank, Seven Bank, Jibun Bank, Japan Net Bank, Sumishin SBI Net Bank, Sony Bank, Daiwa Next Bank, Rakuten Bank, and each company.

[10]See materials prepared by Japan Payment Service Association in the Financial System Study Group of the Financial System Council (the second session of the business year of October 25, 2018).

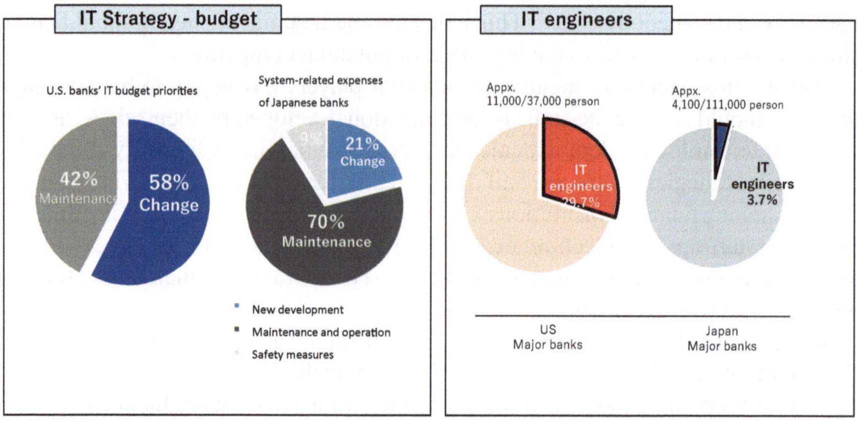

Source: Technology Businesses Research.
Note 1) As of 2014
2) The research targeted about 200 executives from major financial institutions and IT vendors in North America, with total assets of more than $ one billion.
2013) As of 2014
Source:
1) Explanatory Material of the Japan Research Institute, Ltd. at the Financial System Council Study Group on Enhancement of Payment Services (2nd Meeting)
2) FISC Questionnaire Survey on Systematization of Financial Institutions (March 2014)

Fig. 6 Comparative study on IT adaption [Differences between Japanese and U.S. financial institutions]

Taking into account these natures inherent in Japan, it is rather important to forge new environments for positively deploying the innovation by FinTech as an "opportunity" and cultivating more innovative financial services.

(2) Proactively Take Policy Responses to Environmental Changes by FinTech "Opportunities"

In Japan, further collaboration and cooperation between old and new players is of importance to facilitate innovation in an open manner. To attain this, JFSA set out with the goal of creating better regulatory environments and a key conceptual pillar for "open innovation" to flexibly adapt the regulatory frameworks to recent financial environments made by Fintech. One of the specific policy responses is relating to amending the Banking Act in recent years.

While it is of importance to facilitate open innovation, current non-agile style of the bank's IT strategy that is bound to self-IT-adaption (in-house developments) are not enough to adapt to the evolution and speed of today's technology developments. Rather, facilitating collaborations with third parties such as technology-oriented firms will be necessary in Japanese financial services. Thus, JFSA amended the Banking Act to facilitate agile investments by banks to financial-related IT companies,[11] and thereby banks can strategically integrate IT developments into the managerial sources and to enable agile business compositions throughout the financial group.

[11]The Act on Partial Amendment of the Banking Act to Respond to Environmental Changes such as the Advancement of Information and Communications Technology (enacted on May 25, 2016, promulgated on June 3, 2016).

Under the Banking Act, banks are generally prohibited from other businesses than core bank-related ones and from acquiring more than a total of 5% of the voting rights of any specific firm. Similar regulatory cap limitation has applied to bank holding companies to a level of 15% of such voting rights. It has been argued that numerical cap limitation may undermine the flexible investments by banks for collaboration with FinTech companies. Through amending the Banking Act, banks become capable of investing Fintech firms without specific cap limitation, provided that such bank's investments will lead to innovation of banking business and further improvement of user convenience and so forth.

In addition to the facilitation of banks' flexible investments, further amendment of the Banking Act has been made for the purpose of open engineering using the bank open-API initiative while we are mindful of user protection.

In the data sharing structure between financial institutions and FinTech companies in the current PFM services, customers provide passcodes and thereby FinTech companies can access the personal bank account data in the internet banking on behalf of customers. This "screen-scraping" technology underpins the data aggregation services and makes this scheme possible. However, under this method, this is likely to be at risk in customer information by an unauthorized access or data leakage without establishing proper legal contracts between banks and Fintech firms. There is also a risk by unclear legal responsibility between them and therefore they should legally establish the risk allocation mechanism when accidents occur.

As the proper and efficient data sharing is quite important agenda in today's digitized society, the Banking Act was amended in order not to hinder the motivation to it, while taking into account the possible risks on the user side. We are also mindful of securing the safe use of data between relevant parties.[12]

In order to safely connect to the financial institutions by FinTech companies, the amendment necessitates that Fintech firms that provide services of account aggregation and payment order requests shall be subject to registration requirement as the status of "Electronic Payment Service Provider.[13]" And they are also subject to governance-related and financial-related requirements as well as the requirement of establishing proper legal contract with a bank in terms of customer protection and proper information usage, loss compensation to customers and so forth. On the other hand, banks are required to make every efforts to facilitate unleashing API scheme and must disclose their own policies for API strategy and technical standard on their websites.

If they have any specific reasons where banks are not able to respond to releasing policies, they are also required to disclose the reasons why it is unable. This framework essentially comprises a mechanism of "compliance or explain" for banks and promote API collaboration between them. At the moment as of December 2018, 130 out of 139 Japanese banks, which exclude foreign branches, have announced their

[12]The Act on Partial Amendment of the Banking Act, etc. (enacted on May 26, 2007, promulgated on June 2, 2007).

[13]See the FSA website for the status of registration of electronic settlement agents.

policy for opening API and 122 banks have announced that the API scheme will be implemented by June 2020.

With regard to API-related initiatives, the Japanese governmental growth strategy has laid out the specific KPI and incentivized the API implementation by targeting 80 banks implementation till 2020. The current level of policy commitment by banks is now far beyond the prescribed level. In line with the process of implementation, collective efforts have been made among API stakeholders to establish industry standards by publishing reports and technical standards specifically through the Advisory Council of the Japan Bankers Association.[14]

(3) Proactively Take Policy Responses to Revitalize the Payment Infrastructures and Modernize the Payments

The historical developments by the Zengin System has already been described in the Section above. On the other hand, emerging motivation for enhancing "digitalization" of data has encouraged to use electronic information for further analysis and improve their operations by companies. Especially, if the existing payment infrastructure has become more sophisticated in light of smooth data sharing, this will give rise to efficient operations especially for corporate's back-office.

Further upgrading Japan's financial infrastructure is of importance. Thus, JFSA has taken policy responses flexibly to modernize the payment system.

A typical example of the initiative is the transition to an XML format e-messaging in interbank payments and remittances. In Japanese interbank settlements, banks could only send information by a fixed length within 20 characters. However, the newly developed "Zengin EDI system" (called as the "ZEDI"), which operationalized in December 2018, allows almost unlimited transmission of e-massages using the XML format (Fig. 7).

Japanese banking settlement infrastructure is recognized as the core function in financial system and its further functional developments will lead to the user convenience, as well as the efficiency of cooperate activities that will result in the growth of whole Japanese economy. However, there is crucial bottlenecks in smooth information sharing currently limited under a fixed length e-message in Zengin-system, as the current fixed format lacks of information in order to check the detailed commercial data between mutual counterparties. If sales information made by front-office (such as order details etc.) is to be directly linked to the information handled in back-office for settlements, then operations that have been separated in the sales and finance divisions will be streamlined. If enough data is shared using the unlimited e-message format, it is also expected that the financial division will be able to automate the data matching without having to check between counterparties. For companies, improving the efficiency will lead to create a virtuous circle to save

[14]The JBA established the Review Committee on Open APIs, published the "Report of Review Committee on Open APIs: Promoting Open Innovation" (released in July 2017; also published in English), and also published the "Message Specification Standards." In addition, the Open API Promotion Study Group was established to design the template of the API agreements between two parties and published it in July 2018. For details, see JBA website.

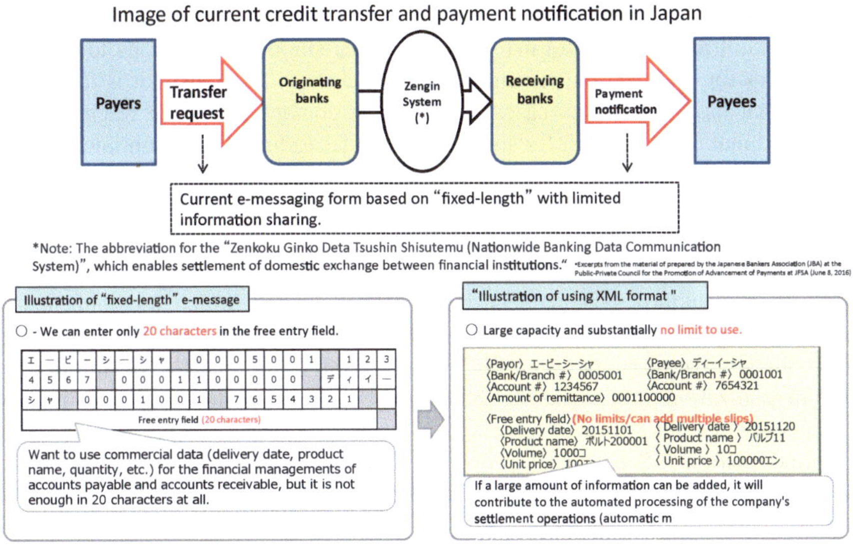

Fig. 7 Reforms of payment infrastructure (Transition to XML format)

resources and spare it more productive fields, and attain to yield benefits through efficient digitization of information.

In order to support these efforts, the "Public-Private Council for the Promotion of Advancement of Payments", was established within the Financial System Council in June 2016 to design the initiatives and monitor the current financial infrastructure environments.

In addition to the issue of "transition to XML format," the council has been addressing various issues, such as modernizing retail payment services and the promotion of the aforementioned "Open-API" and so forth. The council is also playing a role in promoting digital solutions such as the "digitalization of bills and checks" and "digitization of tax payments and public payment services".

In addition to the ZEDI, the Zengin System has begun the 24/7 (services in all days and all times) operations since October 2018. This is expected to increase the convenience of payment and remittances, especially by enterprises.

(4) Flexible Support the Firm's Deployments by JFSA's Supporting Tools—"FinTech Support Desk", "Fintech Proof-of-Concept (PoC) Hub", and "Bilateral Cooperation", under the "Fintech Innovation Hub"

For facilitating FinTech developments, JFSA has set out programs to support the efforts of FinTech start-up companies. The "Fintech Support Desk" is one of supporting program for these efforts, which was established in December 2015, and thereby JFSA can flexibly counsel them in light of compliance-related issues and concerns from FinTech related start-ups.

A major feature of the Desk is that it provides the one-stop service channel for various inquiries relating to FinTech and advises smooth interactions to required procedures for certification, registration, and licensing. Previously, it is frequently argued that there have been cases in which the contact points are fragmented at JFSA and making it difficult for start-up companies to find the appropriate desk for consultation. The effect of creating a one-stop channel is to integrate the fragmented points of contact in a transparent manner. The Desk has accepted many queries so far, and is working to respond quickly and flexibly within a week on average.

Another supporting program is the "Fintech PoC Hub" which is the similar program of "sandbox system" seen in other jurisdictions, which was launched in September 2017. More specifically, this aims to support projects in the stage of PoC and collaborative phase between FinTech companies and financial institutions for commercialization. Projects are selected after a certain screening process in light of possible service innovation or securing user protection. Thereafter, a dedicated team is formed within JFSA for each project and, in some cases, JFSA will collaborate with relevant ministries and agencies if necessary. The results of the applied POC are to be published[15] in a report from the project where PoC activities have been completed.

Furthermore, JFSA is building mutual cooperative relationships with relevant foreign authorities to facilitate the interactions of inward and outward FinTech companies to expand operations in Japan or relevant jurisdictions. In this framework, a mutual referral system has been applied. If a FinTech company wishes to expand overseas, JFSA will act as a liaison and introduce the company to the partner authority. In addition, this also attains a framework for candid exchange of information with foreign authorities relating to FinTech developments and thereby we are conducting effective interactions between authorities.

Recently, JFSA has developed a partnership with FINMA in Switzerland, ACPR and AMF in France as well as Dubai's financial authority. JFSA's portfolio of FinTech partnerships has been already extending to FCA in the U.K., MAS in Singapore, and ASIC in Australia and so forth.

In addition, JFSA has established the organizational function for extensively addressing FinTech matters, namely the "Fintech Innovation Hub" established in July 2018, to holistically support the challenges of innovation as well as abovementioned supporting programs. Through this function, members of the Innovation Hub conduct on-site meetings with FinTech start-ups if necessary and capture the latest technological trends and new issues of financial services. Through this process, JFSA is able to reflect next policy agenda in FinTech into the process of policy-making and setting policy priorities which JFSA should handle. JFSA has been making every efforts to create "opportunities" and necessary "venues" for smooth interactions with industry side, and addressing new issues, which will become next agenda in the coming future, in timely manner.

[15]As of February 2019, five cases had been tested through the PoC Hub, four of which have already been published on the FSA website.

3 Proactively Design the Regulatory System in Coming Phase (Function-Based, Cross-Sectoral Financial Regulations)

As stated in the Section above, designing the next phase of legal system suitable for the new era of finance made by FinTech is the key policy agenda and priority in the FDA (Finance Digitalization Strategy).

As described, the current financial environment continues to change by unbundling financial services and re-bundling with another non-financial services to provide the services through a combination of two. This motivation will be expanding more than ever. As the integration of incumbent financial and non-financial services develops, it is anticipated that the boundaries between these services have become increasingly blurred.

For example, new players in various forms have come into the market for some of the services formerly provided by banks. There are some cases where such players accept users' money in the form of e-money, make payments on customer requests and provide funds while operating the e-commerce market.

Under these diverse circumstances, the current legal system basically comprises laws and regulations for each business category, and even if each player's services have the same functions and risks, they may be subject to the different regulations according to the business category to which the player belongs. The current legal structure made by each business category may impede the choice of business between different business categories, and it has been frequently argued that there is a risk of arbitrary behaviors in manner of avoiding regulations by moving to less regulated business category.

Taking into account these circumstances, the Study Group on the Financial System was established under the Financial System Council at JFSA and has been designing the state of finance regulation in coming periods since November 2017.

In such circumstances, it is important that each player flexibly select a business model or a service and financial authorities adapt appropriate rules to the players according to the functions and risks of the selected business model or service, rather than regulating diverse players by applying each business law which currently exists. In addition, this should be reviewed from the viewpoint of promoting innovation, improving user convenience, and ensuring user protection and fair competitive conditions.

Current financial regulations comprise the Banking Act, the Payment Services Act, the Money Lending Business Act, the Financial Instruments and Exchange Act, and the Insurance Business Act and so forth. In contrast, through the consideration by the Study Group, it is argued that the functions have been divided into four categories, namely "payment and settlement," "lending," "investments," and "risk undertakings and transfer," without necessarily being constrained by the framework of existing acts. In June 2018, the "Interim Report by Study Group" was released titled the "Toward a Function-based, Cross-sectoral Financial Regulations"[16] as a deliberation.

In September 2018, the Study Group was resumed to enter the next phase in which concrete and proactive considerations should be taken on areas where rapid progress is being made.

The Study Group set out four issues that should be immediately covered: (1) appropriate use of information, (2) cross-sectional payments and settlement legislation, (3) response to the financial platformers, and (4) a review of regulations on banks and banking groups, are set out and reviewed. In particular, taking into account the rapid progress in the data digitization and its practical uses, the Study Group issued the "Report on the Development of Regulations for Financial Institutions regarding Data Utilization" in January 2019, based on the principle of summarizing issues in timely manner right after the review of discussing agenda is closed and subsequently requesting the actions quickly".[17]

4 Proactively Address the Challenges of the Decentralized Financial System—Toward the Establishment of New Global Collaboration Mechanism

As stated, blockchain is technically based on cryptography and is underpinning technology of crypto-assets, such as Bitcoins. Although the technology is still immature in terms of scalability and so forth, new use cases and various technological improvements have been proposed.

Furthermore, the inherent natures of blockchain technology will fundamentally give rise to the shift to be a more autonomous and decentralized financial system in the future. While current crypto-assets have underlying technical challenges including less scalability and the lack of finality in settlement and so forth, it will become a useful settlement function in the next phase of financial transactions if proper improvements and new proposals are made to resolve its underlying challenges and properly deploy it.

On the other hand, if specific technical or cypher problems occurs in blockchain-based transactions, financial authorities might not be able to solely solve it by themselves. This is also applicable to the cases even in the current crypto-asset transactions. If autonomous and decentralized financial system based on blockchain which do not exist any human interventions or economic agents becomes a reality in coming period, financial authorities will face the issue of losing the specific regulatory targets and its enforceability, as well as the issue of range of regulatory perimeters which would become ambiguous.

[16] See FSA website (https://www.fsa.go.jp/singi/singi_kinyu/tosin/20180619.html).

[17] See FSA website (https://www.fsa.go.jp/singi/singi_kinyu/tosin/20190116.html).

Since 2017, JFSA has highlighted issues, as a research agenda, on technical and security issues and the possible effects of the decentralized financial system thorough the initiative of "Multilateral Joint Research Project on Blockchain."

To date, JFSA has extended the researches in light of vulnerability issue on blockchain including technical risks such as the issue of "cryptographic compromise" (the risk of decryption over time or lapse of the strength in encryption over time). Furthermore, JFSA has organized an ad hoc global conference group of the "Blockchain Round-Table [BCRT]" to create a discussing platform for various blockchain stakeholders, including experts from foreign financial authorities and central banks, as well as experts from cryptography and security from academia, corporate professionals and developers (Fig. 8).

Recently, in the field of crypto-assets, we frequently encounter the emerging cyberattacks, such as "selfish-mining" or "51% attack" that can be used for constituting fraud transactions. In addition to the study of such attacks, the BCRT has also discussed the issue of balancing privacy and traceability of transactions (issues on privacy-enhancing or anonymizing technologies) and blockchain governance issues as well as the future possible deployments on layer-2 technologies and issue of CBDC etc.

In March, 2018, nine (9) foreign and Japanese regulatory and supervisory authorities have participated in the BCRT and now the participation has been extended to sixteen (16) authorities in March 2019 including the international organization such as FSB, OECD and IMF-OAP. The BCRT has various folks of security experts

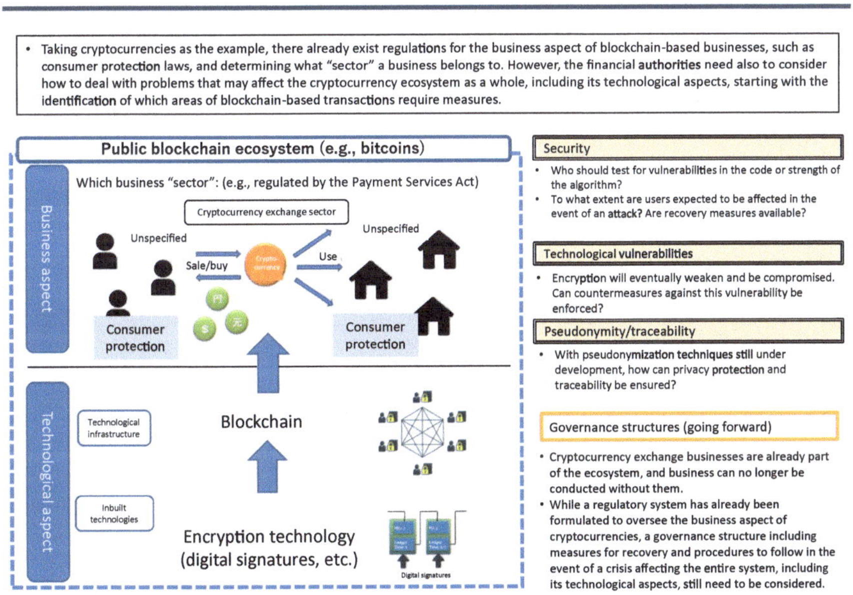

Fig. 8 "Multilateral joint research"—Research agenda

from universities in Japan, such as the University of Tokyo and Keio University, as well as the director and experts from the MIT Media Lab, experts from Georgetown University in the U.S. and Cambridge University in the U.K. The BCRT has been building the capacity as a concrete conference body for multi-stakeholder activated in the blockchain community.[18]

The issues discussed in the BCRT were re-addressed in the panel sessions at the FIN/SUM,[19] a global FinTech conference co-hosted by Nikkei and JFSA. The conference recently held in September 2018 invited experts from various fields, and they discussed the potential challenges and further applicability of the blockchain. In particular, there is a mutual understanding in the discussion on the necessity of establishing a community in which a wider range of stakeholders, such as regulatory authorities and engineers, could participate to organically resolve the technical problems in which current blockchain technology embeds.[20]

At the Keio University, "Scaling Bitcoin[21]" was held in October 2018. Many developers and experts from academia from global space have discussed the latest proposals to resolve the scaling issue of Bitcoin and recent technological developments and proposals. Participants in the Scaling Bitcoin have also attended the FIN/SUM, which was held prior to the event. At the FIN/SUM, there was a collaboration session with Scaling Bitcoin.

JFSA has been making efforts to create a new form of global cooperation by providing a series of "fora" that will cultivate the opportunities and deepen the cooperation not only with financial regulators but with the technical communities as well. In fact, these fora are acting as venues to create a virtuous circle for having future-oriented discussions and opportunities to create potential agenda.

As stated, the issues on crypto-assets draw attentions at the G20. Last year, Japan, under the presidency, has raised issues on decentralized financial system and gain the consensus on the necessity of various stakeholder dialogues in light of decentralized financial system at G20 Fukuoka in finance track and G20 Osaka. JFSA will continue to develop such a virtuous circle using the momentum gained in the G20 and create a mechanism that will help solve new issues among various stakeholders, while leading the material discussions that are globally addressed.

[18]See JFSA website.

[19]See http://www.finsum.jp.

[20]See FSA website: Minutes of "FIN/SUM2018 (https://www.fsa.go.jp/singi/finsum2018/finsum2018.html).

[21]See https://tokyo2018.scalingbitcoin.org/ja.

Chapter 10
Blockchain Basics

Masahiro Fukuhara and Sahoko Kaji

1 What Is a Blockchain?

(1) Birth of Blockchains

Blockchains and cryptocurrencies[1] are often discussed in the same context, partly because they were developed together. However, while blockchains can exist independently of cryptocurrencies, cryptocurrencies cannot exist independently of blockchains as of the present.[2] Blockchains have many uses and a wide range of applications, so their invention has had a broad impact. The main aim of this chapter is to shed light on these applications by providing an elementary-level understanding of blockchains.[3]

[1] In December 2018, the Financial Services Authority of Japan began to use the term "crypto assets" for cryptocurrencies, but in this chapter, we use the more familiar term cryptocurrency.

[2] The Internet of Things Application (IOTA) has been proposed as a non-blockchain-based cryptocurrency. IOTA is said to use a system whereby each node is expected to arbitrarily validate two previous transactions to create not a "chain" but a "tangle" (https://www.iota.org/get-started/what-is-iota). This system, however, is still under development, and some, such as Heilman et al. (2017), are skeptical of the system, citing its fragility. The IOTA system is also sometimes categorized as a type of blockchain by calling it "the IOTA blockchain."

[3] There are also what are called "permissioned blockchains," which are blockchains that involve the participation only of entities that share information. These have been proposed as a means of ensuring the protection of corporate secrets and other confidential information without depending on a central authority even in an environment where mutual trust is not guaranteed. This chapter will only mention and refrain from going into the details of such blockchains.

M. Fukuhara (✉)
Institution for a Global Society Corporation, and Faculty of Economics, Keio University, Tokyo, Japan
e-mail: m.fukuhara@i-globalsociety.com

S. Kaji
Faculty of Economics, Keio University, Tokyo, Japan

S. Kaji et al. (eds.), *The Economics of Fintech*,
https://doi.org/10.1007/978-981-33-4913-1_10

The world was introduced to blockchains through a paper[4] written under the pseudonym Satoshi Nakamoto in November 2008. The paper simultaneously proposed the world's first cryptocurrency, the Bitcoin, and the blockchain, a novel system on which the Bitcoin would be based. A software program based on the concept outlined in the paper became available for use in 2009, and the creation and use of blockchains began soon afterward. It was in 2011 that cryptocurrencies other than the Bitcoin began to emerge. Etherium (which uses coins called Ether),[5] the most famous cryptocurrency after the Bitcoin, was launched in 2016.

It was in a climate of distrust regarding existing financial institutions and public institutions that the Bitcoin was born. The birth of the Bitcoin around the same time as the collapse of Lehman Brothers was no coincidence. The financial crisis that began with the collapse of Lehman Brothers and which went on to severely impact not just the U.S. but also the global economy, was caused by financial products developed by financial institutions. Those institutions were not made to take responsibility for the crisis, however, but were rescued using people's hard-earned tax money. This naturally led to widespread anger, and tech-savvy people, especially on the U.S. West Coast, decided to try and establish a financial system that would not depend on Wall Street (on the East Coast) or on the government that rescued it, and would, moreover, be perfectly trustworthy. The most prominent example of such a system is the Bitcoin system, based on blockchain technology.

(2) Present Status of Blockchain Technology

The word "blockchain" refers to a distributed ledger that is based on encryption technology. The blockchain is not a physical object. It is simply an amalgamation of various technologies—a peer-to-peer (P2P) network, a distributed ledger, transaction blocks, encryption technology (such as the hash function), and so on—required for building a network of contracts on the blockchain. The most important characteristic of blockchain technology is that, not only does it not require public institutions, clearing houses, market makers, or other commonly trusted third parties, it does not even require trust between the parties entering a contract. Transactions take place on what is called a "decentralized network" of nodes. A blockchain is a computational algorithm for maintaining and using distributed ledgers, and it is fast becoming indispensable not just in fintech, but also as a General-Purpose Technology (GPT) for the 21st century, similar to the Internet.

In a blockchain P2P network, files are shared and stored on each computer or server (called a "node") on the network, which is interconnected through the Internet. The word "peer" describes each individual computer or node on the network, and peer-to-peer indicates that these nodes are interconnected and files are mutually shared among them. This is in significant contrast to a client-server network, where files

---

[4]https://bitcoin.org/bitcoin.pdf.

[5]Ethereum can be seen as a platform featuring smart contract (a computer-based mechanism for enforcing contracts) functionality, where the contract takes the shape of a program on the blockchain. It is revolutionary because it allows anyone to program a contract over the blockchain for a small fee, and a large number of businesses have been set up on the basis of Ethereum.

are stored on a server at the center of the network, and all users access the files by connecting to the server.

The distributed ledger is a database of records with timestamps that can be viewed at any time by any member of the network.[6] Transactions take the form of commands over the network, and blocks are like boxes in which multiple transactions are stored by time slot. Blocks are linked one after another in the form of a chain, which is why they are called blockchains. The act of creating a new block is called "mining," and those who mine blocks are called "miners."

The current state of blockchain technology overall resembles that of the Internet at its dawn. While the possibilities are numerous, there are still challenges that need to be overcome with respect to each part of the technology. However, blockchains may eventually become a GPT infrastructure we take for granted in our day-to-day lives, just like the Internet today.

(3) Problems with Blockchains

There are many criticisms of blockchains,[7] and the following are among them.

1. They consume enormous amounts of electricity.
2. A conflict between two groups of miners can cause the blockchain to split into separate paths (a fork).
3. Blockchains are vulnerable to hacking by quantum computers.

Several studies have come up with concrete figures on how much electricity is consumed by blockchains. Hileman and Rauchs (2017) points out that annual Bitcoin-related power consumption is equivalent to the annual power consumption of Uruguay, a country with a population of 3.3 million.

A potential solution to this voracious energy consumption in cryptocurrency mining is the use of an algorithm resistant to application-specific integrated circuits (ASIC). If miners were to use algorithms that are resistant to computers optimized for solving hash functions (through the use of ASIC chips), it would eliminate the difference between personal computers and specialized computers in terms of hash-function solving capabilities.

Right from the beginning, it has been noted that hash functions are "memory-hard" puzzles, and the speed of solving them depends not just on CPU power, but also on the memory available. A hash function called scrypt, which cannot be solved by brute force, is ASIC-resistant.

Another initiative for reducing the amount of energy consumed is to give "mining power" to coin holders in proportion to the quantity of a given currency they own

---

[6]BIS (2018) presents an easy-to-understand diagrammatic representation of the difference between distributed and centralized ledgers.

[7]For instance, Roubini (2018) called the blockchain "one of the most overhyped technologies ever." Many consider cryptocurrencies themselves to be a "scam," and there is the problem of bitcoins being used for criminal purposes. Further, cryptocurrencies replacing regular currencies would create other potential problems, such as their potential impact on monetary policy efficacy and the question of who would be the lender of last resort.

(a type of proof-of-stake system), rather than allowing all miners to compete freely and, thereby, to competitively consume power. The first cryptocurrency to use proof of stake is the Peercoin. Peercoin uses coin age (a type of proof of stake) and makes it easier for miners in possession of coins with higher "coin age" to compete for the next block through the proof-of-work process. However, such initiatives go against the essential idea of the blockchain as an open and democratic system, instead resulting in a trend toward centralization.

A fork arises when there is conflict between major players in an existing cryptocurrency network causing the associated currency to split into two new cryptocurrencies. In other words, a fork is a split in a blockchain that results in two new blockchains.

A soft fork takes place if the majority of miners agree to make a switch, and systemic compatibility is maintained between the new and original chains. In this scenario, the problem is limited. A hard fork, however, is a scenario in which a new chain is created that, though acknowledging the existence of the original chain, is not systemically compatible with it and may even operate on a completely different protocol. This is a much bigger problem.

One regular-currency analogy to this is a hypothetical scenario in which almost all government and central bank employees are replaced, and the transition to currency operations managed by the new staff severely undermines confidence in the currency.

Another problem with blockchains is that quantum computers can easily crack their cryptographic codes. Though this problem is not limited to blockchains, it is a serious problem in the case of blockchains. This is because, in contrast to encryption processes that involve human intermediaries, encryption in blockchains is a fully digitized operation that does not involve humans. In overseas bank transfers, for instance, the need for human intermediaries may make the process inefficient, but is an advantage from the perspective of risk management because human beings cannot be controlled by quantum computers. But if the encryption codes for pseudonymous public keys and private keys in a blockchain are cracked, the entire system's risk management would fall apart.

(4) Advantages of Blockchains

The following are some of the advantages of blockchains.

1. Blockchains increase economic efficiency and create an environment conducive to innovation.
2. They ensure transaction irreversibility and prevent duplicate-spending.
3. They offer a new model of decision making by groups.

Blockchains enable consensus-formation over the open Internet, which can be accessed by anyone, without a mediator or owner of the system. They also sustain an information history that cannot be falsified and that can be traced back in time by anyone, thereby maintaining transaction transparency and eliminating the incentive to engage in fraudulent practices. This can help lower costs related to commissions, intermediary fees, and verification (for confirming that a product or service meets the conditions required by regulations or specifications).

Blockchains also confer network externalities[8] at lower costs, which can increase economic efficiency and create an environment conducive to innovation.

The second advantage applies to cryptocurrency transactions on blockchains, and relates to the question of how to ensure transaction irreversibility and preventing duplicate-spending.

With currency notes and coins, once the appropriate amount is handed over by the buyer to the seller, a transaction is complete. It cannot be reversed unless the same amount of money in notes and coins is returned to the buyer. However, if the payment is made electronically, its irreversibility cannot be guaranteed so long as digital records can be falsified.

In addition, once notes and coins are physically handed over for a specific transaction, they cannot be spent again by the same person. However, electronic records can be rewritten and the same money can be used again for a different transaction, which is duplicate spending.

It is natural to assume that we need public institutions with legal authority to act as intermediaries to ensure the irreversibility of transactions and to prevent duplicate-spending. Blockchains ensure transaction irreversibility and prevent duplicate-spending even in a decentralized system comprising only private entities with no central authority. Moreover, they do away with the need for mutual trust between the transacting parties.

The third advantage of blockchains arises from the fact that they are decentralized. Companies like Google, Amazon, Facebook, and Apple (GAFA) or Baidu, Alibaba, and Tencent (BAT) currently have monopolistic power over information of users. This problematic situation could be alleviated by making intelligent use of the decentralized system of blockchains, because it makes information ownership more democratic. The profits earned by monopolistic corporate giants through rent-seeking can be returned to the users, and this could promote additional innovations. In Europe, the EU has enacted the General Data Protection Rule (GDPR) to reduce the risk of companies making unfair use of individuals' private information. However, with blockchains, private entities can themselves protect their information.

From a broader perspective, the emergence of a model that is in extreme contrast to the current centralized model is probably a good thing. It could be said that blockchains provide a new answer to the age-old question related to the choice between dictatorship and democracy.[9]

---

[8]"Network externalities" refer to the benefits to original users of a network as a result of an increase in users of that network. Since the original users of a network do not pay for the benefits obtained from the participation of other users in the network, such benefits are "externalities" (a term in economics that indicates economic effects that are not paid for).

[9]Former British Prime Minister Winston Churchill is often quoted as having said, "Many forms of government have been tried, and will be tried in this world of sin and woe. No one pretends that democracy is perfect or all wise. Indeed, it has been said that democracy is the worst form of government, except for all those other forms that have been tried from time to time." Arrow's impossibility theorem, which is well-known in economic theory, states that it is only in a dictatorship that both the fair-voting principles of independence of irrelevant alternatives and Pareto efficiency can be simultaneously met. Independence of irrelevant alternatives exists when the preferred order

A system that can function without the need for a central authority or even mutual trust among participants has major implications and could offer valuable hints for the political decision-making process involving multiple entities. Blockchains and bitcoins provide a brand-new solution to the problem of market design using public registers, the right kind of incentives for miners, a P2P network, and encryption technology (private and public keys, hash functions, etc.).

However, there are potential risks. One example is a "51% attack," a scenario in which 51% of those participating in the blockchain decide to propagate fallacious data that could derail the effort to preserve the chain of blocks containing correct information. Ultimately, there may be no easy escape from the fundamental human tendency to want to benefit from propagating untruths.

2 Blockchain-Based Money Transfer Example

Let us take a look at the mechanism by which bitcoins are transferred over the blockchain as a way to elucidate how blockchains work in practice.

Consider a hypothetical scenario in which Tokyo-based Alice wants to send money to London-based Bob. Using the conventional (pre-blockchain) financial system, where banks act as intermediaries, the only way for Alice to transfer the funds to Bob would be by visiting her bank or using its website. From Alice's perspective, some of the problems with this system are the high bank transfer fees (overseas transfer fees typically exceed JPY 5000) and the risk of bank failure (not rare in some countries). There are other problems, such as time constraints (bank operating hours and bank holidays), the inability to transfer funds over the weekend, and the fact that the bank is now in possession of Alice's transaction history.

By contrast, blockchains make fund transfers possible through the following mechanism.

Phase 1: Alice, Bob, and a cryptocurrency exchange

> Alice and Bob open accounts with a cryptocurrency exchange (for example, BitFlyer in Japan). An account, called a "wallet" in Bitcoin terminology, comprises a set of two encryption keys—a private key and a public key. The "wallet" is a location that stores a variety of files that give the owner access to a variety of Bitcoin addresses.
>
> A public key is generated from the private key, as a pair to the latter. Keeping the private key safe is a matter of priority, because there is simply no way of accessing the wallet without it. A wallet for which the private key is stored in an offline environment is called a "cold wallet." A cold wallet is a safe option, away from the reach of hackers and so on, but losing a key stored in this manner will result in the irreversible loss of all the cryptocurrency in the wallet. There is, however, also the option of storing a wallet's private key online, such as at the exchange itself. Such a wallet is called a "hot wallet." It offers a simpler method of storing the key, but it is risky in the sense that the key is stored in the same online environment as the cryptocurrency itself.

---

of two alternatives, X and Y, is not affected by any other alternative (Z). Detailed explanations are found (in Japanese) in Sakai (2015), especially p. 113, and https://www.coindeskjapan.com/4012/.

To make a fund transfer using bitcoins, Alice would encrypt the transaction data and her private key together to create what is called a digital signature. Alice's digitally signed fund-transfer information is then sent by her bitcoin exchange along with her public key to the transfer destination (usually the bitcoin exchange used by Bob). In other words, Alice's transaction data digitally signed using her private key is sent along with her public key to the recipient over the blockchain.

After this point, anyone on the network can access this transfer information using the pubic key sent with it.

Phase 2: Blockchain and miners supporting the Bitcoin system

Bitcoin transactions on the blockchain are maintained by investors called "miners." Miners compete with each other to compile all the transactions on the blockchain, including Alice's fund transfer to Bob, into a single block once every 10 min. Miners compete with each other to input a range of "nonces" or "numbers used only once" into hash functions, which are cryptographic codes, in an effort to come up with a hash value that meets certain conditions. The first successful miner to come up with the desired hash value gets to add a new block to the blockchain—this happens once every 10 min—and win the reward of a fixed number of bitcoins (the block reward decreases over the medium-to-long term, but is 12.5 bitcoins as of the present).

A hash function is a function that replaces the large amount of information contained in a block with a string of digits of fixed length. Because the hash function can convert a large volume of information into a uniquely determined string of digits, from which the original information cannot be deduced, it is a "one way" function.

To prevent falsification of data, miners create a new hash value for each block by hashing together the hash value of the previous block, information regarding the new block, and the nonce given to that block by the miner. If the hash output of the nonce is smaller than a certain threshold level, the miner wins a certain number of bitcoins. (This could be seen as a type of lottery.)

Readers are encouraged to visit MIT's simulation website,[10] which makes it very easy to understand how this process works.

Phase 3: Finalization

Once a miner builds a block and the block is validated, the transaction between Alice and Bob is complete. This validation work can take anywhere from 30 min to an hour or so. Taking some time is not a big problem in the case of most overseas transfers. However, it must be noted that the blockchain mechanism as it is at present is not well-suited to deal with making a variety of transactions in quick succession. Bitcoin transfer fees can differ depending on the desired speed of validation, but are lower than bank transfer fees regardless.

As already mentioned, cryptocurrencies are not widely used for making overseas bank transfers except in emerging market economies (EMEs). Legal hurdles are one of the reasons for this. In Japan, for instance, there are many laws preventing such transfers, including the Foreign Exchange and Foreign Trade Act, and the Criminal Proceeds Transfer Prevention Act, and settlement-related laws.

---

[10] http://blockchain.mit.edu/how-blockchain-works.

The reason blockchains consume so much energy is because of the large amount of computing power required for competing to make this calculation.

3 Possibilities of Blockchains

(1) Possibilities in Business

Blockchains have the potential to create major new businesses, and even issues that need to be resolved regarding blockchains offer business opportunities. The issue specifically referred to here is what is called the last-mile problem.

The last-mile problem relates to the issue of who will put the details of a physical transaction on a blockchain in digital form and how. In other words, how can digitized data and real-life activity be synchronized? How should one design incentives using cryptocurrency in order to achieve synchronization? Is there no way to use sensing or other IoT technology to do away with human intermediation altogether? Taking these issues into account in designing markets presents both challenges and opportunities to create new businesses. The following sections provide an overview of specifically what kind of business applications there might be in this regard.

(2) Financial Services

Given that blockchains were developed in conjunction with Bitcoins, it seems natural that the application of blockchains in financial services will gather momentum. BitGold Inc. (currently Goldmoney Inc.) developed a product that provides an example of such an application.

> Josh Crumb, the co-founder and former chief strategy officer of BitGold believes that blockchain technology will revolutionize money transfers and payments, so that people around the world can have access to lower transfer and settlement costs as well as highly transparent and safer financial services. He says his company sees gold as an "assetized bitcoin," and hopes to give it a hugely important role to play in this revolution.[11]

BitGold was founded on this idea of giving gold an important role to play as digital currency technology evolved, and it has become a success. The company saw gold as an alternative to both fiat money, which is exposed to inflation and devaluation risks, as well as cryptocurrencies, which have no inherent value and could undergo major price fluctuations or face the risk of regulation.

BitGold's patented technology, Aurum, is based on blockchain technology. As Bitcoin users would know, transactions conducted over the blockchain are irreversible and preclude duplicate-spending. But unlike the blockchain used in the Bitcoin network, Aurum is not a decentralized tool. Blockchains are used in Aurum mainly for their ledger function and for determining the exchange rate with the gold market. The role of Aurum is to show that customers' gold holdings are safely preserved at BitGold.

Aurum plays the role of auditing the gold held at all storage facilities in real time and confirming that this is consistent with the actual gold holdings of account

[11] Vergne and Burke (2015) "BitGold: Turning Digital Currency into Gold?", December, Ivey Publishing.

holders. It uses three methods to provide gold-related ledger information to related parties.

(a) Electronic and paper reports are sent several times a day to the recovery center to provide for contingencies.
(b) An encrypted electronic copy of information is safely sent to a third-party auditing firm every 24 h.
(c) The third-party auditing firm conducts regular as well as surprise audits of the holding facilities and sends out reports to customers on whether BitGold's gold holdings are consistent with their reports.

BitGold has leveraged the electronic settlement revolution to enable gold to be safely acquired, stored, and used with an ease never before possible. The company issues debit cards to make payments easy. Its ATMs allow customers to withdraw cash from their gold accounts. Opening an account is free, and customers can withdraw their gold holdings in the form of one-kilo gold bars or branded 10-gram gold cubes at any time. BitGold has in place all the processes necessary for allowing customers to acquire, store, and use gold with ease.

Apart from the aforementioned B2C (customer oriented) services, blockchains are now being used also for B2B services, back-end financial operations, trade financing, and other applications.

(3) Blockchain-based Cryptocurrencies' Role as Currencies

In Japan, following a cabinet decision on March 15, 2019, the FSA submitted a bill to the Diet for the partial revision of laws governing payment services, etc., in response to the diversification of financial transactions with the evolution of information and communication technology. As part of this bill, the Payment Services Act (PSA) was partially revised to change the term "virtual currency" to "crypto asset." In view of this, the term was revised from "virtual currency" to "crypto asset" in the Income Tax Law as well, as provided in Article 18 of the aforementioned bill.[12]

In fact, cryptocurrencies are rarely used as a transaction medium in developed countries. By contrast, in Emerging Market Economies, especially those that do not have much confidence in their central banks, the situation is ripe for the adoption of cryptocurrencies as a transaction medium. In Venezuela, where inflation remains at an annualized rate of 2 million percent as of 2019, the government has issued a cryptocurrency called the petro. This currency has been labeled a failure by the U.S. government, but the people of Venezuela have begun using it to buy food. The Nicolas Maduro administration moreover established a money transfer system that used both the Bitcoin and another cryptocurrency called the Litecoin.

Efforts are also underway toward establishing cryptocurrencies as units of account by stabilizing their value. Issuers of stablecoins, for instance, are required to fully back coins with central bank reserves, and more innovation in this area is expected going forward. Meanwhile, at the March 2018 G20 meeting of finance ministers and

[12]https://www.fsa.go.jp/common/diet/198/02/houritsuanriyuu.pdf (in Japanese).

central bank governors held in Buenos Aires, Argentina, it was stated that cryptocurrencies were not "currencies" but "crypto assets," and problems were pointed out in terms of their impact on market health and their use in crime (including tax evasion, money laundering, and terrorism funding). Subsequently, the Financial Action Task Force (FATF, a committee of financial supervisors) contemplated cryptocurrency-related regulations. These regulations were announced in June 2019, and their legal enforcement in countries around the world has been called for.

If we think about the reason blockchains and cryptocurrencies emerged in the first place, it is quite understandable why policymakers would be against them. However, as mentioned above, blockchains can be used for purposes other than providing cryptocurrencies. Also, as already noted, in countries where confidence in domestic currency authorities is not firm, there is not just the incentive but even the need to use cryptocurrencies as currency. Of course, regulations to protect consumers and investors are necessary, but it is also important for the authorities to make sure they do not nip beneficial innovation in the bud.

(4) Examples of Other Applications

Many companies including IBM have developed and are offering platforms built on blockchains that are fundamental to the business application of blockchains. Moreover, a large number of new businesses have begun to actively provide non-financial services using such platforms.

Since blockchains do away with the need for middlemen, the possibilities will expand for all businesses where intermediaries are a part of the current ecosystem. For instance, new blockchain-based businesses could replace intermediaries such as travel agents and media companies such as newspapers.

Apart from this, initiatives are underway in the healthcare industry to lower social security costs by using blockchains to facilitate the sharing of information among the relevant entities including the government, hospitals, patients, and pharmacies. Some hurdles remain, including legal ones and the challenge of preserving the anonymity of patient information, but it can be said that this is a promising area for the application of blockchain technology. For a country like Japan, especially, where social security expenses are expected to continue rising while their burden falls on fewer shoulders amid declining birthrates, it will be important to see new initiatives that leverage blockchains to increase transparency, lower medical costs through the use of big data, and raise the overall efficiency of the healthcare process.

Another example of the use of blockchains is the Georgian government's use of a blockchain-based platform for real-estate registration in Georgia. This platform was built by a venture company called Bitfury. If a large amount of data is accumulated on blockchain networks, it will be possible to glean new knowledge using machine learning and other AI technologies, which are powerful tools for analyzing big data. Incorporating machine learning into smart contracts will open up new possibilities for society.

Blockchain technology is expected to make rapid progress as a General-Purpose Technology (GPT) going forward. As blockchain technology becomes more widespread, it seems very likely that all intermediary businesses in Japan—not just in the financial industry—will progressively evolve as they find ways to use the technology. This platform has great potential for facilitating innovation, and many companies, especially startups, are expected to utilize it.

One of the challenges we will be facing in the near future is a shortage of human resources capable of promoting further progress in this field. In Japan, especially, there is a severe shortage of data scientists and other skilled professionals who can work in fields related to big data, leave alone blockchains. There is an urgent need to encourage people—regardless of whether they have science or humanities backgrounds—to boldly take on the challenge of working in and contributing to innovation in this field.

References

Bank for International Settlements (2018) V. Cryptocurrencies: looking beyond the hype, Annual Economic Report 2018. https://www.bis.org/publ/arpdf/ar2018e5.pdf. Accessed 19 Feb 2019

Hileman G, Rauchs M (2017) Global cryptocurrency benchmarking study. https://www.jbs.cam.ac.uk/fileadmin/user_upload/research/centres/alternative-finance/downloads/2017-global-cryptocurrency-benchmarking-study.pdf. Accessed 23 Feb 2019

Heilman E, Narula N, Dryja T, Virza M (2017) IOTA vulnerability report: cryptanalysis of the Curl Hash function enabling practical signature forgery attacks on the IOTA cryptocurrency. https://github.com/mit-dci/tangled-curl/blob/master/vuln-iota.md. Accessed 25 Feb 2019

Roubini N (2018) The big blockchain Lie. https://www.project-syndicate.org/commentary/blockchain-big-lie-by-nouriel-roubini-2018-10?barrier=accesspaylog. Accessed 19 Feb 2019

Sakai T (2015) Questioning majority decisions (in Japanese). Publishers, Iwanami Shoten

Vergne J, Burke B (2015) BitGold: turning digital currency into gold? Harvard Business Review, 23 December. https://hbr.org/product/bitgold-turning-digital-currency-into-gold/W15608-PDF-ENG

Chapter 11
Machine Learning Principles and Applications

Teruo Nakatsuma

1 Problem-Solving by Thinking Machines

In the First Industrial Revolution, which began in England and took place from around the mid-18th through the nineteenth centuries, mass production by machines was introduced to the manufacturing industry, which had until then relied heavily on human labor. The technological innovations that made this possible include the invention of manufacturing equipment such as spinning and weaving machines, the improvement of power sources (steam engines) to run these machines, and new steam-powered modes of transportation (steam locomotives and steamships) for transporting raw materials and finished products. This industrialization dramatically improved labor productivity and converted predominantly agrarian societies into societies that revolved around factory labor.

The Information and Communications Technology (ICT) revolution, which began in the second half of the twentieth century, gave rise to the computer—a thinking machine—and the Internet—a network of interconnected computers that can exchange information with each other. Since then, the processing and storage capabilities of computers have increased exponentially, and it has become possible to perform a variety of tasks involving numerical operations—from basic arithmetic operations to complex simulations and sophisticated graphics processing—within practical timeframes and at reasonable costs.

Ever since the emergence of "thinking machines", researchers have been attempting to develop computers that may some day be able to take over the reasoning and decision-making processes currently performed by humans. (In other words, they have been attempting to create artificial intelligence or AI.) AI research dates back to the 1950s, but there have been ups and downs in its progress, with alternating periods of significant progress and stagnation. However, with the proliferation of

T. Nakatsuma (✉)
Faculty of Economics, Keio University, Tokyo, Japan
e-mail: nakatuma@econ.keio.ac.jp

S. Kaji et al. (eds.), *The Economics of Fintech*,
https://doi.org/10.1007/978-981-33-4913-1_11

parallel computing systems and the development of efficient algorithms, especially starting around 2010, AI research has made great strides, suddenly making practical applications a reality. That was the beginning of the recent boom in AI research.

In the first industrial revolution, machines replaced humans in the simple task of spinning yarn, thereby greatly increasing productivity in the spinning industry. High-performance computers developed as a result of progress in ICT are expected to take over the currently human task of problem-solving in the broader sense. "Problem-solving" in this context refers to finding the most efficient method or means of executing a given task. What amounts to the "most effective way to execute a task" depends on the nature of the problem. For instance, let us see what kind of problem-solving is involved the process of driving a car. Assume that you are driving a car to work. In this scenario, your aim is to drive safely while paying attention to various changing situations. Some of the things you must do are to make sure you are on the right route to your destination, keep to the speed limit, pay attention to the signal at the upcoming intersection, avoid cars from the on-coming lane that may be turning right, and be vigilant of pedestrians walking out in front of your car from behind something. Your given task is to "arrive" at the destination, and arriving sooner can be considered more efficient. However, it would be counterproductive to have an accident on the way while attempting to arrive sooner, so safety must be considered alongside speed. In this way, even though driving a car may seem like a mechanical task, it is in fact quite a complex problem that requires the driver to anticipate what will happen next and choose the best course of action in each situation.

For a computer to be able to perform a task, the task must first be reframed as a problem that can be solved by a computer. If the problem is ambiguously defined, it cannot even be solved by a human, leave alone a computer. What computers are good at is solving "well-defined" problems. Mathematical equations, for instance, are clearly defined problems, and there are a number of algorithms for rapidly solving them. This makes mathematical equations very easy for computers to solve. Computers have also become sophisticated enough to beat professional players in games such as Go and shogi, which are easy games for a computer to play mathematically because their rules can be phrased as well-defined problems. In extreme scenarios, a computer can use brute force to anticipate its opponent's move(s) and find the best countermove(s). Of course, actual games have time controls, so this would take a high-speed computer and, needless to say, an optimal search algorithm.

More practical examples involve something called the "traveling salesman problem" (TSP). TSP asks the question, "Given a predetermined set of customers, what is the shortest route a salesman can take to visit every customer and return to the point of origin?" There are many practical applications of TSP, such as in planning optimum routes for delivery services or in wiring electronic parts. TSP is a clearly defined problem, as the number and location of customers is predetermined, but the time required to find the shortest possible route increases with an increase in the number of customers, necessitating the use of high-speed computers. TSP is a type of mathematical optimization (or mathematical programming) problem, and is usually formulated as follows. First, a constraint condition is established that determines the set of values for the selectable variable (a variable that can be selected by the decisionmaker). In TSP, for instance, the travel route is the selectable variable, and the constraint condition applied is that the salesperson visit every single customer. Next, the objective function, the value of which depends on the value of the variable, is decided. In TSP, the travel distance is the objective function, the value of which changes depending on the travel route taken. The objective here is to find a travel route that will minimize the travel distance. The value of the selectable variable that can minimize (or maximize) the objective function is called the optimal solution (or simply the solution). Note that the solution to an optimization problem must also fulfil the constraint condition. To summarize, the task involves:

- Taking all possible selectable variable values that fulfil the constraint condition.
- Finding the value that optimizes (minimizes or maximizes) the value of the objective function.

For relatively simple optimization problems, the exact solution can be found. For example, the minimum (or maximum) values of quadratic equations can be found easily because there are formulas for doing so. With more complex problems, however, there is no guarantee that a solution can be found even if the problem is well defined.

It is known that foolproof strategies for winning in Go and shogi exist, but even with current computer capabilities, it is practically impossible to discover the precise set of moves that form these foolproof strategies. If, however, the aim is merely to win in a given game, all one needs to do is to find the winning moves in each scenario of that particular game. Therefore, there is no need to find a foolproof winning strategy in the first place. TSP is also a difficult problem in the sense that it takes a long time to find the most precisely optimal solution. But if all one needs is a route that can sufficiently shorten the travel distance, then even a slightly less precise solution would have sufficient practical use. Solutions that may not optimize the objective function's value in the most precise terms, yet provide sufficient optimization from a practical standpoint, are called quasi-optimal solutions.

2 Data-Based Learning

Optimization problems may seem difficult at first glance, but they are mathematically well-defined problems. By contrast, there are other problems that have very obvious answers but are difficult to define. For instance, encountering a cat or a dog on the street, humans can tell at a glance whether it is a cat or a dog, but may find it surprisingly difficult to explain in words what distinguishes the two animals. This task of discriminating between cats and dogs is an example of something that involves "pattern recognition." In our day-to-day lives, we are effortlessly able to discriminate between people, electric poles, and other common things, but this is a task that is quite difficult for machines to perform (and without it, self-driving cars are not possible).

Various methods (discussed in detail later) have been proposed for teaching a machine to perform pattern recognition, but first, let us make note of the fact that a computer or smartphone screen is made up of color pixels, and photographs and other images displayed on these screens are no more than collections of pixels. A set of photographs of cats and dogs can technically be seen as collections of pixels that are possible to interpret differently depending on the angle of view. The only reason we humans can group them into cat pictures and dog pictures is because we can use our past experiences to tell cats and dogs apart based on their facial contours, the shapes of their eyes and ears, and other attributes.

One way to teach a computer how to do the same thing is to first feed various features of cats and dogs, such as the shapes of their eyes or ears, into the computer in numerical format (which is the only format a computer can understand), and then train the computer to tell the two animals apart using pictures that have features similar to the input numeric features (feature values). For this method to work, the operator must first find effective feature values (feature values that are effective for the task—in this case, discriminating between the given set of cat and dog pictures) and feed them into the computer in advance. Unfortunately, effective feature values are different depending on the pictures used, and there is no way to find them except by trial and error. Moreover, the discriminating accuracy is not as high as expected even when feature values discovered in this way are used.

Deep learning emerged as an alternative method for training computers in pattern recognition. Deep learning is the general term for a machine learning method that uses a multi-layered neural network model. The advantage of deep learning is that the neural network model itself automatically generates feature values when it is trained with a large input data set of photographs. The word "learning" in the context of machine learning means using data to adjust the model parameter values so as to increase discrimination or prediction accuracy. This corresponds to the task of estimation in statistics. With deep learning, instead of humans extracting feature values and feeding them to the machine, the machine is programmed to autonomously learn feature values. This change in modeling strategy dramatically improved discrimination accuracy and increased the practical utility of machine learning.

Recognizing image data is not the only application of pattern recognition. If applied to voice data, the machine can automatically transcribe human speech and convert it into text data. Handwritten documents can also be scanned to produce image data, which a machine can read using pattern recognition and convert into text data. Natural language processing (NLP) is another technology that has evolved alongside the technology for recognizing and converting speech or handwriting into text data. NLP enables machines to analyze said text data to understand the details of a conversation or document. A familiar example of the application of NLP is conversing with machines that became famous for their (simulated) AI speech function.

These developments have facilitated efforts to replace human customer service representatives at call centers with machines. There are also services that use machines to automatically retrieve corporate accounting reports, generate summaries, and distribute them. In the sense that these trends aim to replace human workers rather than use machines to help humans with problem solving, they resemble the mechanization trends seen during the first industrial revolution. Technologies such as the above, which aim to automate various office processes, are called robotic process automation (RPA) technologies. Natural language communication was traditionally considered an area of human monopoly, but it has now become possible to entrust some aspects of human communication to machines, thanks to NLP. The trend of replacing humans with machines using RPA technologies is, therefore, spreading in all directions, including in areas where human monopoly used to be unchallenged.

Returning to image recognition, anyone can picture a Shiba Inu even though no two Shiba Inus look exactly alike. If we compile a large volume of Shiba Inu image data, we will find that there are many differences in shape and form from one Shiba Inu to the next. In other words, there are distortions. For a computer, these distortions are an obstacle when it comes to accurate recognition of a Shiba Inu, but that obstacle can be overcome through skillful machine learning of feature values. The reason humans can discriminate between a Shiba Inu and a poodle or read handwriting is because we have the ability to process distortions. From a different standpoint, distortions can be seen as noise or error contained within the data. Then, by reframing machine-based pattern recognition as a problem of selecting the discrimination method that minimizes the error, the pattern-recognition problem can be turned into an optimization problem similar to the one described in the TSP example above. To use optimization-problem terminology, the image recognition error is the objective function, and the parameters within the neural network model are the variables that determine the value of the objective function. Given their flexible structures, neural network models can freely generate feature values for recognizing a Shiba Inu or the shape of the letter "a" by changing the parameter values within the model. All that remains to do, then, is to get the computer to make the necessary calculations for solving the optimization problem, which is something a computer is quite good at. To summarize, machine learning (specifically, "supervised learning," which will be discussed in detail later) merely solves an optimization problem by (i) building a model for pattern recognition; (ii) defining a function for quantifying the error, which is the gap between the correct answer and that produced by the model; and (iii) adjusting the model's internal parameters to solve an optimization problem in which the function defined above is the objective function. Because adjusting the model parameters based on the data is inseparable from solving an optimization problem (to minimize the error), machine learning treats "learning" as synonymous with "solving" an optimization problem.

Pattern recognition is not the only type of problem that can be solved by machine learning. In some cases, the solution to a given problem may be a specific numerical value. Take used apartment pricing as an example. What price should a real-estate agent offer when considering the purchase of a used apartment? From a common sense standpoint, the apartment's price should depend on factors (or "features") such as its floor plan, floor area, age, whether it is on a higher or lower floor, whether its main windows face south, and how far away it is from the nearest station. Using data related to used apartments purchased in the past, the real estate agent could find a way to identify the relationship between an apartment's features and its price, and use this relationship to assess what a reasonable buying price would be for the apartment in question. The methods of machine learning can be put to use for this purpose.

Here again, a model is first built to express the price of an apartment in terms of its features. Say there are "m" number of features to be considered ($\text{Feature}_1, \text{Feature}_2 \ldots \text{Feature}_\text{m}$). It can be assumed, then, that the sum of each feature multiplied by its coefficient would produce an appropriate price for the apartment. In other words,

$$\text{Appropriate price} = \text{Constant term} + \text{Coefficient}_1 \times \text{Feature}_1 + \ldots + \text{Coefficient}_\text{m} \times \text{Feature}_\text{m}$$

In the above equation, the constant term adds a certain amount to the price irrespective of the feature values. It is common to add a constant term in models such as the above. Of course, the above formula for calculating the appropriate price would not apply exactly to all past purchases. There will, inevitably, be some errors. The problem will, therefore, have to be reframed as a pattern recognition problem, using the error as the objective function, and solving to minimize the error. In other words, one will have to:

(i) Build a model to generate an appropriate price for an apartment based on its features
(ii) Define a function for quantifying the error, which is the gap between the correct answer and that produced by the model, and
(iii) Adjust the model's internal parameters to solve an optimization problem in which the function defined above is the objective function.

3 The Principles of Machine Learning

As seen above, machine-based decision-making techniques for the purpose of problem solving can often be converted into optimization problems of some sort. In particular, data-based adjustment of the model's internal parameters in the process of finding the solution to the optimization problem—a process that is accompanied by "learning"—is called "machine learning." The previous sections explained these concepts using specific examples, but in this section, the principles of machine learning will be explained at a greater level of abstraction. As the first step to that, the following terms (many of which have already been introduced) must be defined:

(i) Entity: People, animals, real-estate agents, corporations, and other objects regarding which data is observed or collected
(ii) Feature: Data that expresses the characteristics of an entity (for instance, floor plan or floor area in the case of an apartment)
(iii) Target: A feature of the entity that needs to be inferred (for instance, price in the case of an apartment)
(iv) Model: A function that expresses the relationship between the target and the other features
(v) Parameter: A variable that determines the relationship between the target and the other features within the model.

The main goal of machine learning is to infer the target based on data regarding many other features of the entity. In the previous example about apartment pricing, the price of the apartment was the target, and the goal was to infer it based on data regarding the other features of the apartment. Usually, the process of machine learning starts with the collection of data set that shows the relation between the target and other features for a large number of entities of the same category. The feature values are then input into the model, and the theoretical value of the target vis-à-vis other features is calculated. The gap between the theoretical value and the measured value is calculated as the "error," and the model adjusts its parameters to minimize the error. This is all there is to the machine learning process. Adjusting the parameters takes the form of solving an optimization problem in which the error is the objective function. The above type of machine learning is called "supervised learning," because the correct value (measured value) of the target is provided as part of the data set right at the beginning of the learning process.

By contrast, learning under conditions where the correct target value is unknown is called "unsupervised learning." In unsupervised learning, the target value is an indicator (called "label") of the affiliation of each entity with a group. Take, for instance, the task of categorizing users of a video distribution service into groups with various characteristics. Here, there is no accurate label information that tells us which group any particular user belongs to. The groups themselves are defined quite vaguely. However, users can be divided into a few different groups based on behavior patterns such as the type of video most commonly viewed (music, sports, gaming, news, etc.), viewing frequency, or viewing time slot, and this information can be used to determine which videos to recommend next, and what advertisements to show. Unsupervised learning is used to divide entities into an unspecified number of groups based on their features (in this example, their video viewing behavior and history). Unsupervised learning may optimize some specific objective function to determine labels under which to classify entities, or it may measure some specific criterion for grouping together similar entities. An example of the former is an expectation–maximization (EM) algorithm to classify entities in a mixture-distribution model, while a k-nearest neighbors (KNN) algorithm is an example of the latter.

Many types of data are used in machine learning, but they can be roughly categorized as quantitative or qualitative data. With quantitative data, the data points change in a linear manner (strictly speaking, they can take integer values), and the values themselves have meaning. In the example of apartment pricing, floor area or apartment age are examples of quantitative data that changes linearly. Other examples of quantitative data may include images, audios, or location information (latitude and longitude). With qualitative data, however, the data points change in a discrete manner (they are often given integer values for convenience). In this case, the values themselves have no significance, except perhaps for ordering the data in a certain way. For instance, it is common to represent the gender of individuals within a dataset by numbers (say, 1 for women and 0 for men), but the values in this context are useful only for separating and categorizing the entities. The magnitude of the numbers has no significance and can even be reversed without any loss of information. In the case of consumer brand selection in marketing, brands are numbered (1, 2, 3, etc.) for the purpose of classification, which is, again, merely for the purpose of distinguishing between the brands. The specific sequence has no other significance. In the case of corporate credit rating, however, the sequence has a significance even though the data is qualitative. A company with a higher credit rating can be said to have greater creditworthiness than a company with a lower credit rating. However, the numbers are not significant in terms of their exact magnitude, so it would be incorrect to say that a company with a credit rating of 2 is twice as creditworthy as a company with a credit rating of 1. Essentially, quantitative data often represents an entity's assignment to or affiliation with a particular group. For instance, in assessing creditworthiness (the risk of a corporate loan or housing mortgage going bad, for example), one could obtain qualitative data such as assignment to the Bad Debt group. Say, assignment to the group is represented by 1, non-assignment to the group is represented by 0, these numbers can be seen as representing the entity's affiliation with a particular group.

Regardless of whether the data is qualitative or quantitative, its handling is not that different so long as it is seen as expressing a feature of the entity. In the example of apartment pricing, whether the data is quantitative (floor area) or qualitative (window direction), the way this data is incorporated into the apartment price inferring model is essentially the same. However, what is of much greater importance is whether the target is qualitative or quantitative. This is because the method for inferring the target value is very different depending on whether it is qualitative or quantitative. In many cases of supervised learning, the main goal is to infer the target value. If the target is quantitative, inferring its value is called "prediction," and if the target is qualitative, inferring its value is called "classification." However, this categorization is also no more than a matter of convenience, because the task of "classifying" can be seen from a different perspective as "predicting" which group an entity with an unclear affiliation should be assigned to. For instance, at the time of assessing the credit risk of a corporate loan, the company seeking the loan is not yet in default, so it is unclear whether it should be assigned to the default group or not. Consequently, predicting whether or not the candidate company could go bankrupt is essentially the same as judging whether it should be assigned to the default group.

A linear model is often used in supervised learning for the prediction of a quantitative target's value:

$$\text{Predicted target value} = \text{Constant term} + \text{Coefficient}_1 \times \text{Feature}_1 + \ldots + \text{Coefficient}_m \times \text{Feature}_m$$

A linear model of this type is trained using either (a) the sum of the squared residuals (difference between the predicted and measured values of the target) or (b) the sum of the absolute values of the residuals as the objective function. In statistical analysis, the former is called the least squares estimation method, while the latter is called the least absolute deviations (LAD) method.

On the other hand, logistic regression and support vector machine (SVM) are examples of models used to predict the value of a qualitative target. The only difference between the methods for predicting qualitative and quantitative targets is in the manner in which the error is calculated. Both methods, however, involve adjusting the model parameters to minimize the error.

In neural network models used in deep learning, activation functions (sigmoid functions, ramp functions, and so on) are used to generalize the linear model. In other words, if f is taken to be the activation function, then expressing the predicted target value as a function of the right side of the equation in the aforementioned linear model as.

$$\text{Predicted target value} = \text{f (Constant term} + \text{Coefficient}_1 \times \text{Feature}_1 + \ldots + \text{Coefficient}_m \times \text{Feature}_m$$

allows the relationship between the feature values and the predicted value of the target to be expressed flexibly. Further, in a neural network model,

$$\text{Feature}_j = \text{f (Constant}_j + \text{Coefficient}_{j1} \times \text{Feature}_{j1} + \ldots + \text{Coefficient}_{jm} \times \text{Feature}_{jm}), \ (j = 1, 2, \ldots m)$$

In this way, it is assumed that each individual feature can be expressed as an activation function of other features. The features within the activation function on the right side of the above equation can further be expressed as an activation function of other features, and so on and so forth, creating many layers of activation functions nested one inside another.

The actually observed features of an entity are used as inputs for the top layer's activation function. Features in the hidden middle layers are complex functions of the entity's observed features, so if the layers go deep enough and the coefficients are skillfully adjusted, the information contained in the entity's features can be combined to flexibly generate feature values. This is the advantage of a neural network model. Such a model is called a "deep learning model," because it is trained using many layers that are nested deeply, one inside the other. However, in the end, deep learning is also doing no more than adjust the coefficients within the neural network model with the goal of minimizing the prediction error of the objective function. The method used for solving the optimization problem is called a backpropagation algorithm.

In general, the greater the number of features used in a prediction model, the smaller the error in the training data, but excessive focus on minimizing the error in the training data increases the risk of dramatically reducing prediction accuracy if the prediction model is applied to new, unseen data. This problem is called overfitting, and it is avoided by imposing penalties for increasing the number of features.

$$\text{Objective function} = \text{Error in training data} + \text{Weight} \times \text{Penalty}$$

Commonly used penalties are (a) the sum of squared coefficients of features in the prediction model or (b) the sum of their absolute values. In statistics, the former is called ridge regression, while the latter is called Linear Absolute Shrinkage and Selection Operator (LASSO). The weights used for the penalty term are adjusted by cross validation (a method that trains the model by splitting the training data into several subsets in order to find the right weight for minimizing the objective function).

4 Recommendations for Further Study

This chapter gave an overview of machine learning in the limited space available. Many of the explanations inevitably lack rigor because of the effort to avoid using mathematical expressions to the extent possible. However, machine learning cannot really be understood without some knowledge of mathematics. There is no need for advanced mathematics. Knowledge of high-school mathematics and a basic understanding of university-level calculus and linear algebra would be sufficient at least for *understanding* machine learning equations, even if it is not sufficient for rigorous proofs. In addition to reviewing mathematics, reading books that explain machine learning rigorously using mathematical expressions is recommended. Bishop (2006), Hastie, Tibshirani and Friedman (2009), and Murphy (2012) are a few books that cover a wide range of machine learning methods. There are, of course, many other books on the subject that are also worth reading.

Some knowledge of programming is also necessary for applying the methods of machine learning to actual data. A programming language widely used in the field of machine learning is Python (https://www.python.org). Python itself has no machine learning functions to speak of, but several machine learning functions can be used in Python programs by loading packages such as.

- scikit-learn (https://scikit-learn.org)
- statsmodels (https://www.statsmodels.org)
- TensorFlow (https://www.tensorflow.org)
- PyTorch (https://pytorch.org).

Python is a convenient programming language for mastering machine learning because it can be downloaded and used free of charge—using Anaconda (https://www.anaconda.com) makes it relatively easy to install Python plus other essential packages for beginners. Many useful handbooks are available for machine learning with Python, including Raschka and Mirjalili (2017). Another popular programming language for machine learning is R (https://www.r-project.org), which can, again, be downloaded and used free of charge. Books on machine learning with R include James, Witten, Hastie and Tibshirani (2013). There are two things one must do to master machine learning. The first is to try programming in Python or R to gain the experience of performing analyses using actual data. With the wide range of machine learning packages available these days, it is possible to perform analyses of often-used techniques by writing just a few lines of code. The second thing one must do is to try developing one's own machine learning algorithms. Programmers capable of developing their own algorithms have an advantage over those who simply use existing Python or R codes.

References

Bishop CM (2006) Pattern recognition and machine learning, Springer

Hastie T, Tibshirani R, Friedman J (2009) The elements of statistical learning: data mining, inference, and prediction, 2nd edn. Springer

James G, Witten D, Hastie T, Tibshirani R (2013) An introduction to statistical learning with applications in R, Springer

Murphy KP (2012) Machine learning: a probabilistic perspective, MIT Press

Raschka S, Mirjalili V (2017) Python machine learning: machine learning and deep learning with python, scikit-learn, and tensorFlow, 2nd edn. Packt Publishing

Chapter 12
The Mechanism of HFT and Its Merits and Demerits—The Information Efficiency Challenge

Teruo Nakatsuma

1 Is Speculation Bad?

What impression does the word "speculation" conjure up for you? Let us use the example of real estate to consider the difference between investment and speculation.

If a real estate developer buys land with a view to developing a shopping mall or commercial complex and earning revenues through rents, for instance, this would widely be viewed as an honest investment. By contrast, a company that buys up idle land when land prices are soaring during a real estate bubble with a view to reselling it for the highest price it can obtain, or buys up real estate at rock-bottom prices from companies that have collapsed with the bubble is criticized or viewed with contempt. This behavior is branded "land speculation," and those who engage in it are compared to vultures. Both the above are commercial activities involving the buying and selling of land or buildings, but people have a bad impression of the latter as "greedy profit-seeking through the resale of assets such as land and property" or "making excessive profits by simply passing things along from one hand to another."

It is not just in Japan that people have this negative impression of speculation. This kind of impression is common all over the world. However, Milton Friedman, one of the great economists of the twentieth century, argued that speculation had the effect of stabilizing the financial markets.[1]

It is a counterintuitive opinion at first glance, but Friedman had a good reason for holding it. Let us try to understand it using the analogy of the stock market and defining speculation as "the act of buying shares at rock-bottom price and selling them off when they have recovered and risen to their full potential." When the price

[1]The original paper, Friedman (1953), mentions this in the context of speculation in foreign exchange markets.

T. Nakatsuma (✉)
Faculty of Economics, Keio University, Tokyo, Japan
e-mail: nakatuma@econ.keio.ac.jp

S. Kaji et al. (eds.), *The Economics of Fintech*,
https://doi.org/10.1007/978-981-33-4913-1_12

of a particular share begins to decline, ordinary market participants, including both individual and institutional investors, expect it to continue weakening and refrain from buying it. This could cause the price of that share to fall even further as it loses buyers. Speculative investors (speculators), however, look for and buy up shares that are on the decline, because they consider it a good opportunity to buy them cheaply. As a result, a share on the decline finds buyers, bottoms out, and begins to recover.

On the other hand, when a particular share is rising sharply, market participants expect it to rise further and rush to buy it, thereby causing that share to continue rising, and its market to potentially overheat. In these cases, speculators, gauging that a specific share is overvalued and will probably peak out soon, begin selling it off in large volumes. These sell orders cool the market down.

In other words, speculators play the role of checking unilateral price movements in the market by adopting the strategy of going against market trends. This is why Friedman considered speculation to play a stabilizing role in the markets (by the same logic, the land speculators described above help stabilize land prices).

Going further, one could say that it is in part because of speculators' attempts to profit by bucking the trend that financial market transactions proceed smoothly. Assume, for instance, that all market participants share a common understanding of the appropriate prices for different shares. Under this assumption, shares would only be traded at their appropriate prices. In such a scenario, an investor may not be able to sell his shares in return for cash at a time of his choosing, because there may be no buyer for those shares at their appropriate price at that particular time. There do, in fact, exist some such shares in the stock market that do not trade well because of the lack of potential buyers or sellers.

However, the scenario is different when the market includes a large number of speculators with different speculations regarding future share prices. Speculators who consider a particular share to be undervalued at a given time will snap it up when it is offered for sale at that price. This makes for a successful transaction. The seller is happy to have been able to sell the share at what she considers to be the appropriate price, and the speculator, who expects the share's price to go up in the future, is happy to have been able to buy it cheaply. The technical term for this ease of buying and selling in the market is "liquidity," and the existence of speculators with different price speculations increases liquidity in the market and contributes to robust trading activity. In the sense that speculation—an action based on selfish motives—helps make market transactions smoother, the role of speculators in the stock markets may be compared to the role of miners in the functioning of cryptocurrency.

It has been a long introduction, but the aim of this chapter is to explain the means of pursuing profits through short-term speculative transactions mainly using high-frequency trading (HFT), which has become increasingly significant in the financial markets in recent years. HFT is the general term for large-volume asset trading performed by computers over the short term at speeds impossible for humans. It is a representative example (although just one example) of algorithmic trading, which is performed mainly by computers capable of high-speed computation and processing.

By contrast, there are investment funds that use artificial intelligence (AI) to perform long-term asset management. These will be discussed in detail in Chap. 13.

HFT and other kinds of algorithmic trading can apply to a variety of financial products, but this chapter will focus mainly on the stock market to explain it.

2 Stock Market Trading Mechanism

First, let us take a look at the modern system of stock markets that has made HFT possible. The main market where stocks are traded is called a stock exchange. The largest and central stock exchange in Japan is the Tokyo Stock Exchange (TSE), operated by the Japan Exchange Group (JPX). Making shares available for trading on a stock exchange is called "listing," and the process of listing on the stock exchange and beginning trading is called an Initial Public Offering (IPO). There are as many as 2128 companies listed in the First Section of the TSE alone, with as many as 3655 companies listed if one counts the Second Section, Mothers, JASDAQ and other markets (as of the end of 2018).

A trading session is when the stock exchange is open and stocks can be traded. Different stock exchanges and financial products have different trading sessions, but in general the TSE has a morning session from 9:00 a.m. to 11:30 a.m. and an afternoon session from 12:30 p.m. to 3:00 p.m. on business days.

There are two ways to submit an order to buy or sell shares on the stock exchange—limit orders and market orders. With limit orders, the trade will be executed at the price specified by the person placing the order (the order price). Market orders, however, are placed without specifying an order price. The successful purchase or sale of a share through the execution of an order placed with the stock exchange is called a "trade," and the price at which a successful trade takes place is called the trade price.

For an order to become a trade, the bid price (price offered by a potential buyer), the ask price (price asked by the seller), and the number of shares being bought/sold must match. In Japan, two clearing methods are used for matching buy and sell orders—the *itayose* method and the *zaraba* method.

The *itayose* method is used to match buy and sell orders that were either submitted before the beginning of a trading session, or were unable to be cleared before the end of a trading session. At the TSE, the *itayose* method is used to determine opening and closing prices—prices at the beginning and end of a session.[2] The stock price mentioned in financial news, for instance, is often the closing price, which is the trade price of the last order cleared after the end of the afternoon session using the *itayose* method. Meanwhile, of the various orders placed before the opening of the morning session, the trade price of the first trade executed after the session opens, again calculated using the *itayose* method, is called the "opening price."

Itayose clearing is implemented according to the following rules to determine the market price:

---

[2]The *itayose* method is also used to determine the opening and closing prices if trading resumes after a temporary halt for some reason.

(i) First, all market orders submitted to the exchange are cleared.
(ii) Next, all limit buy orders with order prices higher than the market price, and limit sell orders with order prices lower than the market price are cleared.
(iii) Third, either all limit buy orders or all limit sell orders at the market price are cleared.

These rules may appear complicated at first glance, but they are simply a verbal representation of the economic principle of finding the market price at the point where the supply and demand curve meet. Consider a coordinate of axes, with order price plotted along the y-axis, and order volume (number of shares) plotted along the x-axis. On this coordinate, first plot the limit buy order price along the y-axis, against the total limit buy order volume for orders below that price along the x-axis. (For the sake of convenience, assume that the market buy order price is infinity.) This will ordinarily result in a downward-sloping graph, because market participants tend to want to buy shares as cheaply as possible, with the result that the order volume decreases with an increase in order price. This graph represents the demand curve.

Next, on the same coordinate, plot the limit sell order price along the y-axis, against the total limit sell order volume for orders above that price along the x-axis. (For the sake of convenience, assume that the market sell order price is 0). This will ordinarily result in an upward-sloping graph, because market participants tend to want to sell shares as lucratively as possible, with the result that the order volume increases with an increase in order price. This graph represents the supply curve.

From the above, it is clear that the supply and demand for a share coincides at the point where the two graphs intersect, and this is the point at which rules (i) and (ii) of the *itayose* clearing method have been executed.

However, in actual share trading, order prices do not change in a smooth continuum, so the supply and demand "curves" actually look like steps. This makes it difficult to find a precise point of intersection for the two curves, leaving open the possibility that the buy order and sell order volumes do not coincide at the price where rules (i) and (ii) have both been executed. Consequently, trades can be executed only for the smaller of the two volumes, which is why we need rule (iii).

Consider the following concrete example to better understand how the market price is determined in the *itayose* method. Chart 1a shows the order status before *itayose*. The "Price" column shows different order prices. The top-most entry in this column says "market," which indicates the market order price. The "Sell order volume" and "Buy order volume" columns show the number of shares ordered.

At the order price of JPY 3002, for instance, the sell order volume is 6000, indicating that sell orders for 6000 shares have been submitted at the price of JPY 3002. Of course, the sell order for all 6000 shares may not have been submitted by the same market participant—it is both possible and acceptable for there to be several such market participants.

The "Supply curve" column shows the number of shares for which orders have been submitted to sell even if the price is lower than the indicated price. For instance, the number in this column corresponding to the price of JPY 2999 is 4700, which is arrived at by adding.

market sell orders: 2000 shares
+ limit sell orders at JPY 2997: 300 shares
+ limit sell orders at JPY 2998: 400 shares
+ limit sell orders at JPY 2999: 2000 shares.

Meanwhile, the "Demand curve" column shows the number of shares for which orders have been submitted to buy even if the price is higher than the indicated price. For instance, the number in this column corresponding to the price of JPY 3001 is 5500, which is arrived at by adding.

market buy orders: 3000 shares
+ limit buy orders at JPY 3002: 1000 shares
+ limit buy orders at JPY 3001: 1500 shares.

Following the rules of the *itayose* clearing method, the price in the gray-highlighted row on Chart 1 (JPY 3000) is obtained as the market price. Let us see how. In Chart 1a, for prices higher than JPY 3000, the supply curve is higher than the demand curve, while for prices lower than JPY 3000, the demand curve is higher than the supply curve. However, the two curves appear to meet at around JPY 3000. However, since the lowest unit of price change in this case is JPY 1, one cannot find the exact point where the demand and supply curve meet with greater precision. Instead, rule (iii) of the *itayose* method is applied to clear either all limit buy or all limit sell orders at JPY 3000. In the example in Chart 1, the demand (8000 shares) is higher than the supply (7700 shares) by 300 shares, so after rule (iii) has been executed, there will still remain limit buy orders for 300 shares at JPY 3000, so ultimately, one will be left with the order status described in Chart 1b.

Moving on to Chart 1b, it is obvious that all sell orders lower than the market price and all buy orders higher than the market price have already been cleared. This method of clearing sell (buy) orders of lower (higher) prices first is based on the "principle of price priority." In other words, the *itayose* method determines the market price based on the principle of price priority.

Chart 1 Determining the market price using the *itayose* method

(A) Before *itayose* clearing.
Supply curve.
Sell order volume.
Price.
Buy order volume.
Demand curve.
(B) After *itayose* clearing.
Supply curve.
Sell order volume.
Price.
Buy order volume.
Demand curve.

Note that the limit orders that remain after *itayose* clearing, as in Chart 1b, will be cleared using the *zaraba*[3] method when the next trading session begins.

The *zaraba* method is used for matching orders that come in during a trading session, as and when they come in, with orders that have already been submitted and are yet to be cleared. Orders from market participants keep coming in even after *itayose* clearing. Chart 1b summarizes the limit orders placed with a stock exchange that remain after *itayose* clearing. The chart is an example of what a Limit Order Book (LOB) may look like. The lowest sell order price in the LOB is called the "best ask," while its highest buy order price is called the "best bid." Since market participants would ideally prefer to buy shares at the lowest price possible and sell them at the highest price possible, the best ask is always higher than the best bid, and the difference between the two is called the bid-ask spread (or simply "spread").[4]

The *zaraba* method for clearing market orders is different from that for clearing limit orders. In the case of market orders submitted during a trading session, buy orders are matched with the best ask, and sell orders are matched with the best bid.

In a scenario portrayed by Chart 1b, assume that a market buy order for 1000 shares comes in. Since there already exists a sell order for 4000 shares at JPY 3001, which is the best ask, the aforementioned buy order will be cleared at JPY 3001. However, what if a market sell order for 2000 shares comes in? In this case, since there are only 300 shares remaining in the buy order at the best bid (JPY 3000), the remaining 1700 shares in the sell order will be matched with the buy order at the next best bid (JPY 2999, 3000 shares).

Market buy orders that come in are similarly matched with sell orders, starting with the best ask (lowest ask price) and moving on to the next lowest ask price until the entire order has been cleared. In this way, the *zaraba* method also follows the principle of price priority. For orders at the same price, the *zaraba* method additionally follows the principle of time priority, in the sense that orders are cleared sequentially, on a first-come-first-serve basis.

Meanwhile, limit orders that come in during a trading session are added to the line of limit orders on the LOB waiting to be cleared at a particular price. These orders are cleared sequentially, as and when they match any market orders that come in during the session. Naturally, the principle of time priority is applied here too, as orders that come in earlier take precedence.

3 HFT Merits and Demerits

Once a trading session begins, orders start pouring in and are cleared sequentially. As a result, the LOB, which might look like Chart 1b when the session opens, changes

[3]The word "*zaraba*" refers to the period between the opening and closing of a trading session (for example, the period from 9:00 a.m. to 11:30 a.m. in the case of the TSE's morning session).

[4]A "bid" refers to the price specified for a buy order, while an "ask" refers to the price specified for a sell order.

continuously through the course of the session. In fact, given the increasingly rapid processing systems employed by exchanges (some exchanges have achieved speeds of up to several trades per microsecond or even nanosecond), it is no longer unusual for the LOB to become completely unrecognizable in the blink of an eye, literally speaking. Consequently, market participants who place market buy or sell orders based on the best bid or best ask displayed on the LOB at any given moment run the risk that the best price will have shifted to an entirely different place by the time their order arrives at the exchange.

To put it differently, the trader whose order arrives at the exchange first gets the most advantageous bid or ask price on the LOB and makes a profit. This is the concept behind HFT.

HFT is a type of algorithmic trading that aims to generate profits through a series of speculative transactions made at frequencies too high for humans to achieve. In HFT

- Orders are placed via a high-speed line directly connected to the exchange,
- High-speed computers are used to automatically execute algorithm-based trading strategies,
- High volumes of orders and cancellations are submitted at high frequencies, and
- The aim is to get all orders processed (either cleared or cancelled) within trading hours.

Liquidity supply and arbitrage are examples of trading strategies used in HFT. In the former, large volumes of limit sell and limit buy orders are placed, and the spread resulting from the execution of these trades is retained as profit. In the latter, products that should be identically priced in theory but end up with different prices for various reasons are exploited for profit by making what are called "arbitrage transactions."[5]

As only very small profits are obtained from single transactions based on the aforementioned strategies, HFT relies on a "small profits, quick returns" principle, aiming to make as many transactions as possible within trading hours. Naturally, since there are only a limited number of trading hours, low-latency (low-delay) trades are the key to securing profits.

For instance, HFT uses servers that are set up within the stock exchange (a practice known as "colocation") in an effort to minimize communication time. The optimization of HFT programs and the use of high-speed computers to execute these programs are also essential. HFT entered popular consciousness through Lewis (2014) book *Flash Boys*, which gave a raw glimpse into the various tactics employed by HFT trading firms. Here is a simple example.

Assume that a big investor has placed a large buy order targeting the current best ask. In this scenario:

(i) An HFT trader is already prepared with a specially prepared limit sell order at a price higher than the current best ask
(ii) The trader will then go ahead and buy up all the sell orders at the best ask price targeted by the big investor

[5]Hosaka (2014), Adachi (2018), and others discuss the subject in detail.

(iii) The big investor's buy order will end up being matched with the specially prepared sell order at the higher ask price
(iv) The difference between the best ask price and the higher ask price of the specially prepared sell order is the profit margin earned by the HFT trader.[6]

However, this method of earning a profit margin causes a considerable deviation of the original function of financial markets. In the beginning, there were very few HFT traders, and they were able to make big profits, but as more and more such traders enter the market with the purpose of making a quick profit using similar techniques, competition has intensified, and the profit margins originally possible have become difficult to come by.[7] Regardless, HFT traders insatiably continue to pursue ever dwindling profit margins at a rapid pace,[8] and HFT is now too big a trend to ignore.[9]

The demerits of HFT were highlighted by the May 6, 2010, U.S. stock market flash crash. This was an incident in which major U.S. stock indices, including the Dow Jones Industrial Average and the S&P 500, plummeted and then recovered rapidly, all within the space of 30 min or so. The incident came as a bolt from the blue (no major event had taken place that could explain the crash), so HFT was originally suspected to have been responsible.

Similar flash crashes have taken place in several financial markets since the 2010 incident, and discussions are continuing on the possible relation between these incidents and HFT.[10] While no clear conclusions have been arrived at regarding the relationship between HFT and this destabilization of the markets, countries around the world have now begun to regulate HFT. In Japan, for instance, the Financial Instruments and Exchange Act was revised in May 2017 to require the registration of HFT traders[11] starting April 2018.

In this way, HFT traders are generally treated as "bad guys," but the role of HFT in increasing stock market liquidity (making it easier for trades to be executed) cannot be denied. As one can tell from the system for determining the market price using the *zaraba* method, a large order that comes in at a time when there are only a few orders waiting to be cleared tends to be cleared at a price very different from the best price originally available. This effect of large orders on the market price is called "market impact."

If HFT traders targeting the bid-ask spread place a large number of orders in the neighborhood of the best price, they will easily be able to absorb the large order, thereby facilitating the smooth clearing of orders while preventing large price

---

[6] This is a technique called front running. For details, please see Adachi (2018).

[7] Meyer, Bullock and Rennison (2018).

[8] Tett (2019) introduces the various efforts to improve communication speeds undertaken by HFT traders.

[9] According to Hosaka (2014) and Meyer, Bullock and Rennison (2018), HFT is thought to account for around 5% of all stock market transactions in the U.S. and Japan.

[10] Please see Kirilenko, Kyle, Samadi and Tuzun (2017), Wigglesworth (2019), etc.

[11] The legal term used is "High-Speed Trader.".

movements due to market impact.[12] It is important, therefore, to remember that HFT also has considerable merits.

4 The Information Efficiency Wall

Excuse me for introducing a personal story here. My father was an avid follower of the stock markets, as was common among middle-aged Japanese men in the Showa era. My family's bookshelves were lined with books on stock market investment (with titles such as *Never Lose in the Stock Market*), along with the *Japan Company Handbook* (which provides detailed corporate information) and other similar publications. My father read the financial papers every morning, tuned in to shortwave radio for the latest share prices, made his own share price chart in a notebook, and predicted the following day's share prices. Growing up watching my father do this sort of thing every day undoubtedly influenced my choice of career in a big way.

The method my father used to predict share prices was an elementary form of technical analysis using a moving average. As there were no personal computers in those days, my father calculated the moving average of share prices every day on an abacus and entered the results in his chart, which he used for making decisions on when to buy or sell specific shares.

My reason for relating this story from my childhood is to point out that modern trading methods such as HFT and algorithmic trading are also, at their core, no more than my father's technical analysis plus a little something extra. Of course, the data collection tools have changed from shortwave radios to computers, the order-placement tools have changed from NTT-issued black rotary dial phones to high-speed dedicated lines, and the calculation and processing tools have changed from abacuses to super computers. These changes have made trading more convenient, but they have not changed the essential nature of it. Algorithmic trading uses much more sophisticated mathematical techniques than moving averages,[13] but these techniques also ultimately perform the same function—predicting future prices based on past price movements.

A fundamental question that arises here is—can future prices be predicted based on past price movements? From the point of view of economics, this boils down to a question regarding the stock market's information efficiency. According to Fama (1970), stock market information efficiency can be categorized as follows:

- Weak-form efficiency (future prices cannot be predicted based on past price movements)
- Semi-weak-form efficiency (future prices cannot be predicted using all publicly available information including past price movements)

[12] This skillful clearing of large orders while preventing market impact is called an "optimal execution strategy." Implementing optimal execution strategies is one of the important applications of algorithmic trading.

[13] Adachi (2018) introduces these mathematical techniques in detail.

– Strong-form efficiency (future prices cannot be predicted even using unpublished insider information).

In a weak-form efficient market, technical analysis based on past price movements is ineffective. In a semi-weak-form efficient market, fundamental analysis based on publicly available information including corporate financial information is ineffective. In a strong-form efficient market, even insider trading is ineffective.

Given that insider trading does, in fact, generate considerable profit (which is why it has been made illegal), it is unlikely that stock markets are strong-form efficient markets. However, empirical studies conducted in the past attest, by and large, to their being weak-form efficient markets. Putting a variety of statistical models to the test, one may be able to find some models that are able to predict price movements during some periods, but none of these models guarantee sustained accuracy of prediction sufficient to make it worthwhile if transaction costs are also taken into account. In other words, there is no guarantee that low-latency HFT based on advanced algorithmic transaction techniques will be worth the investment.

Meanwhile, the time taken for corporate financial information to be updated, which is relevant for fundamental analyses used in semi-weak-form efficient markets, is almost an eternity from the perspective of HFT. Consequently, it may be possible to break the wall of information efficiency if one can use oft-neglected but publicly available corporate financial information to accurately predict companies' future financial conditions. Attempts are being made to predict corporate performance using unconventional data (alternative data) such as social media postings and satellite imagery, and these attempts can be seen as efforts to beat information efficiency.

In sum, stock markets are currently midway between weak-form and strong-form information efficient, and HFT traders are battling it out in a narrow arena that may or may not fall into the space of semi-weak-form efficiency by refining their algorithms on a daily basis. HFT traders are merely pursuing profits through ultra-short-term speculative trading, but their activities supply liquidity to the markets and facilitate smooth transactions.

References

Adachi T (2018) Algorithmic Trading (in Japanese). Asakura Publishing Co Ltd

Fama EF (1970) Efficient capital markets: a review of theory and empirical work. J Finance 25:383–417

Friedman M (1953) The case for flexible exchange rates, essays in positive economics, University of Chicago Press

Hosaka G (2014) An analysis of high-frequency trading on the Tokyo Stock Exchange (in Japanese). Securities Anal J 52:72–82

Kirilenko A, Kyle AS, Samadi M, Tuzun T (2017) The flash crash: high frequency trading in an electronic market. J Finance 72:967–998

Lewis M (2014) Flash Boys. Norton & Company, W.W

Meyer G, Bullock N, Rennison J (2018) How high-frequency trading hit a speed bump, Financial Times, January 1, 2018. https://www.ft.com/content/d81f96ea-d43c-11e7-a303-9060cb1e5f44

Tett G (2019) Finance v Physics: even 'Flash Boys' can't go faster than light, Financial Times, February 21, 2019. https://www.ft.com/content/c529809a-349f-11e9-bd3a-8b2a211d90d5

Wigglesworth R (2019) Volatility: how 'Algos' changed the rhythm of the market, Financial Times, January 9, 2019. https://www.ft.com/content/fdc1c064-1142-11e9-a581-4ff78404524e

Chapter 13
Asset Management and Robo-Advisors

Teruo Nakatsuma

1 Asset Management in the Era of 100-Year Lifespans

Thanks to medical advances, Japan's average life expectancy has continued to increase, giving rise to the mantra "era of 100-year lifespans." This has prompted discussions on increasing the retirement age, but the reality is that people cannot continue to work until the day they die. Our intellects and physical strength have their limits, and we are all forced into a life of retirement on a pension at some point or the other. Meanwhile, thanks to declining birth rates, the working population, which contributes to pension funds, continues to shrink. Under such circumstances, it becomes necessary to get an early start on making one's own financial arrangements for retirement in order to feel confident about the future.

However, it is not just for retirement that one must put aside money. There are other major expenses, such as children's educations and home ownership, that require hefty savings. Therefore, in order to live a 100-year long life in comfort, one has to start saving systematically right from the time one begins working, taking into account income and expenditure levels at each stage of life along with expenses associated with marriage, childbirth, parenting, buying a home, and retirement.

However, thanks to the BOJ's long-term low-interest-rate policies, it has become impossible to obtain a sufficient return on investment from savings and other bank and postal deposits alone. For instance, even at an annual compound interest of 2%, it would take 35 years to double the principal. At a rate of 1%, it would take 70 years. This is in contrast to an annual rate of 5% or 7%, which would double the principal in 15 and 10 years, respectively. In order to achieve this magical doubling of one's savings, one must choose assets that offer high investment returns. This is the idea behind the slogan "from savings to investment," which many enthusiastically aspire to but never actually implement.

T. Nakatsuma (✉)
Faculty of Economics, Keio University, Tokyo, Japan
e-mail: nakatuma@econ.keio.ac.jp

S. Kaji et al. (eds.), *The Economics of Fintech*,
https://doi.org/10.1007/978-981-33-4913-1_13

The main aim of this chapter is to consider how to select assets for investment, mainly focusing on such financial products as savings and other deposits, stocks, and bonds. Of course, it is also possible to discuss a wider range of assets including real estate. Broadly speaking, an "asset" can be defined as something that earns a revenue for its holder (dividends in the case of stocks, interest income in the case of bonds or bank deposits). The act of holding an asset is called "investment," and an entity engaging in investment is called an "investor." In the context of economics and business management, the word investment may bring to mind "fixed investment," but in this chapter, the word will be used simply to mean the possession of assets.

Investors holding assets could be individuals or even corporations, including companies and other types of organizations. Individuals who invest are called individual investors, while corporate investors are called institutional investors. Investment income for investors is defined as the sum of capital gains and interest and dividend income for the investment period. Capital gain is the profit earned as a result of the value of the asset itself increasing, and is derived by subtracting the asset's value at the beginning of the investment period from the that at the end of the investment period. Obviously, capital gain is positive or negative depending on whether the asset's value increases or decreases over the course of the investment period. The return on investment is derived by dividing the investment income by the asset value at the start of the investment period.

2 Long-Term, Diversified Investments

Ordinarily, investors (especially institutional investors) invest in a variety of assets. Together, these form the investor's investment "portfolio." Of course, it is also possible to invest in a single stock of one's choice, but this is a bad investment strategy that amounts to putting all one's eggs in one basket. If the basket falls, all the eggs will break. Similarly, investing all one's funds in a single stock is risky because, if the associated company were to go bankrupt and the price of its shares were to crash, one could lose the majority of one's capital.

One way to avoid this is to invest in several companies. Take the case of an individual investor, say Alice, who invests half her funds in Company A's shares, and the other half in Company B's shares. Companies A and B would each have allocation ratios (portfolio weights) of 50% in Alice's portfolio. Should Company A go bankrupt, and its shares become worthless, Alice would not lose all of her funds, because Company B is likely to continue operating. If Alice were to further increase the number of companies she invests in, the portfolio weight of each company would correspondingly decrease within her portfolio, so the collapse of any one company would not result in any significant loss for Alice.

Assume that Alice has n types of assets in her possession ($Asset_1$, $Asset_2$, … $Asset_n$). If the funds are allocated equally among the assets, each asset would have a portfolio weight of 1/n. Consequently, if any one asset becomes worthless, the loss to Alice would amount to $1/n^{th}$ of her total funds. The greater the value of n, the smaller the loss. This, in essence, is the reasoning behind a diversified investment strategy.

In reality, it is not common for a company to collapse or its shares to become worthless. What does happen more frequently is share price volatility, which could cause the value of assets in one's portfolio to rise or fall significantly. However, unlike the risk of corporate bankruptcy, this kind of risk can be considerably mitigated with sufficient diversification and does not cause significant losses to investors except under special circumstances, such as a global financial crisis or other event that causes the entire stock market to crash. Of course, investors would still like to structure their asset portfolios so as to avoid extreme price volatility risks, and the next section will discuss in detail how this volatility risk can be managed.

Although avoiding asset price volatility is an important factor to take into consideration when building one's investment portfolio, the main purpose of investing is to secure a sufficient return on the investment over the medium and long term. There would, consequently, be no point to prioritizing safety above all else and ending up with nothing but low-yielding assets. Further, if the purpose of the investment is to ensure sufficient retirement funds after a few decades, it is important to have a long-term perspective of investment returns rather than focusing too much on short-term asset price fluctuations.

Those who have studied statistics have probably heard of the law of large numbers. According to this law, the sample mean of a data set approaches the true mean as the data set becomes larger.

If we apply the law of large numbers to return on investment, the average monthly return will approach the expected average return with an increase in the number of months. In other words, the longer the investment period, the more likely it is for the return on investment to approach the expected average return.

On could say, therefore, that while diversified investment is a technique for spreading risk out among a range of assets, long-term investment is a technique for spreading and smoothing out the volatility risk along the time axis. In other words, if the purpose is to steadily grow one's funds for future requirements, it is important to adopt a prudent stance toward portfolio selection and investment amounts, making sure to manage risks through diversification and secure solid returns through long-term investment, rather than attempting to make a fortune overnight.

3 Formulating the Portfolio Selection Problem

This chapter will demonstrate the way to build an asset management portfolio to minimize the volatility risk while maximizing the average return on investment (hereafter: "expected return") through long-term investment. The problem at hand can be expressed in terms of an objective function as follows:

$$\text{Objective function} = \text{expected return} - \text{risk aversion coefficient} \times \text{volatility risk}$$

where the value of the objective function can be seen as the level of desirability of a particular portfolio for an investor. Selecting the best investment strategy then boils down to an optimization problem in which portfolio weights are selected in a way that maximizes the objective function.

In the above objective function, expected return and volatility risk are functions of portfolio weight. Here, if the expected return of Asset_j is expressed as Return_j and the portfolio weight of Asset_j is expressed as Weight_j (where $j = 1, 2, \ldots n$), the expected return of the portfolio could be expressed as:

$$\text{Return} = \text{Weight}_1 \times \text{Return}_1 + \ldots + \text{Weight}_n \times \text{Return}_n$$

The variance of portfolio's return on investment (the average dispersion of the returns of individual assets in a portfolio around the expected return) is used as an indicator of volatility risk. The usual formula for portfolio variance (expressed as "Variance" in equations below) is more complex,[1] but in a case where there are only two assets in the portfolio,

$$\begin{aligned}\text{Variance} =& (\text{Weight}_1)^2 \times \text{Variance}_1 + (\text{Weight}_2)^2 \times \text{Variance}_2 + 2 \times \text{Weight}_1 \\ & \times \text{Weight}_2 \times \text{Covariance}_{1,2}\end{aligned}$$

where Variance_j ($j = 1, 2, \ldots n$) is the deviation of Asset_j's return from the expected return, and $\text{Covariance}_{1,2}$ is the average deviation of the returns pertaining to Asset_1 and Asset_2 from the expected return.

Further, the correlation coefficient of the returns on Asset_1 and Asset_2 (expressed as $\text{Coefficient}_{1,2}$) is given by:

$$\text{Correlation coefficient}_{1,2} = \text{Covariance}_{1,2} \div (\text{Standard Deviation}_1 \times \text{Standard Deviation}_2)$$

Here, $\text{Standard Deviation}_j$ (where $j = 1, 2, \ldots n$) is the square root of Variance_j. By definition, the correlation coefficient can only take a value between 1 and -1. When $\text{Covariance}_{1,2}$ is 0 (in which case, the correlation coefficient is also 0), the equation becomes simpler:

$$\text{Variance} = (\text{Weight}_1)^2 \times \text{Variance}_1 + (\text{Weight}_2)^2 \times \text{Variance}_2$$

To understand this better, let us use a concrete example to visualize the relationship between expected return and volatility risk. Assume that Asset_1's expected return is 1% with a standard deviation of 1%, while Asset_2's expected return is 8% with a standard deviation of 3%.

Figure 1 shows how the expected return and standard deviation of each asset affects its portfolio weight and the correlation coefficient.

[1] For details, please see Ikeda (2000) and Nakatsuma (2018).

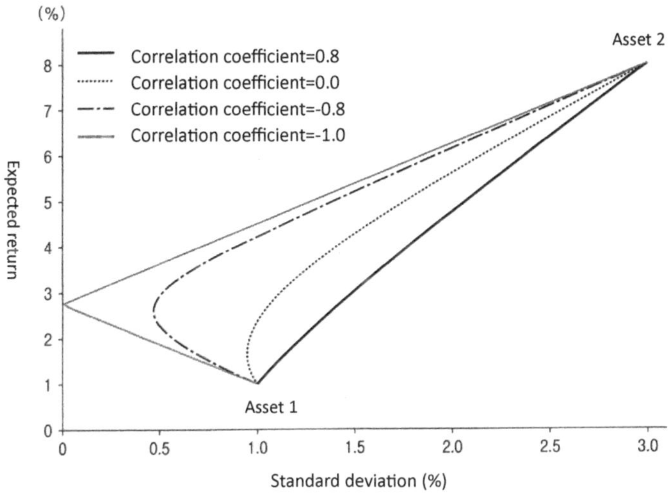

Fig. 1 The relationship between expected return and volatility risk

The first thing that is obvious from the figure is that, no matter what the correlation coefficient, the portfolio's expected return would be 1% with a standard deviation of 1% if it was comprised entirely of $Asset_1$, and its expected return would be 8% with a standard deviation of 3% if it was comprised entirely of $Asset_2$. Changing the portfolio weights of the two assets will cause the expected return and standard deviation to move along one of the curves joining points (1, 1) and (3, 8) in the graph.

The smaller the correlation coefficient, the more the curve veers to the left in the graph. For instance, when the correlation coefficient is -0.8, it is possible to minimize the standard deviation to around 0.5% while raising the expected return to almost 3% by optimizing portfolio weights. This shows how a portfolio's volatility risk can be minimized by combining multiple assets – more evidence of the benefits of diversified investment.

Further, when the correlation coefficient is -1 (the lowest value), the standard deviation becomes 0% for a certain portfolio weighting. This is the weighting at which risk can be avoided (hedged) completely.

ところで目的関数の中のリスク回避度は、期待リターン(運用利回りの平均)と変動リスク(運用利回りの分散)のバランスを決める正の値をとるパラメータであり、基本的に投資家が自由に決めること Incidentally, the risk aversion coefficient in the objective function is a parameter that takes a positive value and signifies the balance between expected return (average return on investment) and volatility risk (portfolio variance), and investors are free to decide their risk aversion level. Investors who are not concerned about risk ("risk-neutral" investors) choose a risk aversion coefficient of 0. Risk-neutral investors tend to build aggressive portfolios aimed at maximizing expected returns.

On the other hand, an investment portfolio with a high volatility risk would be undesirable for investors who are averse to asset price volatility. Such investors,

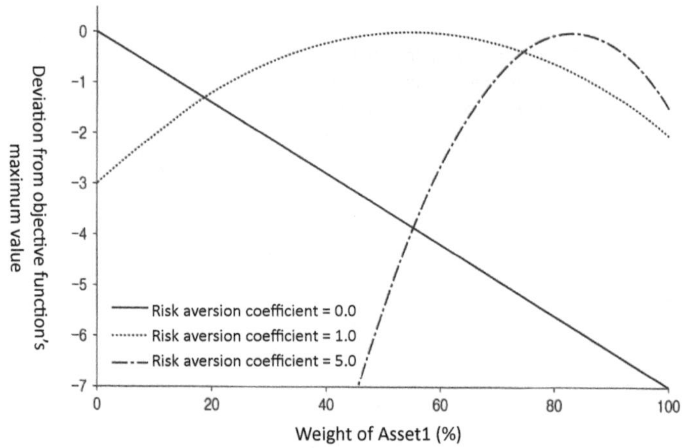

Fig. 2 Portfolio selection

called "risk averse" investors, would do well to choose a positive risk aversion coefficient. Unfortunately, it becomes difficult to achieve high expected returns in such cases, because high returns come with high volatility. For such investors, therefore, a portfolio with a high expected return is not necessarily a desirable portfolio.

Maximizing the objective function would ideally involve (i) maximizing expected return, and (ii) minimizing portfolio variance, but there is no guarantee that (i) and (ii) can be simultaneously achieved, as both expected return and portfolio variance are functions of portfolio weighting. The objective function will, therefore, have to be maximized by finding the portfolio weighting that best balances expected return and portfolio variance. This is the basic principle on which the solution to the portfolio selection problem is based.

Let us look at this problem (Fig. 2) using the same portfolio as in Fig. 1. To recap, this portfolio comprises two assets, namely Asset_1 with an expected return of 1% and a standard deviation of 1%, and Asset_2 with an expected return of 8% and a standard deviation of 3%. Additionally, assume a correlation coefficient of 0. In such a scenario, how will the shape of the curve representing the objective function change with a change in the risk aversion coefficient from 0 to 1 to 5?

In the graph, the portfolio weight of Asset_1 is plotted along the x-axis while the deviation from the objective function's maximum value is plotted along the y-axis. Naturally, the most desirable portfolio weight for Asset_1 is at the point where the curve's y-coordinate is 0. For a risk-neutral investor, who chooses a risk aversion coefficient of 0, the portfolio weighting with the highest expected return is optimal. Since the expected return of Asset_2 is higher than that of Asset_1, the best portfolio for such an investor would comprise entirely of Asset_2, which gives Asset_1 a weight of 0.

For a somewhat risk-averse investor who chooses a risk aversion coefficient of 1, the standard deviation of the portfolio can be lowered by including some amount of Asset_1, which has a smaller standard deviation than Asset_2. Naturally, this will lower the expected return, but the disadvantage of a lower expected return will be offset to some extent by the advantage of a lower standard deviation. As is obvious from Fig. 2, therefore, the optimum portfolio for this investor would include both Asset_1 and Asset_2 in almost equal weights.

For an even more risk-averse investor who chooses a risk aversion coefficient of 5, the optimal weight of Asset_1 is substantially higher, at over 80%. In this way, although the portfolio of all three hypothetical investors includes the same two assets, the optimal weighting of the two assets changes simply due to each investor's preferred level of risk.

Something that has not been stated explicitly so far is that the following constraint condition is applied to the portfolio selection optimization problem:

$$\text{Weight}_1 + \ldots + \text{Weight}_n = 1$$

In other words, the sum of all the weights in the portfolio should be equal to 1. Given the definition of portfolio weighting, this equation invariably holds true, and it is a constraint condition that is applied to almost all portfolio selection problems. In practice, the constraint condition.

$$\text{Weight}_\text{j} \geqq 0, (\text{Where j} = 1, 2, \ldots \text{n})$$

also applies in most cases. This constraint condition amounts to not holding a short position. One way of holding a short position is by selling shares one does not own (certain types of shares are available for selling short for the purpose of margin trading). In the case of savings and other bank deposits, a negative weight corresponds to a loan. However, going back to our constraint condition $\text{Weight}_\text{j} \geqq 0$, this applies to scenarios where there are only two options, having assets ($\text{Weight}_\text{j} > 0$) or not having assets ($\text{Weight}_\text{j} = 0$). Apart from the above, it is possible to add various other constraint conditions to the portfolio selection problem, such as setting upper limits for portfolio weights.

In finance, this approach to portfolio selection, where the expected return is used as an indicator of profitability while portfolio variance is used as an indicator of volatility risk, is called the mean–variance approach.[2] The mean–variance approach is still widely used in practice, but there are also newer approaches to portfolio selection that use other indicators of volatility risk: (i) the mean absolute deviation approach (which uses the mean of the absolute deviation of return on investment from expected return as the indicator of volatility risk) and (ii) the expected shortfall approach (in which the average return on investment is used as the indicator of volatility risk under conditions of extremely poor returns on investment). The expected shortfall (also called conditional value at risk) approach, in particular, is gaining popularity

---

[2]This is the classic approach to portfolio selection, proposed by Markowitz (1952, 1959), and is also known as the Markowitz model.

for its ability to calculate risk during periods of significant downturn in the financial markets.[3]

In explaining the portfolio selection problem so far, this chapter has assumed that, once a portfolio has been weighted, it will not be revised until the end of the investment period (for instance, until retirement). However, in actual practice, it is important to consider changing portfolio weights (rebalancing the portfolio) midway through the investment period. To implement portfolio rebalancing, the portfolio selection optimization problem needs to be reformulated and solved as a dynamic optimization problem, but this chapter will refrain from addressing that, as it is mathematically quite advanced. Those who are interested can refer to Hibiki (2001) and others.

4 Robo-Advisors as Asset Management UI/UX Tools

From what has been discussed thus far, it is clear that amateurs cannot hope to easily solve portfolio optimization problems to invest their assets wisely. Financial institutions, however, have begun to offer convenient services that help make investment decisions, especially for individual investors, in an effort to improve the user interface/user experience (UI/UX). The general term for such services in the world of fintech is "robo-advisors." Most robo-advisors take the form of conveniently accessible smartphone apps, and such apps are now being developed not just by fintech startups but also by major conventional banks and securities companies, resulting in fierce competition.

Services provided by robo-advisors include:

(i) Functions related to the purchase of financial assets
   (a) Order placement using chat boxes or AI customer service representatives
   (b) Internationally diversified investments using exchange-traded funds (ETF)
(ii) Graphs and other visualization aids
   (a) Easy-to-understand visualizations of the tradeoff between expected return and volatility risk
   (b) Visualizations of funds required in the different stages of life
   (c) Visualizations of the roadmap for accumulating the required funds (for leisure activities or expensive purchases)
(iii) Systems for making small cumulative investments
   (a) Automated systems for withdrawing small amounts from one's bank account each month to progressively add to one's investment fund

[3]Please see McNeil, Frey and Embrechts (2015) and others for a more detailed discussion of various types of risk indicators.

  (b) Systems for meticulously saving shopping points or small change left over from shopping

(iv) Information for individual investors

  (a) Share prices
  (b) Economic new
  (c) Elementary courses on investment for inexperienced investors.

Easy to use even for inexperienced investors, robo-advisors are remarkable tools that could encourage the channeling of funds from savings and other bank deposits to investment in financial assets—something the Japanese financial industry has been trying unsuccessfully to promote right since after the collapse of the asset price bubble in the early 1990s.

References

Hibiki N (2001) Financial engineering and optimization (in Japanese). Asakura Publishing Co., Ltd
Ikeda M (2000) Basic monetary economics (in Japanese). Asakura Publishing Co., Ltd
Markowitz H (1952) Portfolio selection. J Finance 7:77–91
Markowitz H (1959) Portfolio selection: efficient diversification of investments, Wiley
McNeil AJ, Frey R, Embrechts P (2015) Quantitative risk management: concepts. Revised Edition, Princeton University Press, Techniques and Tools
Nakatsuma T (2018) Introduction to finance using Python (in Japanese). Asakura Publishing Co., Ltd

Chapter 14
New Risks from Fintech (1) Cyber Security

Yuta Miyauchi

1 Asset Protection in the Age of Fintech

Every year, cyberattacks targeting countries and corporations are becoming more sophisticated and intense. In a 2017 survey by Japan's Ministry of Internal Affairs and Communications (MIC), around half of all Japanese companies reported "some kind of loss resulting from a security breach (…) in the past year."[1] Chart 1 lists some of the major cyber security incidents that have taken place in the past few years. In recent years, attacks have frequently targeted information assets or systems owned by the state or corporations, in particular, causing damage on a large scale. Most of these attacks are thought to be by criminal organizations or nation states and are sophisticated, organized attacks.

With the spread of fintech, companies will be able to provide financial services through a variety of new channels. For instance, an open API (application programming interface) is a system that allows payment services, which were only available through financial institutions until recently, to be provided by third-party non-financial entities (NFEs). As the numbers of companies and people involved in the provision of these services rise, there will also be an increase in risks and points of vulnerability. Cyber security problems are one of the risks inherent in fintech and a common challenge for all entities involved in the provision of services.

This chapter discusses the cyber security risks faced by companies offering fintech services (fintech companies) and existing financial institutions that offer similar services along with some countermeasures against such risks.

[1]MIC (2017), "Communications Usage Trend Survey."

Y. Miyauchi (✉)
Armoris Co., Ltd, Tokyo, Japan
e-mail: miyauchi@armoris.jp

S. Kaji et al. (eds.), *The Economics of Fintech*,
https://doi.org/10.1007/978-981-33-4913-1_14

Overseas	2013	Three major South Korean banks	ATM and payment services were suspended for a few hours following simultaneous attacks targeting several banks.
	2015, 2016	Ukraine power companies	Power companies' information systems were attacked, which shut down substations and disrupted electricity supplies for several hours.
	2017	UK, National Health Service (NHS)	Data on infected computers in the network was encrypted and 34% of NHS trusts had to suspend services temporarily.
Japan	2015	Japan Pension Service (JPS)	The JPS network was breached using targeted emails, and around 1.25 million personal data records were leaked.
	2016	Major travel agent	The company's network was breached using targeted emails, and around 6.78 million personal data records were leaked.
	2018	Major cryptocurrency exchange	The cryptocurrency management system was hacked and cryptocurrency worth JPY 58 billion was stolen.

Chart 1 Major cyber security incidents in recent years

Unauthorized access	Parties without appropriate permissions gain unauthorized access into the system. The main *modi operandi* include unauthorized use by impersonating a legitimate user and unauthorized entry exploiting system vulnerabilities.
Illegal money transfer	Money transfers noti ntended by legitimate users are made to bank accounts oft hird parties. The main *modi operandi* include impersonating a legitimate user to make unauthorized transactions and falsifying communication details to make transactions noti ntended by legitimate users.
Denial of Service (DOS) attack	The aim oft hese attacks is to disrupt service provision. The main *modi operandi* include heavily burdening the server or network and exploiting vulnerabilities to bring down the system. Distributed DoS (DDos) is a type of attack in which the attack is carried out using multiple devices connected to the network.
Targeted attacks	These are persistent and sustained cyberattacks targeting a specific organization with the aim of destroying and/or stealing information or money. The attacks tend to be conducted secretively and in stages to preventt he target organization from realizing thati ti s under attack.

Chart 2 Main forms of cyberattacks against fintech companies or financial institutions

2 Fintech-Related Cyber Security Risks

The Ministry of Economy, Trade, and Industry (METI) defines cyber security as an effort to forestall leaks or falsification of electronic data and IT system malfunctions that prevent them from functioning as they are expected to.[2] In modern society, where everything is connected to networks, the use of networks to steal money or information by persons or entities with malicious intent, also known as cyberattacks, are a major threat that can take place anywhere, anytime, and against any organization. The main forms of cyberattacks possible against fintech companies or financial institutions are listed in Chart 2.

[2] METI (2017) "Cybersecurity Management Guidelines Ver 2.0" (Japanese only).

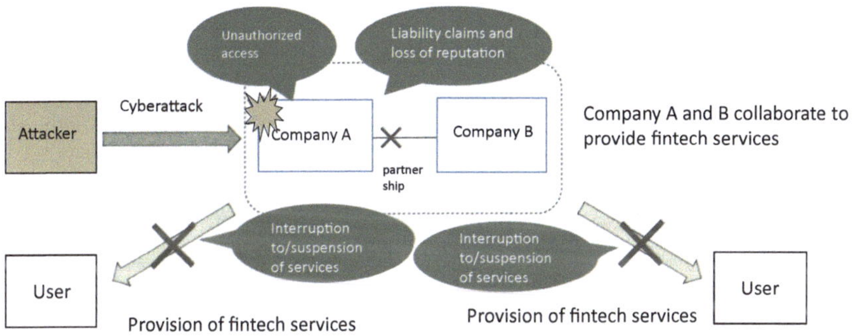

Fig. 1 Main cyber security threat in fintech

Cyber security risk is a company's measurement of the possibility of cyber security problems occurring and impacting its management.[3] Below (Fig. 1) is an explanation of the main types of cyber security risks faced by fintech companies and financial institutions as a result of cyberattacks. Please note, however, that this chapter will not go into the specifics of risks related to the various individual technologies involved in the provision of fintech services, such as the risk of fraudulent transactions following a 51% attack on a blockchain, or unauthorized access through theft of access tokens from clients in an open API.

(1) Unauthorized Access

As fintech services are typically provided via the Internet, there is always the risk of unauthorized access to a system by someone without the appropriate permissions. The main reason attackers gain unauthorized access to systems is to steal money or information, so, organizations that fall prey to unauthorized access are very likely to suffer a series of illegal money transfers or information leaks.

In a recent incident involving unauthorized access to a major Japanese cryptocurrency exchange, customers' private keys, which the operating company had stored in an online environment, were stolen by the attackers and used for the unauthorized transfer of funds. In addition to the direct targets of such attacks, which are fintech companies and their customers, companies or people related to the direct targets are also at risk. They could become indirect targets, used as stepping stones to get to the direct targets. In other words, those who are victims of unauthorized access could become the unwilling facilitators of attacks against others.

There are many ways to gain unauthorized access, but the main ways are stealing legitimate users' IDs or passwords and exploiting system vulnerabilities. A summary report by the National Police Agency (NPA)[4] revealed that in around 65% of unauthorized cryptocurrency transmissions during the first half of 2018, the victims had used the same ID and password for their cryptocurrency wallet they had used for

[3] See previous footnote.

[4] NPA (2018), "The situation of threats in cyberspace in the first half of 2018."

other services. Using the same ID or password for multiple services increases the risk of unauthorized access to other services when there is an information leak related to any one service.

The provision of fintech services is not handled by the fintech company all by itself, but rather in collaboration with several other financial institutions as well as NFEs. Payment services or personal financial management (PFM) services, for instance, are composite services brought to users as a team effort by multiple service providers. If any one of these service providers falls victim to unauthorized access, the entire service is likely to be impacted. It is therefore important for each service provider to take thorough measures against cyberattacks.

(2) Interruption to or Suspension of Services

Cyberattacks pose a risk to the uninterrupted provision of services. Service disruption is achieved mainly through DDoS (Distributed Denial of Service) attacks, which overwhelm network bandwidth and shut down systems, or by infecting computers and servers with ransomware (malware that forcibly encrypts files on computers or servers and then demands a ransom to decrypt them). Service interruption or suspension do not just prevent users from using the services of a company, they could also damage the company's reputation.

Such attacks could be motivated by a variety of things, but some of the main assumed motives include extortion (of money) or political activism. The *modi operandi* of such cyberattacks may include notifying the victim of an imminent attack and demanding ransom for not going ahead with it, using the attack to manipulate volatile cryptocurrency rates for profit, or targeting government agencies or financial institutions in protest against the enforcement of some law or business activity. In particular, numerous DDoS attacks on cryptocurrency exchanges resulting in an interruption of services are coming to light.

Attacks have become increasingly wide-reaching and sophisticated over the years, and complete protection against attacks is considered difficult. A new type of DDoS attack that emerged in 2016 used a variety of devices and unmonitored servers connected to the internet to assist in the attack, flooding a major domain name system (DNS) provider with assault traffic and bringing down the websites of major U.S. service providers one after another. There have also emerged agents that execute DDoS attacks for an affordable fee, so that anyone can carry out a DDoS attack by proxy at any time.

(3) Liability Claims and Loss of Reputation

Unauthorized access or the interruption or suspension of services could lead to liability claims, the loss of customers, and damage to reputation resulting in a fall in share prices. In past incidents involving unauthorized access into the systems of major cryptocurrency exchanges in Japan, claims for compensation were filed by victims, and the companies had to pay damages, which ultimately resulted in those companies going bankrupt or being acquired.

In recent years, the privacy and protection of personal information has become a hot topic of discussion. In 2018, the EU enforced the General Data Protection Regulation (GDPR), which stipulates legal requirements related to the transfer or processing of personal information and imposes large penalties on violators. As fintech services are tailored to individual customers' needs, there are inevitably many situations in which personal information is handled. In light of this, all fintech companies need to be aware of the various rules and regulations, not limited to the GDPR, that may apply depending on information ownership and acquisition routes.

3 Cyber Security Risk Management

Cyber security risks have existed since before the age of fintech, so in dealing with them, it is possible to use approaches similar to those used when dealing with other risks. ISO 31,000, a family of international standards related to risk management, defines seven ways to deal with risks (see Fig. 2). This section will discuss cyber security risk management from the perspective of risk assessment and risk treatment, which are two of the core processes.

(1) Risk Assessment (Risk identification/risk analysis/risk evaluation)

Risk assessment is the process of identifying risks and ranking them according to the need for action. Risk assessment can be divided into three main steps.

(i) Risk identification

This step involves determining all the assets that need to be protected, identifying all the risks they are exposed to, and gauging the impact of risk occurrence in each case. There is no established procedure for identifying risks, but doing so at the corporate

Fig. 2 The risk management process

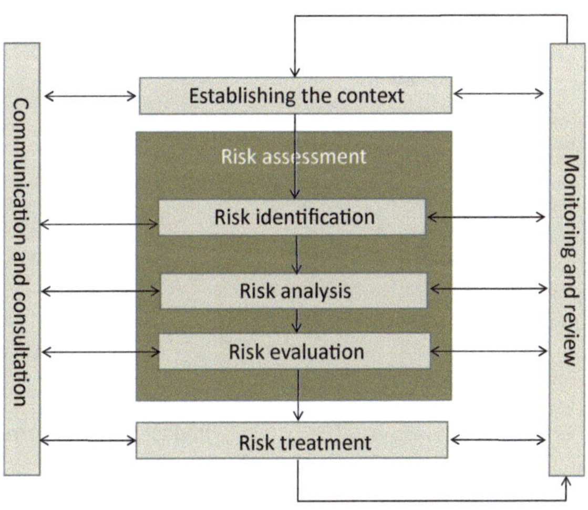

strategy and daily work management levels and based on data gathered over the years can help improve the comprehensiveness of the process.

(ii) Risk analysis

This step involves quantifying the magnitude of each risk. Some key indicators used are the magnitude of the threat to the asset, the vulnerability of the asset to risks, and the impact of risk occurrence.

(iii) Risk evaluation

This step involves comparing the magnitude of each risk against risk standards formulated based on such factors as environmental requirements and corporate policy, then determining which risks need to be addressed and in what order of priority.

(2) Risk Treatment

Risk treatment is the process of revising existing measures and considering new measures to deal with new risks. A treatment policy is determined based on the magnitude and nature of risks that are considered necessary to address based on risk assessment.

There are four main ways to respond to risks: (i) risk avoidance, which involves eliminating risky assets, activities, and processes in order to lower the likelihood of risk occurrence, (ii) risk transfer (or sharing), which involves sharing the cost of risks with other entities by purchasing cyber security insurance against liability claims or security incidents, (iii) risk reduction, which involves lowering the likelihood of risk occurrence or its impact by taking action to manage vulnerabilities, and (iv) risk acceptance, which involves retaining risks that have a low risk occurrence likelihood or impact without taking any action to counter them (Fig. 3).

In the case of cyber security risks, one of the risk factors is the presence of malicious entities with intent to attack, so risk treatments must be considered and

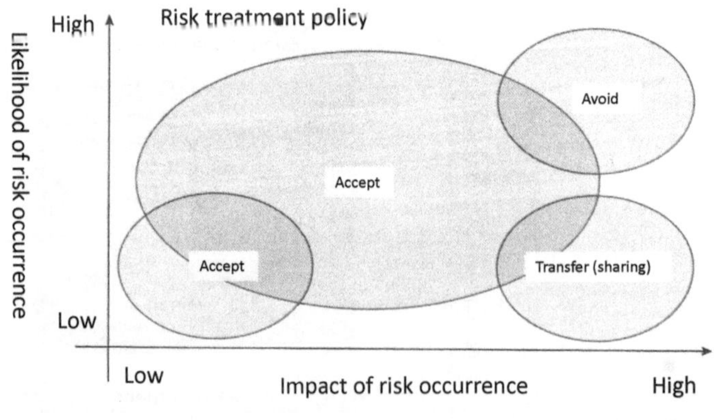

Fig. 3 Risk matrix

organized from the perspective of preventing attacks. There are three main types of measures depending on the objective: (i) entrance control measures, which prevent attackers from gaining entry into the organization and carrying out an attack, (ii) exit control measures, which prevent assets from leaving the organization, and (iii) internal measures, which detect suspicious activity and prevent unauthorized searches and other behavior within the organization. This approach, involving multiple layers of security controls, is called "defense in depth," and the idea behind it is to position the organization to detect and deal with suspicious activity at one of several stages before the attack can be completed.

However, as cyberattacks intensify and become more sophisticated, complete protection from all attacks may be impossible. There are no cyber security products that offer comprehensive protection against all threats, and budgets allocated for cyber security tend to be limited. An effective way to deal with security threats, therefore, is to assume that security incidents will take place and put in place organizational, technological, and human countermeasures that can be implemented both before and after an event. Concrete examples of each type of countermeasure are given below.

(i) Organizational Countermeasures

One of the reasons cyberattacks have intensified and become more sophisticated is because attackers are increasingly organizing themselves and promoting division of labor. For instance, there are different sets of people or entities specializing in malware development, distribution, and application. Attackers also appear to share information within their own networks on methods of attack and vulnerabilities that can be exploited. In other words, the attackers have an advantage over the defenders, who implement countermeasures on individual bases.

To defend against organized attacks, defenders also need to organize themselves in establishing protective measures. In 2014, the U.S.-based National Institute of Standards and Technology (NIST) published its Framework for Improving Critical Infrastructure Cybersecurity (Cybersecurity Framework), which defines five core functions regarding cyber security initiatives (Fig. 4).

The framework provides a comprehensive set of guidelines, rules, and points that are key means of protecting against security incidents both before (Identify, Protect, and some of Detect) and after (some of Detect, Respond, and Recover) the fact, and it is an effective tool for considering organizational response functions or evaluating an organization's preparedness even outside the critical infrastructure sectors.

Organizations are increasingly establishing Computer Security Incident Response Teams (CSIRTs) and Security Operation Centers (SOCs) to respond to security incidents on an organization-wide level. A CSIRT is an incident response team that specializes in dealing with cyber security problems, while the SOC is a specialized team tasked with the prediction or early detection of security incidents.

If a security incident takes place, the CSIRT cooperates with the SOC and systems department in taking of the situation, ascertaining the cause of the problem and the damage incurred, and sharing information with concerned persons both within and outside the organization. The SOC ordinarily monitors and analyzes security logs

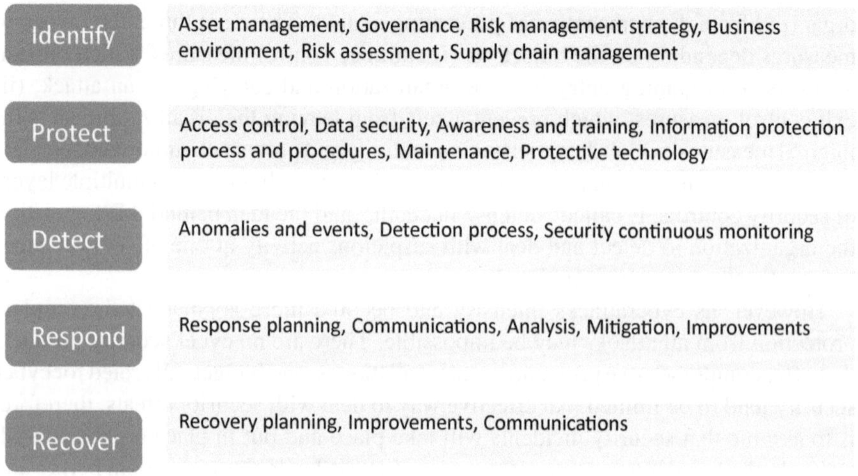

Fig. 4 NIST cyber security framework core structure

and equipment including firewalls and proxy servers, but when the organization is under attack, it implements initial response by blocking communications from the source of the attack and isolating and securing compromised equipment.

It has also become quite common for multiple organizations to closely cooperate with each other in their efforts to bolster organizational countermeasures in preparation for security incidents. A concrete example of this kind of initiative is the establishment of industry-wide Information Sharing and Analysis Centers (ISACs), especially in critical infrastructure sectors. ISACs share information about threats, vulnerabilities, and other trends; implement joint training exercises to share expertise; and adopt a range of initiatives toward resolving common challenges faced in the business world.

(ii) Technological Countermeasures

Numerous cyber security products are available these days, but haphazardly introducing everything that becomes available is neither an effective nor a feasible way to deal with threats. When considering technological countermeasures, therefore, it is important to take stock of the situation from two different standpoints—revising existing measures and introducing new measures.

Revising existing measures

The security response level can be improved even without introducing new technologies or products. For instance, it is possible to reduce risk by revising network settings, access permissions, and authentication methods with a view to limiting the number of persons with access to the organization's assets.

Improving authentication methods is an effective way to deal with unauthorized access through impersonation. The three main factors used for authentication include

(i) something you know, such as a password or other information, (ii) something you have, such as a card or token, and (iii) something you are, such as fingerprints or iris patterns. NIST's 2018 *Special Publication 800–63-3* offers guidelines for digital authentication, which is defined as the practice of combining appropriate authentication methods based on the level of confidentiality or importance of an asset.

Specifically, there can be three levels of authentication in terms of strength, with the lowest level requiring authentication by one of the three factors mentioned above (something you know, something you have, or something you are), and the highest level requiring two-factor authentication, of which of which one of the factors is biometric identification or something that is difficult to duplicate.

Biometric identification is extremely effective in preventing impersonation, but it must be handled with extreme caution as it is also highly sensitive information that cannot be altered. Organizations must also closely monitor technological trends, because even highly effective authentication methods could be rendered ineffective by new technologies.

Introducing new measures

Having brought the organization's existing technological measures up to date, it is important to introduce new ones to make up for functions or roles not covered by the existing technology. In examining new measures, it is important to categorize them by whether they are entrance control, exit control, or internal measures, and by whether the format/location of introduction should be the cloud, servers, or endpoints. Doing this will make an organization's cyber security measures more comprehensive.

Physical measures must also be considered in addition to technological measures. For instance, in the context of cryptocurrency, measures to protect keys stored in online environments would not be effective for protecting cold wallets, where the keys are stored in an offline environment. In the case of cold wallets, unauthorized access through theft, eavesdropping, and physical contact are conceivable, so physical measures such as installing security cameras or limiting the number of people with access to the asset must also be implemented.

(iii) Human Countermeasures

Attacks that target people, such as service users or employees, are difficult to prevent using organizational or technological measures and must involve measures taken by the people themselves. For instance, phishing, which involves e-mails or websites that steal the IDs and passwords of users by mimicking financial institutions, or social engineering, which involves exploiting human error or weaknesses to steal important information through conversations or physical contact, often take place as a prelude to unauthorized access attacks and are difficult to detect or prevent even for organizations that employ highly sophisticated organizational or technological measures. They are, therefore, considered easy attack points.

Human countermeasures must be considered from the perspective of both service users and service providers. Service users, for their part, can refrain from using the same ID or passwords for multiple services, proactively use multi-factor authentication, and remain vigilant against phishing emails and websites.

Service providers, in addition to urging users to take precautions, can enforce more effective measures such as mandatory multi-factor authentication for important operations including sign ins and money transfers. It is also important for organizations to conduct periodic employee drills on how to handle suspicious emails or respond to a security incident in order to strengthen their human countermeasures.

4 Indispensable Security Measures Going Forward

This chapter provided an overview of the cyber security risks faced by fintech companies and financial organizations. As society promotes the use of fintech, it will be vital for all concerned entities—from fintech companies and financial institutions to service users—to take appropriate measures against cyber security risks in order to continue enjoying safe and secure services going forward. Given that underlying technologies such as blockchains and artificial intelligence are interconnected, there is a tendency to focus mainly on technological measures, but it is important to recognize that organizational and human measures are equally necessary.

Cyber security is a rapidly changing field. Attack methods and countermeasures are constantly evolving, and new rules and regulations are constantly being introduced. One must thus strive to maintain a high level of vigilance on a day-to-day basis.

Chapter 15
New Risks from Fintech (2) Financial System Destabilization

Kazuhito Ikeo

1 The Next Financial Crisis?

In September 2017, an opinion piece titled "The Next Crisis Will Start in Silicon Valley: Forget Wall Street. Worry about Fintech" was featured on Bloomberg,[1] a news media company primarily focusing on business and financial news. The article, written by Texas A&M University School of Law associate professor William Magnuson, was quite well thought out and spurred vigorous debate. There have also been other reports in American media on the risks of Fintech.

This chapter will address the question of whether fintech could cause the next financial crisis, but before diving right into the topic, one needs a fundamental understanding of what a financial crisis is and how it takes place. Without that, the discussion would end up being quite superficial. Let us, therefore, first take a look at the phenomenon of a financial crisis and the mechanism by which it takes place.

2 Mechanism of a Financial Crisis

To understand the mechanism behind a financial crisis, let us go back and take a look at the last financial crisis, which took place in 2007–08 and is commonly referred to as the Global Financial Crisis. Though described as "global," it must be noted that this crisis did not directly affect Japan. Nevertheless, the shrinking of U.S. markets

[1] https://www.bloomberg.com/opinion/articles/2017-09-18/the-next-crisis-will-start-in-silicon-valley.

K. Ikeo (✉)
Faculty of Economics, Rissho University, Tokyo, Japan
e-mail: kikeo.a5@ris.ac.jp

S. Kaji et al. (eds.), *The Economics of Fintech*,
https://doi.org/10.1007/978-981-33-4913-1_15

brought Japanese exports aimed at the North American markets to an almost complete standstill, causing conditions in the Japanese economy to deteriorate sharply. In Japanese circles, therefore, the crisis is commonly understood to have been imported from abroad. Also, in Japan, the crisis is predominantly referred to as the "Lehman Shock," though the rest of the world knows it as "the Global Financial Crisis."

(1) Trigger and Amplification Mechanisms

The subprime mortgage crisis acted as the trigger for the Global Financial Crisis. The word "prime" in this context means high quality, as in "prime loans," which are housing loans that meet certain standards. By contrast, "subprime loans" indicate loans that do not meet those standards. In other words, they are substandard or low-quality housing loans, typically offered to low-income borrowers with poor credit scores. As financial products, subprime loans are only feasible in a market where housing prices are on the rise and expected to continue rising.

Housing prices in the U.S. had been rising continuously for many years starting around the year 2000. This resulted in a bullish market with strong expectations of continued price rises and an increase in the number of subprime loans being given out. Around 2006, however, the trend began to lose steam and housing prices started to peak, causing subprime loans to turn delinquent, then non-performing one after another in large numbers. This is what triggered the financial crisis, although no one realized it at the time.

Then Federal Reserve Board (Fed) chairman Ben Bernanke, for instance, told the U.S. Senate Committee on Banking, Housing, and Urban Affairs, "Some estimates are in the order of between $50 billion and $100 billion of losses associated with subprime credit problems." Mr. Bernanke went on to say that the losses, though significant, were not large enough to cause serious damage to the U.S. financial market, given its scale, and that they were within the limits of what the U.S. financial system was capable of absorbing.

Though true that the U.S. financial market is colossal in its entirety, the subprime mortgage crisis still ended up becoming a full-blown, general financial crisis. The key to understanding why this happened is to distinguish between the trigger, which is the event that set off the crisis, and the amplifying mechanism, which is the process by which the problem was exacerbated and escalated internally, thereby turning it into a financial crisis. It is because the amplifying mechanism was activated that the losses snowballed and surpassed levels that could be absorbed, thus resulting in a financial crisis.

(2) Systemic Risks

Let us take a look at a phenomenon called chain bankruptcies. Assume that Bob, anticipating payment from Alice, schedules a payment to Carol. However, Alice goes bankrupt, and Bob is unable to receive the payment he was expecting, thereby preventing him from making his scheduled payment to Carol. This domino effect is what causes chain bankruptcies.

The phenomenon is quite common in the business world at large, not just in the financial sector. In fact, there are government programs to support subcontractors supplying materials and parts to large enterprises over a certain size to ensure that the subcontractors don't fall victim to a chain reaction in the event of the large enterprise going bankrupt and being unable to pay them.

Chain bankruptcies can, therefore, happen in any commercial context, but they are a particularly serious problem in the financial sector. This risk in the financial sector is that chain bankruptcies can spread widely, causing the entire system to collapse, thereby making it a "systemic risk."

The reason the financial sector is especially vulnerable to such chain reactions is because of the nature of business in this industry. There are inevitably very close-knit networks of debtor-creditor relationships among financial institutions. For instance, payments are one of the core functions in the banking business and a primary factor contributing to the formation of debtor-creditor relationships.

Let us use the example of remittance or wire transfer, which is a type of payment function. Assume that Alice wants to remotely transfer some money to Bob. Alice would go to her bank, call it Bank X, and complete the procedure for remittance. Following this, Bank X, rather than physically transferring the money itself, would simply pass along a message to Bob's bank, call it Bank Y. This is equivalent to Bank X requesting Bank Y to pay Bob on behalf of Bank X, to be reimbursed later.

Bank Y will grant the request and deposit the specified amount into Bob's account on behalf of Bank X. Consequently, there arises a debtor-creditor relationship between Bank X and Bank Y as a result of the wire transfer from Alice to Bob, with the requestor bank (Bank X) becoming the debtor and the requestee bank (Bank Y) becoming the creditor (See Fig. 1).

Remittances are a core banking function, and banks facilitate several tens of thousands of them each day. Some remittances may be from Bank X to Bank Y, while others may be from Bank Y to Bank X. Banks do not physically transfer the funds for each remittance, but simply send messages pertaining to each remittance.

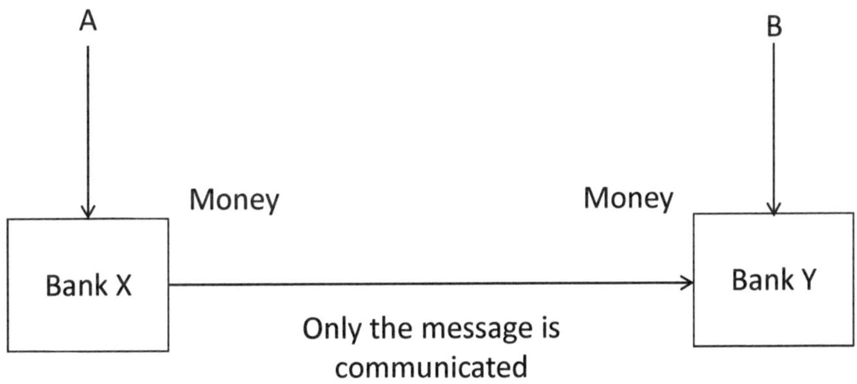

Fig. 1 Inter-bank transfers

Then, at a designated time, such as the end of the business day, all the transactions that took place are taken stock of, the total debt and credit amounts pertaining to each bank are calculated, and the amount due is aggregated into a single payment. This is called netting. The amount arrived at as a result of netting is then paid, and the settlement is completed.

This is the most commonly used system, called Designated Time Net Settlement (DTNS). The debtor-creditor relationships that arise between banks under the DTNS system are a risk factor for chain bankruptcies, which, as mentioned before, are a systemic risk.

To lower this systemic risk, a different system called real-time gross settlement (RTGS) has also begun to be used for large payments, which involves settling those payments on an individual order basis. However, interdependent relationships between banks still arise as a result of their other businesses, for example inter-bank transactions, making it very difficult for problems in the financial sector to be contained. Anything bad that happens in the financial sector is highly likely to spread due to a chain reaction, and the use of RTGS does not change the essential nature of this problem.

The debtor-creditor relationships that exist between banks are the root cause of what are traditionally understood as systemic risks, but in the wake of the Global Financial Crisis, there arose the specter of a different type of systemic risk—market risk, which is a systemic risk affecting the entire market. Even if there were no debtor-creditor relationships between financial institutions, if a number of financial institutions invest in the same class of assets, they will be exposed to the same kinds of risks and are liable to be simultaneously impacted if the relevant asset's value plummets or its market crashes. Such a situation also results in widespread problems and is considered another type of systemic risk.

(3) Amplification Mechanism 1—Bank Runs

As we just saw, the financial sector is exposed to several types of systemic risk that promote chain bankruptcies or deliver a blow to multiple organizations simultaneously. There are various mechanisms by which this systemic risk can eventuate and the problem be amplified. Of these, the mechanism that has traditionally been considered most likely to amplify a problem and lead to a financial crisis is a bank run.

Figure 2 provides a simplified illustration of a bank's balance sheet (B/S). The liabilities side reflects fund procurement primarily through deposits. Banks also have net worth equivalent to a small percentage of deposits. A very small portion of the bank's deposits are set aside toward repayments and other contingencies. These take the form of cash on hand or deposits with the central bank (the Bank of Japan) and are called the bank's "reserve," which is listed on the assets side. A large portion of the assets side of a bank's B/S comprises investments. The figure shows these investments as "loans," but strictly speaking, they also include securities and other investments.

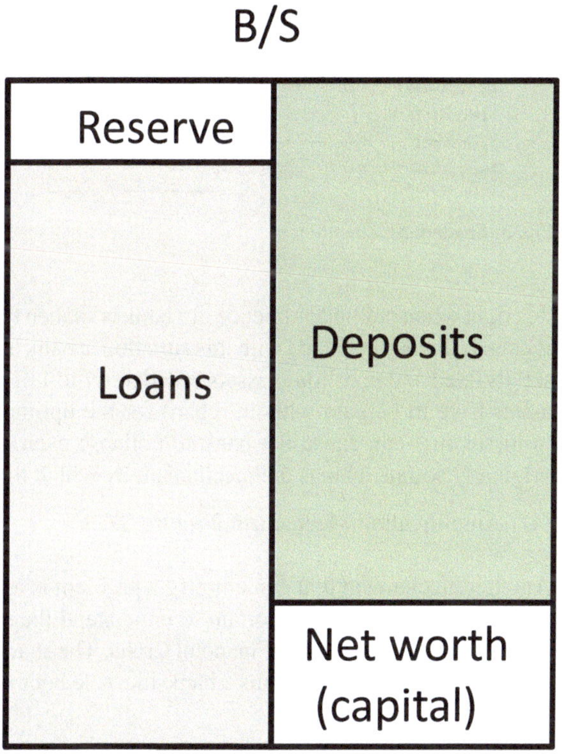

Fig. 2 Balance sheet of a bank

Bank deposits are repayable on demand, but the fact is that banks invest a large portion of their deposits in loans and other fixed or non-liquid assets. Fixed or non-liquid assets are assets that take time to convert into cash commensurate with their original value. This is because the original value of these assets cannot be recovered unless they are sold at the right time. Attempting to cash them on the spot can result in losses.

Banks can use their reserves to repay depositors who want to withdraw money, but as reserves cover only a fraction of the bank's deposits, the system is called fractional reserve banking. Under ordinary circumstances, fractional reserves are sufficient for a bank to function smoothly, because, although deposits are repayable on demand, the need for banks to repay the entirety of their deposits at a given point in time does not generally arise. Customers find it convenient to deposit their money with banks and do not usually demand to withdraw all their money at once unless they have a real need for it. Consequently, banks can afford to take the money procured based on the promise to repay on demand and invest it into fixed and non-liquid assets, and this is not a problem under normal circumstances.

However, if the financial system becomes unstable or rumors start spreading about a certain bank, things change. It is well within the rights of depositors to demand repayment, and a large number of depositors will simultaneously choose to exercise

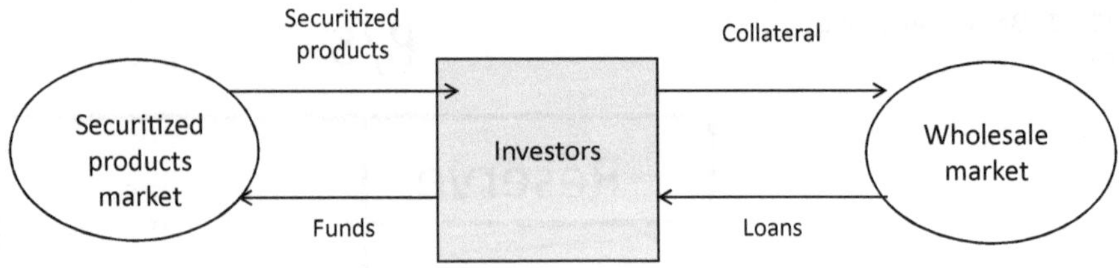

Fig. 3 Shadow banking system

this right when public confidence in a bank is shaken for some reason. Such a situation is called a bank run. Faced with this situation, a bank has no choice but to immediately sell its fixed and non-liquid assets in order to fulfil its repayment obligation. As these assets have to be sold without regard for the optimal timing, the sales often result in losses that can cause the bank to collapse even if its financial conditions were originally sound. This is the mechanism by which the problem is amplified.

(4) Amplification Mechanism 2—Fire Sales

Another mechanism that can amplify a problem is a fire sale. Before understanding what a fire sale is, it is important to understand the shadow banking system, which set the stage for the Global Financial Crisis. The shadow banking system refers to an informal system that performs a bank-like role but exists outside the formal banking system.

The entities pertaining to "banks" in the shadow banking system are the investors in the center of Fig. 3. These investors invest in securitized products and a variety of other financial assets, but only a portion of the funds required for making these investments is their own. The rest of the funds are procured through loans obtained using already-purchased securitized products as collateral.

However, borrowers cannot obtain loans exactly equivalent to the value of the collateral they pledge. Since the value of the asset pledged as collateral could decline, lenders will take this into account when determining how much to loan against a particular collateral. The size of a loan relative to the value of its collateral is called the loan-to-value (LTV) ratio. All secured loans have an LTV ratio, and the size of the loan may be no more than 80% or 90% the value of the collateral. LTV ratios can also be expressed in terms of "haircuts." A 5% haircut indicates an LTV ratio of 95%, meaning that the size of the loan would be 95% the value of the collateral.

Because of the extremely bullish expectations in U.S. markets just before the Global Financial Crisis struck, secured loans with haircuts of 5% were easy to come by. So, for instance, an asset worth 100 could be used as collateral to procure a loan of 95, which could be supplemented with own funds worth 5 in order to invest in new assets worth 100.

This kind of investment using borrowed funds is called "leveraged investment," and investments made using secured loans with 5% haircuts are said to have a 1:20 leverage.

It was against the background of robust leveraged investment activity that the aforementioned subprime mortgage problem came to light, creating a sense of mistrust in securitized products and weakening the securitized products market. As a result, there was a greater risk of these products depreciating, and the haircut rate on loans secured by them increased from 5 to 10%. This meant that leveraged investments now required a 90:10 ratio of borrowed to own funds compared with the previous ratio of 95:5.

As a result of an increase in the haircut rate on secured loans from 5 to 10%, investors became unable to maintain their existing investments unless they managed to arrange for an additional 5% in own funds, which many investors found difficult. Interestingly, the failure to procure the additional required funds meant that investors could only maintain investments worth 50 using a secured loan with a 10% haircut rate, forcing them to sell their remaining investments worth 50. This forced selling of assets is called a fire sale, and as more investors were driven to dispose of their securitized products through fire sales, the prices of these products fell, and the haircut rates on loans secured by these products rose even further, creating a vicious cycle. This vicious cycle is another mechanism by which a crisis is amplified.

(5) Crisis Management Measures

Without the activation of a vicious cycle, a single adverse event would not result in a crisis. In other words, a crisis only happens if an amplification mechanism is activated and triggers a vicious cycle. For this reason, crisis management tends to be a two-tier process.

The first line of defense against a crisis is to prevent isolated events that could trigger chain reactions. This involves minimizing the risk of events that could act as triggers. An archetypal trigger is the soaring of asset prices as a result of credit expansion, which results in what is called a "financial imbalance." In addition to protecting against potential triggers, financial institutions must make sure that their financial conditions are robust and healthy enough to withstand negative shocks.

Nipping the problem in the bud is the best option, but let us assume that the first line of defense has been breached and an individual financial institution has failed for some reason. At this point, the focus of efforts must shift to containment. This involves keeping the problem limited to that institution and preventing a chain bankruptcy or an endogenous vicious cycle. This is the second (final) line of defense. Measures pertaining to the second line of defense are called safety nets. A typical example of a safety net is the deposit insurance system.

If the government guarantees the repayment of deposits through a deposit insurance system, depositors could rest assured of their money being safe even in the event of a bank failure, and they would not rush to withdraw their deposits at the first sign of trouble. Bank runs were eliminated in the U.S. after the U.S. government introduced the deposit insurance system. It is a sign of the effectiveness of this measure that there were no bank runs in the U.S. for many decades.

However, right before the Global Financial Crisis struck, something similar to bank runs took place in the shadow banking system, which the safety nets did not extend to cover. Given that the shadow banking system emerged and grew informally outside the formal banking system, it was not regulated or monitored by the government, nor did it receive government protection. Consequently, it saw the occurrence of bank runs for the first time in 70 years in the U.S.

Another example of a safety net is the lender of last resort (LLR) function of a central bank. In its role as the LLR, the central bank lends money to a bank in trouble by accepting the troubled bank's fixed and non-liquid assets as collateral in an effort to prevent a fire sale. In response to the Global Financial Crisis, the Fed performed a function similar to LLR by implementing credit easing measures (commonly referred to as QE1). As part of QE1, the Fed purchased large amounts of numerous risk assets and supplied liquidity to the market, performing the role of a market-maker of sorts and effectively bringing the crisis under control.

3 Likelihood of Next Crisis

Having gained an understanding of the phenomenon of a financial crisis, let us move on to considering the possibility of fintech being at the center of the next financial crisis. One of the problems with fintech firms, as pointed out in discussions[2] surrounding the Bloomberg article mentioned earlier, is that the majority of these firms are still small-scale startups. They are much more vulnerable to negative shocks than large financial institutions of the traditional kind. Moreover, these startups have never yet experienced a real economic recession.

One cannot truly test the sustainability of a business model or system during a phase of economic growth. Businesses tend to perform well despite flaws when the economy is booming. The true test of a business model or system's sustainability lies in whether it is able to successfully overcome a recession. Consequently, one has to wait and see which of the diverse business models that have emerged recently survive an entire cycle of the economic fluctuations to determine which are truly effective and sustainable.

For better or for worse, the U.S. (as well as Japan) has been experiencing an extremely long phase of economic expansion. This may be the main reason the shortcomings of fintech firms have not yet been exposed, and it is possible that a large number of fintech firms will fail the next time the economy goes into recession.

Secondly, it is more difficult to monitor fintech firms compared with traditional financial institutions, given the novelty and complexity of the technologies they use. Consequently, such firms remain opaque and insufficiently monitored even in cases where policymakers feel something is amiss.

A third problem is that the fintech industry does not yet have a strong foundation for the development of a mutual support system. As described above, traditional financial institutions are very aware of the systemic risks they are exposed to, and

---

[2] See, for instance, https://www.bankingtech.com/2017/09/industry-views-will-fintech-cause-next-financial-crisis/.

have developed support structures they can fall back on in times of trouble. Some of these support structures are informal, but some are institutionalized in the form of mutual support agreements. In Japan, many credit unions and associations have an institutionalized support structure, with the entire industry pitching in to rescue an individual credit union or association that may be in trouble.

Fintech companies, however, do not have this kind of support structure. The reason for this may be because there is no awareness of systemic risks in this industry. In fact, rather than a lack of awareness regarding risks that exist, the view seems to be that there exist no real systemic risks in this industry as yet. The fintech industry is described as being "fragmented," and companies in this industry are not in a position to form networks to create mutual support systems.

Consequently, one would have to say that, as of the present time, fintech companies may not be exposed to the risk of an isolated event snowballing into a crisis. As Polymath Consulting CEO David Parker put it, "The fintech boom is certainly a bubble, and will some people lose money: Yes. But will it cause a financial crisis: No."

The rise in bitcoin prices in 2017, for instance, would be described as a bubble by most people. However, the short-sighted notion that the collapsing of that bubble will result in a financial crisis may not be correct.

Bubbles can be of two types. The first, for lack of a better description, is just a bubble. The other is a credit-fueled bubble. The first type of bubble happens as a result of speculative activity by investors using their own funds. An example of this kind of bubble is the tech bubble, also known as the dot-com bubble, which took place around the year 2000. When this bubble collapsed, it did not result in a financial crisis. Investors suffered losses, but that was the extent of the damage. In other words, when a bubble of this type collapses, concerned parties are affected, but the macroeconomic impact is limited to that.

In the case of bitcoins and other cryptocurrencies (crypto assets), people have been making credit transactions and investments on a personal basis, but there are no cases of large enterprises or financial institutions making leveraged investments in cryptocurrencies using borrowed funds. Consequently, even if the bubble collapses, the only damage will be to the investors.

In fact, some people have already incurred big losses in connection with cryptocurrencies. The value of the bitcoin, for instance, has fallen to about a third of its peak value. In the process, some investors made enormous profits and became multimillionaires, while other investors lost money on a similar scale. While the losses were serious for some of those who were directly involved, the macroeconomic impact was not something that would cause a crisis.

The risk of a financial crisis exists only in the case of credit-fueled bubbles. When the expected rate of return on an investment is greater than the interest rate applied to a loan, investors can increase their profits by leveraging borrowed funds to expand the scale of their investments, rather than limiting themselves to self-funded investments. Therefore, when market expectations regarding asset prices are extremely bullish, investors tend to engage in leveraged investments as a way to increase the profitability of their equity.

In such a situation, if actual profits fall far below the expected level (i.e., the bubble collapses), tragedy ensues. The price of an asset purchased using a loan may halve or quarter, but the loan still has to be repaid in full. In such cases, the loss is not limited to the entity that actually made the investment, but extends to the entity that loaned to the investor. Assuming that the lending entity is a bank, those who loaned money to the bank (depositors) will also inevitably be affected without safety nets, causing the problem to expand in the form of a chain reaction.

Consequently, the presence or absence of leveraged investments is one of the criteria for judging whether a bubble is credit fueled. In light of this criterion, it is easy to see why David Parker does not think fintech could cause a financial crisis, and his view seems reasonable at this point.

4 Future Developments

Fintech may not seem likely to be the cause of the next financial crisis at this point, but there is no telling what could happen in the future. For instance, a new fintech-based shadow banking system could emerge and become the stage for the next financial crisis in the near term.

However, going by recent trends in the U.S. and Japan, existing financial institutions appear to be taking the initiative to introduce new technologies and partner with fintech firms. In the initial days, it was felt that fintech firms were a destructive force and a threat to existing financial institutions, but this perception appears to have changed over the past few years, since around 2016, at least in the U.S. Fintech firms are now evolving in cooperation with existing financial institutions, which have been engaging with fintech firms by either acquiring or partnering with them.

At the moment, therefore, it seems likely that fintech firms will develop within the framework of existing regulations and safety nets. There does not seem to be much need for concern that they will evolve as a shadow banking system, outside the existing order or the reach of regulations and safety nets, at least in the case of the U.S. and Japan. The situation in China may be somewhat different.[3]

In particular, the nature of payment platforms such as WeChat Pay and Alipay is such that they could develop into shadow banking systems. These platforms use what are called digital wallets. Customers charge their digital wallets with cash, which is converted to electronic money within the wallet's system and used to make payments and money transfers. Electronic money that has been transferred to one's own wallet can also be converted to cash and withdrawn.

Electronic currencies in Japan are also different from WeChat Pay and Alipay in a few other ways. Suica, an electronic currency provided by JR-East, offers the convenience of rapidly processed payments, but this requires extensive capital investment

[3]For details regarding the state of fintech in China, see "A FinTech Future—Technologies, Possibilities, and Challenges" by Yuko Kawai and Masafumi Miya (2018) (Chapter 11 of *Financial and IT Policy Studies*, edited by Hiroyuki Kansaku, et al.).

in card readers and so on. By contrast, WeChat Pay and Alipay use a QR-code-based payment method, which makes the payment process slow, but they are very accessible in the sense that they require no additional capital investment. These services can be used by anyone with a smartphone to pay for anything with a QR code, and this accessibility has contributed to their rapid expansion.

Additionally, WeChat Pay and Alipay offer money transfer and payment services that are essentially free of charge. This is because their owner companies (Tencent Holdings Ltd. and Alibaba Group Holding Limited, respectively) use these services to collect information related to consumer behavior and finances, and then put customer usage history data collected in this manner to use in designing advertisements and increasing earnings from their other businesses, including e-commerce and the sale of insurance or loans. They can thereby make a profit in the bigger scheme of things. In other words, customers are paying for money transfer and payment services by handing over their personal information. This business model is only possible because Alibaba and Tencent are "platform business providers."

Banks and other traditional financial institutions cannot operate on this business model because of the fundamental principle of the separation of banking and commerce, which prohibits banks from engaging in other types of businesses. Traditional financial institutions may be able to use their customer usage history data to make financing decisions, but they can only recover costs and make a profit in their payments business by charging fees for payment and bank transfer services. In other words, they cannot afford to offer them free of charge.

Meanwhile, banking and commerce are gradually being merged together in the Chinese fintech industry. The merger facilitates data collection, and this gives platform businesses an edge over traditional banks when it comes to small short-term loans, where data collected from sales channels can be utilized to statistically manage risks. This is not to say, however, that the rationale behind separating banking and commerce, that is, the necessity of limiting contamination with other business risks or conflicts of interest, has ceased to exist.

With services like Alipay, customers can use their funds in the form of electronic money stored in their wallets without converting those funds to cash or withdrawing them. Moreover, these services also offer their customers a form of credit by allowing them to pay in installments. This seems to portend the likelihood of such services evolving into a shadow banking system capable of creating credit. In the future, it seems inevitable that there will be additional debate about how prudent it is to allow the development of shadow banking systems with no separation between banking and commerce. In this context, it will be important to monitor how the Chinese government deals with companies like Alibaba and Tencent.

As the technological revolution brings changes that enable the creation of a data economy, major new benefits to merging banking and commerce are coming to light. However, there also remain concerns that these benefits may be accompanied by new types of risks and that there may arise conflicts of interest. It will be interesting to see how financial system and institutions are redesigned while keeping these tradeoffs in mind.[4] The success or failure of efforts to redesign the financial system as a whole will depend on whether financial system destabilization risks—just one of the many types of risks associated with fintech—can be eliminated in the long term.

[4]In Japan, the Financial System Council's Financial System Study Group has been deliberating on how to redesign financial systems. See https://www.fsa.go.jp/singi/singi_kinyu/base_gijiroku.html#seido_sg for details.